The Scariest Word in the Bible

The Scariest Word in the Bible

Might You Be *Wrong* About Being *Right* with God?

LANCE M. BACON

WIPF & STOCK · Eugene, Oregon

To my beautiful wife, Crystal.
You are the greatest of my countless blessings,
and you hold all my love for all time.

And to our wonderful Bacon Bits:
Kyra, Austin, Braelyn, and Cheyenne.
You have given my life meaning and made my love complete.

Contents

Acknowledgements

I thank God for the ministers who have honed my thoughts and character. I offer special thanks to Revs. Crystal Bacon, David Smith, Cliff West, Michael Ball, and Mark Hambrick. The insights shared in our many (and sometimes long) discussions are invaluable.

I thank God for the professors and students who have honed my theological understanding. I offer special thanks to Drs. Jeffrey Anderson, Diane Chandler, Dale Coulter, James Flynn, Daniel Gilbert, Peter Gräbe, Michael Palmer, and Archibald Wright. Greater than wisdom is the willingness to impart in the individuals we serve. I learned this from you.

I thank God for Dr. Michael Baker, who has contributed in both ways. Your servant leadership strengthened my pastoral ministry; your encouragement and guidance initiated my transition to pastor/professor. Your example continues to inspire.

I thank God for my church family through the years. I have always prayed my ministry would be a blessing to you. Little did I know how greatly you would bless me.

Abbreviations

ABS	American Bible Society
ACCS/OT	*Ancient Christian Commentary on Scripture—Old Testament*
BECNT	*Baker Exegetical Commentary on the New Testament*
CDCP	Centers for Disease Control and Prevention
de	digital edition
ECNT	*Exegetical Commentary on the New Testament*
INT	Introduction to the New Testament
NAC	*New American Commentary*
NASB	New American Standard Bible
NICNT	New International Commentary on the New Testament
NIVAC	*NIV Application Commentary*
NSSL	National Severe Storms Laboratory
WBC	*Word Biblical Commentary*

Introduction

LET'S CUT TO THE chase. The scariest word in the Bible is the word "many."

For many reasons.

But that word is scariest when spoken by our Lord in Matthew 7:21–23: "Not everyone who says to Me, 'Lord, Lord,' shall enter the kingdom of heaven, but he who does the will of My Father in heaven. Many will say to Me in that day, 'Lord, Lord, have we not prophesied in Your name, cast out demons in Your name, and done many wonders in Your name?' And then I will declare to them, 'I never knew you; depart from Me, you who practice lawlessness!'"

Many on that day.

Do you know what that means? According to the Lord, who has the final say on the matter, many think they are going to heaven but are not. Many have a joyful expectation that one day they will step through the gates of pearl and walk in eternal glory but will never take that step. Many speak of loved ones who will meet them there, but will experience no reunion.

It certainly is not for lack of desire. Many dream about mansions on streets of gold and bodies that never grow old. Many long to stand on the shores of the crystal sea and listen as the angelic choir sings praises unto the Lord Most High. Many imagine what it will be like when they meet Jesus.

I have imagined that meeting many times. One of my favorite songs has long been "I Can Only Imagine." In it, writer Bart Millard and his band MercyMe beautifully captured an inexpressible truth:

> Surrounded by Your glory, what will my heart feel? Will I dance for You Jesus or in awe of You be still? Will I stand in Your presence, or to my knees will I fall? Will I sing hallelujah? Will I be able to speak at all? I can only imagine.[1]

1. MercyMe, "I Can Only Imagine," 1999.

Indeed, it is impossible to know the love, joy, and peace that will fill my being when I stand in the presence of my magnificent Savior. I can only imagine, and I like to imagine! It comforts me. It brings me hope. It gives me strength. It makes me feel at home.

In the many times I have imagined, rarely have I considered that day in the way described by Jesus—a day in which my Lord might not welcome, but instead cast me from his holy presence. Chances are you do not imagine this, either.

Yet this will happen to *many* on that day.

Will the expulsions thunder with the volcanic fury of a righteous Judge? Or will these words be painfully whispered by a broken-hearted Savior? I don't know, but this much is certain: The declaration will come as a surprise to many.

Why do I bring this up? It is not to rain down hellfire and brimstone. My goal is quite different. I want to spend eternity in heaven, and I want to spend it with you. To ensure our names are written on the rolls, we must first understand what it takes to gain entry. Let's be clear: Jesus was not speaking to those sinner-types who think they are going to heaven just because they are a "good person." Oh no. Jesus was speaking about churchgoers when he described those who will be turned away. Many Sunday School teachers, many deacons, many choir members, and many ministers. Many who pray wonderful prayers, quote countless scriptures, or belt out beautiful lyrics, but are not saved . . . and don't even know it.

The people of whom Jesus spoke were baffled when they were banished. They thought they were in good standing, perhaps even on the fast track to God's throne. Surely a mistake had been made! Many cited testimonies in their defense: We prophesied in your name! We cast out demons in your name! We did many wonders in your name! Jesus neither questioned nor criticized their displays of divine power.[2] His response (or lack thereof) suggests the testimonies were true, and that is cause for alarm. Many who do powerful things in the name of Jesus are not headed to heaven. Many will experience charismatic grace, but not saving grace.

Who will be shut out of heaven? Many who have led prayer or Bible study groups. Many who have gone on mission trips and fed the homeless. Many who have lived lives of self-sacrifice. Yet they, and many like them,

---

2. It is worth nothing that God can and often does obtain spiritual results from unspiritual men and women. One time he even spoke through a donkey.

are on the wrong path. That scares me, and it makes me want to know whether I am among the many or among the few.

The answer is not hidden. In fact, it is clearly conveyed in Jesus' indictment, in which he identified two reasons why many will fall short. First, many are workers of lawlessness, meaning they have willful sin in their lives (which includes sins of omission as well as commission). Second, many have substituted religious activities for the righteousness and intimate relationship God desires and requires.

How did they get that way? As we shall see, the reasons are many. Before we tackle those reasons, let us consider a critical question: How many will Christ turn away? Is "many" a majority? I don't know, but I do know that a majority is quite possible, even likely. After all, "broad is the way that leads to destruction, and there are many who enter through it" (Matt 7:13).

How few will find themselves in eternal glory? Would you believe that only half of professing Christians may make the cut? Perhaps you are taken aback by such a suggestion, but consider that only one of two had built a home on a foundation capable of withstanding the storm (Matt 7:24–27). Lot and his two daughters were saved, but his wife and their two suitors perished (Gen 19:12–26). Only one of two are raptured in Luke 17:36. Only half of the virgins were able to make the journey with the bridegroom in Matt 25:1–13. Only one of two praying men were justified (Luke 18:10–14). Only one of the two men crucified with Christ stepped into paradise (Luke 23:39–43).

One in two. Whew. It seems hard to believe. It is downright frightening. If you think that is tough to swallow, would you believe perhaps as few as one-in-four churchgoers will make it to heaven? Yes, I know that is a bold statement, but that ratio also has scriptural consistency. Turn to 1 Samuel 4 and you will find that, in one day, God cleaned his tabernacle in Shiloh, and three of four servants died. They were Eli, the priest who had not demanded obedience to God's word, and his two sons, Hophni and Phinehas. The latter two grew up in "church" and even performed ministry, but they were workers of iniquity. Only Samuel survived. One in four.

In Luke 14:15–24, Jesus told of a man who hosted a great supper. His servant was present, but three others allowed personal priorities and possessions to take precedence, and they were excluded as a result. One in four.

Long could we talk about the outpouring of God's Spirit on Pentecost (Acts 2). Jesus told five hundred believers to tarry in Jerusalem.[3] Five

3. Luke 24:46–49; 1 Cor 15:6.

hundred followers would be blessed beyond measure if they simply obeyed Jesus. When the fire fell one week later, only one hundred and twenty were present in the upper room. That is 23 percent, roughly one in four.

Let us not overlook the Parable of Sower (Matt 13:1–23). Jesus described four outcomes when the good seed of God's word is spread. That word takes root, grows, and bears fruit in only one out of the four examples. That is alarming when you consider we are known by our fruit (Luke 6:44). The parable also revealed why so many will fall so short. Many who have received the word will fail to bear fruit because they are hardened, they are weak, or they are worldly. The parable holds profound insight, which is why we will use this parable as the basis for our self-evaluation.

I am hopeful that more than one out of four who call Jesus "Lord" will make it to heaven. I am equally fearful that perhaps as many as three out of four will not. In light of that truth, we would do well to start with a difficult question: Is it possible that you are wrong about being right with God? The answer is not determined by whether you consider yourself a Christian, but whether Jesus considers you a Christian.

May I ask, how is your relationship with the Lord? How is your prayer life? How well do you know his word? How well do you know him? Not know *about* him, but know him?

"I never knew you."

How about your Christian walk? Are you taking up your cross daily? Loving your enemies and blessing those who curse you? Selflessly serving and sacrificing? Have you allowed God to transform you? To use you?

"He who does the will of My Father in heaven."

As we shall see, your eternity rests in rightly defining salvation, and entering into a loving relationship with God that enables our faithfulness to fulfill what Jesus taught. And we must do what Jesus taught! I am in no way advocating a works doctrine, but in the words of Jesus' own half-brother and the first pastor of the Jerusalem church, "faith without works is dead" (Jas 2:26).

Indeed, the Sermon on the Mount (from which our primary passage is drawn) is the antidote to what the great theologian Dietrich Bonhoeffer called "cheap grace," which he defined as

> the preaching of forgiveness without requiring repentance, baptism without church discipline, communion without confession, absolution without personal confession. Cheap grace is grace

without discipleship, grace without the cross, grace without Jesus Christ, living and incarnate.[4]

Costly grace is, well, costly. It cost Christ his life. It comes at a cost to Christians, as well.

As we will discuss, salvation is not a matter of opinion or simple agreement. One is not a Christian because he believes in Jesus, celebrates Christmas, and maybe even goes to church. As the old saying goes, attending a church no more makes one a Christian than entering a garage makes one a car. To claim that gracious title demands we submit to the lordship of Jesus, abide in him throughout our days, pursue the righteous transformation he has in store, and obey his direction and correction. Through Jesus' sacrifice we are able to enter into this phenomenal blessing called salvation. By abiding in Christ, we are able to remain in this blessing and fulfill its true purpose.

Take a look at the Parable of the Sower and you will see that Jesus said the first problem to producing good fruit was that the individual heard the word but failed to understand it. Therefore, I must ask: Do you understand salvation? Do you understand what salvation *really* is? I'm not talking about Willy Wonka's golden ticket, destined to open the door to untold wonders. I'm not talking about mansions in glory over yonder in Beulah land. I'm not even talking about being spared a devil's hell.

I am talking about love.

Salvation is the expression of a love we cannot comprehend. It is the self-giving of God; a willingness to become completely vulnerable in the hopes of a deeper relationship with you.[5] I am not describing the cross of Christ here. That is an unexplainable act of sacrificial love, no doubt about it.[6] While Christ's sacrifice on the cross covered the sin that separates us from God, the goal of the triune God went further still. As Macchia rightly notes, God does not simply accept the sinner. He embraces the sinner.[7] Like the prodigal's father in Luke 15, our heavenly Father desires to draw us into

---

4. Bonhoeffer, *Cost of Discipleship*, 44.

5. See Moltmann, *Crucified God*.

6. It is worth noting that Genesis 22:2 marks the first time the word "love" is used in Scripture, and it is in the context of a father sacrificing his son. This prophetic event saw Isaac ascend Mount Moriah with wood on his shoulder and fire in his hand, but Abraham was not required to sacrifice his son. Instead, the Father provided him with a lamb, and later offered his own Son atop that hill.

7. Macchia, *Justified in the Spirit*, loc. 2576.

his love, restore our authority, clothe us in righteousness, and renew our walk with him.[8]

Think about the most intimate and loving relationships in life. Not the ones that give you butterflies in your stomach, but the ones that grip the very depths of your soul. Many start as a chance encounter, but later grow into a friendly relationship. From there, they progress into a close relationship, then a critical relationship. Eventually, there comes a point when you desire that relationship go to new and perhaps unexplored depths, but this comes at great risk. The only way you can venture into such uncharted territories is to make yourself completely vulnerable to the other individual. You must allow that person access to your deepest hopes and habits, dreams and desires, fears and failures. You must trust that person with the very essence of your being and give with no way of knowing whether that person will accept your gift, violate your trust . . . or one day break your heart. This is a scary moment, and one with which many will struggle. If all goes well, you will have the kind of relationship you desire, that you dream of! If all does not go well, those dreams will be shattered. The consequences could leave you crushed and heartbroken, yet you know that giving yourself is required if you are ever to enter into this richest of relationships. This is salvation from God's point of view.

The almighty and everlasting, the Ancient of Days who stepped onto nothing and created everything, this awesome God willfully opened his heart and made himself fully available and vulnerable to enable a deeper and richer relationship with you. God knew that many would not accept his love, many would violate his trust, and many would break his heart. Yet in the hope of sharing his love, God laid it all on the line.

Do you think it not possible to affect God so deeply? Then why would we be told to not grieve the Holy Spirit in Ephesians 4:30? I like the way Eugene Peterson interprets that passage in the Message Bible: "Don't grieve God. Don't break his heart. His Holy Spirit, moving and breathing in you, is the most intimate part of your life, making you fit for himself. Don't take such a gift for granted."

God's capacity to love is immeasurably greater than ours. Similarly, God's capacity to hurt is immeasurably greater than ours. God is deeply affected by his creation. God's heart was broken when his people chose other

---

8. Salvation is not simply a matter of going to heaven when you die. In fact, eternal life doesn't begin when you die, it begins when you are born again! Jesus came that you may have abundant life now (John 10:10). The life of which he speaks is one centered in a right and loving relationship with God. This is how Jesus defined eternal life (John 17:3).

things than love (Ezek 6:9–10); when his people turned from him, though they referred to him as God Most High (Hos 11); and when his people refused to be drawn into his embrace.[9] This is most evident in the story of Judas.

That name is synonymous with betrayal, and we are often quick to vilify the son of Iscariot but keep this in mind: Jesus referred to him as a familiar friend, and a trusted companion. Judas had been anointed and empowered to do a mighty work for the Lord.[10] And do not look past Judas' proximity to Jesus at the last supper. That Jesus was able to dip the bread and hand it to Judas meant the disciple was seated in a place of honor near Jesus, most likely at his left hand.[11] It was not Peter seated at this place of honor. It was not James, or Andrew, or Matthew. It was Judas. Even when Jesus sent Judas to seal the deal with the religious leaders, none of the disciples imagined Judas was the betrayer of whom Jesus spoke (John 13:28–30).

Despite Judas' proximity to the light, he chose darkness, and it shattered the heart of God. Judas' betrayal marks the third and final time the Greek word *tarasso* is used to describe Jesus' deep anguish (John 13:21). The same word described Jesus' hurt at Lazarus's tomb, where he faced the death of a close friend and the pain of those dearly loved (John 11:33). The same word is used to describe the weight of his coming crucifixion (John 12:27). Our betrayal, our sin, hurts God as deeply as the loss of a loved one; it hurts God as deeply as the cross, where Jesus was abandoned, denied, wrongly accused, ridiculed, and covered in every putrid sin imaginable.

Why point this out? To have a true understanding of salvation requires we have a true understanding of sin. Every sin is a betrayal of God's self-giving; a betrayal of the vulnerability God offers in the hope of a greater love and relationship. Every sin is a betrayal of God's grace. Every betrayal wounds God beyond our understanding. Every sin breaks the heart of God, and most often, that betrayal is accompanied by a kiss, just like the one Judas offered. It was a sign of respect and admiration, but it meant little since Judas was determined to follow his own will rather than God's will.

---

9. Matt 23:37–39; Luke 19:41–44.

10. Matt 10:1; Mark 3:13–19; Luke 9:12.

11. Israelites would recline on their left elbow with their feet extending from the short table while eating the Passover meal. Because John is able to lean on the bosom of Jesus and speak privately with him, we can surmise the beloved disciple was on Jesus' right side. Therefore, since Judas was within Jesus' reach (John 13:6), he was likely on the left side.

To have a true understanding of salvation also requires we have a true understanding of grace. Grace is a result of the divine self-giving and is meant to be given to others. As we enter into God's divine embrace, we become agents of change in the lives of others. We share the love and light of God to help restore others, and the entirety of creation, to God's original plan. As the Apostle Paul put it, "work out your salvation with fear and trembling; for it is God who is at work in you, both to will and to work for His good pleasure" (Phil 2:12b–13).

We are saved to share in God's love, and to be agents of that salvation. Consider the one-out-of-four folks we discussed earlier: God told Samuel (one in four) to venture out and find David, who would bring God's glory back to the church. The servant of Luke 14 (one in four) was commanded to gather people from the hedges and highways. God similarly sent the one hundred and twenty believers (one in four) from the upper room to spread the gospel and turn the world upside down. When we look to the good ground that received the good seed (one in four), we do so knowing our Father will once more call on those who are rooted downward and bearing fruit upward, just as he did with the remnant of Judah (Isa 37:31). This new remnant will be the ones who journey into the hedges and highways and lead many to salvation in Jesus (Luke 14:15–24). They will open the doors to a final revival in which the Spirit of God will once more be poured out on all flesh; a latter rain that will water the seeds you and I have planted.

Sadly, many in the modern church will miss this great move of God. For many reasons.

This is not a cookbook, so don't expect me to sugarcoat anything. Forces beyond your imagination are battling against your spirit, soul, and body. As we will discuss in the pages that follow:

- Many who believe themselves to be saved do not even know what God requires for one to be saved. In fact, the biblical illiteracy in the United States is nothing short of staggering.

- Many churchgoers are familiar with the great deception revealed in the Garden of Eden, but unaware that they feast on that forbidden fruit with regularity.

- Many have been led astray by shallow Enlightenment principles that consider God's word to be an issue of values for the individual, not truth for the world.

- Many churchgoers have hard hearts that (perhaps unknowingly) do not let God's word take root.

- Many have heard God's plan but have let the devil's doubts and deceptions steal their blessing. Many have placed higher priority on pleasures and popularity.

- Many have embraced what God has to offer but allowed hard circumstances to stop God's promise and purpose for their lives.

- Many will enter a terrible period the Bible calls the great "falling away" (2 Thess 2:1–3) and fall short of God's glory.

The Apostle Paul encouraged believers to "consider yourself, whether you are in the faith" (2 Cor 13:5). That is great wisdom. After all, eternity is on the line. Yet few churchgoers heed Paul's guidance. Many prefer thin theologies that are heavy on cheap grace and assurances that God knows your heart and is happy to forgive. There is no need to change; God made you that way and he loves you just the way you are. Happy to oblige, many preachers present Jesus as some kind of wide-eyed orphan who waits in the wings in the hopes you will take him home. For others, Jesus is some celestial Santa Claus. If you make the "nice" list, you will get a blessing (interestingly, a nice little contribution will often get your name on that list). Others present the genie Jesus. Rub the magic lamp the right way, and he will grant your wish. Entire ministries are built on such theologies and stamp them with marketable catchphrases—blab it and grab it, quote it and tote it, tap it and zap it, name it and claim it. Such churches ignore Christ's message to "take up your cross" and "do unto others," as they instead pursue the latest formula for obtaining God's blessing of the week. This is the "con" of conversion. Such approaches are sure to build congregations but fail to build Christians.

I am burdened by the Churchianity that has so easily replaced Christianity. I am burdened by the many CEOs (those who attend church at Christmas and Easter Only) who are comfortable in the belief they will spend eternity in heaven. I am burdened by the fact that, despite the measurable devolution of discipleship that has driven this nation into a post-Christian status, more than three out of four Americans still believe they are going to heaven.[12] Very few, it seems, believe they are among the "many."

---

12. Sussman, "Elbow Room," para. 1.

Jesus wasn't as optimistic. He said "the gate is small and the way is narrow that leads to life, and there are few who find it" (Matt 7:14). I want to be counted among those few. I am sure you have the same desire. Let us then journey together to carefully consider salvation passages and find the way which leads to life.

The Parable of the Sower will serve as our roadmap on this journey. In this parable, Jesus provided remarkable insight on why "many" will fall short on that fateful day—specifically, three reasons many seeds fail to find good ground and bring forth good fruit. Hard hearts and hard heads prevent good seed from taking root. Rocky ground is full of obstacles that stop our spiritual growth and maturity. Thorny ground will see worldly issues steal the fruit of godly growth.

As we make this journey together, keep this in the back of your mind: Biblical salvation requires we respond to God, begin to live for God, and ultimately live from God. Coming to God will break up the fallow ground. Living for God will get us through the hard times that lay ahead. Living from God will ensure that no care of the world can steal our fruit and promises.

By taking an honest, Bible-based personal inventory, this parable will help us determine how well God's word has taken root and grown in our lives. This may challenge your church traditions. It may run contrary to what you want to believe, or what you hope to be true. It may convict, or even correct you. But like the seed held in the farmer's weathered hand, this parable holds unimaginable potential for personal and kingdom growth. Jesus' timeless teaching can equip you to reap a bountiful harvest for the Lord. Yes, it will take some work. After all, a good farmer does not simply expect his seed to take root, grow and bear fruit; he works hard to ensure this happens. He breaks up hardened ground. He removes stones that would prevent the seed from taking root. He drives off birds that would steal the seed. He cuts away the thorns that would choke out the seed.

So shall we.

SECTION I

When Good Seed Hits Hard Hearts

Behold, the sower went out to sow; and as he sowed, some seeds fell beside the road, and the birds came and ate them up. . . . When anyone hears the word of the kingdom and does not understand it, the evil one comes and snatches away what has been sown in his heart. This is the one on whom seed was sown beside the road.

—Matt 13:3b–4, 19

THERE IS ONLY ONE reason so many will be told to depart from the Lord's presence: They think they are saved, and they are not. In Jesus' first example, we see that some seed never took root. It could not penetrate a hardened earth and was therefore an easy target for the devilish hunters that circled above.

The seed is God's word—his promise and purpose for us. The problem, it would seem, is those dive-bombing buzzards bent on stealing our blessed salvation. The solution, it would seem, is to erect some sort of supernatural scarecrow to keep those birds out of our spiritual garden. We need to rebuke this, and bind that, and plead the blood of Jesus over it all!

Not exactly.

We will certainly take aim at those vultures in later pages. Before we put the enemy in our sights, we would do well to look at ourselves. You may be thinking, *Did he just say to look at myself, when these demons are busy stealing God's word from me?* I sure did. After all, had God's word penetrated that hard ground, those devils would have nothing on which to feast.

Good seed is being spread in good churches every Sunday. Many will hear that word but will not let the word be rooted inside of them where it can grow and produce fruit. Many will have church, but will not have change, and these devilish vultures know it. No doubt they circle above church parking lots each Sunday afternoon because they know a bountiful buffet is soon to emerge, a smorgasbord of good seed that has fallen on hard hearts (or hard heads). Both can be much like concrete: thoroughly mixed and permanently set. I know that is a pretty rough statement, but as I said earlier, this isn't a cookbook, so don't expect me to sugarcoat anything. The fact is, we love to blame those buzzards when we lack God's blessings, but the devil can't steal a word that is planted in our hearts. As we shall see, to allow God's word to penetrate is easier said than done, and this is why our discussion must begin here. No individual will experience a breakthrough if God's seed cannot break through. Like the hardened harvest field, which the Bible describes as fallow ground, a hard heart that won't receive God's good seed will remain fruitless and lifeless; it will neither cultivate God's righteousness nor reap his mercy (Hos 10:12). This need not be.

The world sees roughly sixteen million thunderstorms each year. In fact, there are roughly two thousand thunderstorms in progress at this moment.[1] Those storms pour an average of forty inches of rain on our planet annually. Yet no matter how much rain falls, nothing will grow if seed is unable to penetrate a hardened, fallow ground. Likewise, many will hear the countless sermons preached this Sunday, but if those words do not penetrate those hearts, there will be no life and no growth. As the early church father John Chrysostom rightly noted, nothing can be harder than a man who is neither softened by goodness nor turned back by fear.[2] A woeful fate awaits such, for a hard heart leads to a hard reality: "depart from Me."

When I think of hard hearts, my mind goes straight to the Grinch. That green dude had a serious heart problem. His jealousy and anger churned with volcanic fury, and it nearly drove him mad. It also drove him to steal Christmas. One could preach a month of Sundays on the spiritual implications of that analogy alone.

You know how the story goes. As the sound of worship creeped up Mount Crumpit, the Grinch came to realize why he had failed. Christmas

---

1. National Severe Storms Laboratory, "Severe Weather—Thunderstorms," para. 4.

2. Chrysostom, *Homilies on Acts and Romans*, 655.

isn't about getting stuff; it is about love for God and one another. The same can be said for true Christianity (another month of preaching material right there). When the Grinch came to know the truth, his small heart grew three sizes in one day. As awesome as that sounds, the truth is we don't need a bigger heart. We need a new heart. A bigger heart will do you no good, when one considers the heart is deceitful above all things, and desperately wicked (Jer 17:9), and is killing you from within (Matt 15:18–19). That is why I feel a tinge of pain every time I hear someone say, "God knows my heart." Yes, he does, and that is not a good thing. The issue is not whether God knows your heart—it is whether you know your heart, and whether you know the heart of God.

The fact is, most people know little of their physical heart, let alone their spiritual heart. That is why heart disease remains the leading cause of death in the United States.[3] Heart disease claims more than six hundred thousand people every year. That's one in every four deaths. Roughly seven hundred and thirty-five thousand Americans will have a heart attack this year. Nearly one-third will be a repeat attack. Having lost my father and my spiritual father to heart issues, I know this pain all too well.

Can I tell you a secret? Heart disease is the leading cause of spiritual death, as well. Your spiritual heart bears many similarities to your physical heart. Consider this: the human heart is a hollow muscle roughly the size of your fist that weighs about as much as a can of soda (Diet Mountain Dew, if it is truly blessed). The average heart pumps two thousand gallons of blood each day. It will beat thirty-six million times this year, and 2.5 billion times in an average life. The heart supplies blood to your body through a circulatory system of veins, arteries, and capillaries that measure upwards of one hundred miles in length—roughly the distance from New York City to Philadelphia. The blood that flows through that circulatory system brings life-sustaining oxygen and nourishment to all parts of the body. It simultaneously removes waste without contaminating the body and carries antibodies that defend and protect the body from disease and infection.

As we consider this in a spiritual context, let me hit you with a pop quiz: what can wash away my sins? What can make me whole again? The answer, for those unfamiliar with the old hymnal, is "nothing but the blood of Jesus!" There is "power, power, wonder working power in the blood of the Lamb," to quote another classic tune you youngsters should check out some time. While you're at it, read 1 John 1:7 to see how the blood of Jesus

3. CDCP, "Heart Disease Facts," para. 2.

Christ cleanses us from all sin. Then read 1 Peter 1:18–19 to see how you were redeemed with the precious blood of Christ. And Leviticus 17:11 to see how the life in his blood and makes atonement for your soul. Christ's blood sustains Christ's body, which is his church.[4] His blood will remove all waste and protect you from disease and infection. But that blood, as powerful as it may be, is useless without a strong and healthy heart.

Even Jesus' own disciples struggled with hardness of heart. Have you read of the time they shrieked in horror, having seen someone walking on water? Jesus calmly revealed himself and climbed in the boat, there surrounded by twelve speechless disciples. They were not only astonished by his actions, but also the fact that they continually failed to comprehend their Lord. It was hardness of heart that prevented them from recognizing Jesus' true identity (Mark 6:49–52). Flip a few pages and you will see that the disciples later failed to understand one of Jesus' warnings for the same reason (Mark 8:14–21). In both examples, their shortfall was not a matter of faith or intellect, but of the heart.[5]

A hard heart is one that is unaffected; it is uneasy to move, and difficult to impress. Every heart has been hardened to some degree, and it is not hard to understand why. Life is hard and can leave you hardened. Many are hardened by circumstances. Many are hardened by past hurts. Many are hardened by pride, many by preference, and many by indifference. This hardening of the heart has turned many people, and many churches, into fallow ground.

Roughly fifty-two million people, slightly more than 17 percent of the American population, attended Sunday church services in 2006. The same number attended church in 1990. Some may see that as a "glass is half-full" scenario—hey, at least the church is not declining! But it is. In that same sixteen-year period, an additional ninety-one million people came to live in the United States through birth and immigration.[6] Though billions of dollars were spent on outreach programs, multiple channels of Christian television racked up tens of thousands of broadcast hours, more than one thousand Christian radio stations filled the airwaves and thousands of new Christian books hit the shelves, the American church saw a whopping zero in its net growth.

---

4. Rom 12:5; Eph 4:12.

5. For more on hardness of heart, I recommend Jonathan Edwards's timeless classic *Religious Affections*.

6. Olson, *American Church in Crisis*, 81.

God's word is not penetrating the hearts and lives of an increasing segment of the population. Unless the church finds a way to break up this fallow ground, it is projected that only 14.7 percent of the population will attend church services in 2020. This marks a decline of three million attendees while the American population grows from 296 million to 336 million. If the trends continue, fewer than 9 percent of Americans will attend church in 2050.[7]

What follows are key ways to break up this fallow ground so that the good seed of God's word can find good ground and bear good fruit. We must rightly determine how one becomes rooted in Christ. This begins by understanding how we obtain salvation. The two sections that follow will address how we maintain that salvation. Now, don't skip the first section because you think you have mastered the salvation equation. As Jesus warned us in Matthew 7, many think they are saved but are not. Be sure that you are not in that category. As the Apostle Paul put it, examine yourself to determine whether you are in the faith (2 Cor 13:5).

Your heart exam may reveal that you are in right standing with God, and spiritually healthy, to boot. I pray that is the case, and if so, that you will use our discussion to help you better share this truth with someone in need. To throw God's word in their direction is of no use if that precious seed cannot take root. Therefore, let us turn our attention from the buzzards poised to steal those promises, and prepare the hardened harvest fields for the good seed of God's word.

---

7. Olson, *American Church in Crisis*, 371.

1

Many Do Not Understand Their Situation

IF "MANY" IS THE scariest word in the Bible, then the most important question in the Bible is this: "What must I do to be saved?" (Acts 16:30). Many think they have the answer, and with it, a first-class ticket to paradise. With "coexist" the new rally cry of the religious, such assumption is not surprising. In the introduction, we noted a national poll that found three-in-four Americans believe they are heaven bound. The same poll found that three out of five Americans believe heaven is not a "Christians only" club, the idea being that all religions worship the same God, but simply call him by different names. Some Christian leaders have gone so far as to say hell doesn't exist, and everyone is headed to heaven.[1]

Jesus did not hold any of those opinions. In his view (the only one that matters), many are wrong about being right with God. Why the gap? Like the disciples in Mark's gospel, hardness of heart prevents us from fully comprehending Christ, his teaching, and the salvation he offers. Indeed, many people believe they are worthy of heaven (they certainly do not deserve a devil's hell!), but few can tell you how God determines who will enter heaven. Many believe they are saved, but do not understand what it means to be saved, let alone what it takes to be saved.

As a result, many have entrusted their eternity to good works, but good works do not earn God's grace. God is not good with you simply because you attend church or drop some jingle in the offering. Being baptized

1. Most notable is Pastor Rob Bell, though a few others, especially in the emergent church model, have said as much.

16

or taking your first communion does not guarantee the golden ticket. You are not heaven-bound because you recited a prepared prayer or work a ministry. My friend, conforming to Christianity is not the same as converting to Christianity.

Go back and read that last sentence one more time.

It is good that you do good things, but do not mistake good things for God things. Jesus acknowledged that even the Pharisees did many good things (Matt 23:23), yet the vast majority were not in right standing with God. If we are honest in our self-inventory, we will find that even the good we do is motivated by self-interest, self-gratification, and self-glorification. In this, we serve (and worship) our own self, and are further separated from God.

That is how we got in this mess in the first place.

To understand how we obtain salvation, we must first consider why we need salvation. Imagine you met someone who had never seen a Bible or heard about Jesus. How would you explain sin? How would you explain salvation? More importantly, is this how God would define sin and salvation? To rightly answer, let's journey back to the place where everything went wrong—a beautiful and plentiful garden called Eden.

If asked to define Adam and Eve's great sin in Genesis 3:1–9, many would say "disobedience." Yes, they were disobedient, but the problem runs far deeper. Consider the temptation: eat this fruit and you will be like God. Adam and Eve's great error was that they wanted to be God, rather than be godly.[2] They wanted to know good and evil so they could decide for themselves what is right, beneficial, and true. All they needed was a little nudge—and in slithered a serpent who was quick to rationalize the rebellion. You can make your own conclusions and decisions, he said. You can rule, rather than submit to God. Instead of trusting and obeying God, the duo replaced God by becoming Lords of their own lives. The deception opened the door to everything that is wrong in this world, and the thought of it probably makes you want to squash that serpent's head. Before you do, remember the ground rules we set in the introduction: We must look at ourselves before we point a finger at our foe. Adam and Eve were quick to lay blame on others (some things never change), but church father Augustine (354–430 AD) rightly laid full blame on Adam and Eve. In his classic work *The City of God*, he argued that Satan would have had no chance at initiating the rebellion if this was not already the heart's desire of Adam

---

2. For more on this, see McKnight, *Kingdom Conspiracy*.

and Eve. In his words, "the evil act had never been done had not an evil will preceded it. . . . the devil, then, would not have ensnared man in the open and manifest sin of doing what God had forbidden, had man not already begun to live for himself. It was this that made him listen with pleasure to the words, 'ye shall be as gods.'"[3]

The fall of mankind was a heart issue, and Scripture certainly affirms this scenario. "But each one is tempted when he is carried away and enticed by his own lust. Then when lust has conceived, it gives birth to sin; and when sin is accomplished, it brings forth death. Do not be deceived, my beloved brethren" (Jas 1:14–16). Do you know what that means? Satan didn't trick the innocent and naïve garden dwellers. He saw a desire that festered in their hearts, and he acted upon it. In Augustine's words, "[b]y craving to be more, man becomes less; and by aspiring to be self-sufficing, he fell away from Him who truly suffices him."[4]

Granted, there were other factors that led to Adam and Eve's sin.[5] Topping that list is the fact they did not know God's word as well as they should have. Compare God's word in Genesis 2:16–17 to Eve's response in 3:2–3, and you will see that she failed to include some key words. By omitting "freely," she minimized God's gracious generosity. By omitting "surely," she minimized the certainty and severity of God's response. That is exactly what Satan would have you believe: God's not *that* good, and the consequences aren't *that* bad.

It gets worse. Eve failed to say that God commanded their obedience. She also added the phrase "shall not touch it." God never said that. He did say that the tree had a name: the tree of the knowledge of good and evil. Eve did not identify the tree as God did. She called it "the tree which is in the middle of the garden." She lumped it together with all the others (you know, it's really not *that* different).

It gets worse still. Eve did not refer to God by his covenant name, Yahweh (rendered as "LORD God" in the English translation), which was used twenty times in Genesis 2–3. She instead echoed the term Satan used: Elohim, which is a more general title for God. She was not speaking of him as the covenant creator who gave the breath of life, and with whom they walked in deep relationship. He is just, you know, God. Eve then looked at

3. Augustine, *City of God*, 360.

4. Augustine, *City of God*, 361.

5. I include Adam in this because the Hebrew pronoun "you" appears in the plural form throughout the temptation.

the fruit and saw it was pleasant to behold. At this point, she was walking by sight, rather than faith. She took the fruit in her hand and—well, you know the rest of the story. After all, it is your story.

We spend our childhood swearing up and down that we will never be like our parents when we grow up. Then, one day, you look in the mirror and see mom or dad looking back at you. Yikes! Later, you catch yourself speaking to your child with the same words, mannerisms, and tone that you swore you would never repeat. You have become them. If you are not to that point, you will be one day. It's in your DNA. There is no getting around it.

The same is true for our sinful nature. The Apostle Paul tells us that death came to all by one man, Adam (1 Cor 15:21–22). Ours is a corrupted nature; the desire to play the part of God (the very desire Satan targeted in his first temptation) is engrained deep within. We don't want God to be God. We want to be in charge. We are born with a natural disposition to evict God and take residence on his throne; to rule, rather than submit to God's rule. Sometimes it is through ignorance, sometimes it is through arrogance, but it is our nature to choose our own path; to make our own determination of right and wrong, good and bad, truth and lie. Every choice, every assumption, every decision, every perception made apart from God's perfect word and will is a deafening declaration of our independence from God. That is why disobedience is far more than a minor infraction. The heart hardens every time that declaration is sounded; the harder that heart becomes, the more difficult it is for the good seed of God's word to penetrate.

I know, that sounds pretty bad. It is actually worse than it sounds.

The great theologian Athanasius (296–373 AD) described the fall of man as the dissolution of physical, spiritual, and psychological integrity. Because God created everything from nothing, it is necessary to recognize that everything remains suspended over the void of nothingness, held by the God who sustains and gives meaning to all things. Therefore, to turn from God is to cast oneself into that abyss, to turn toward non-being and thus become corrupt.[6] Such refusal of God "constitutes a radical denial of oneself that threatens one's own reason for being."[7] As Miroslav Volf rightly noted, "since our very existence is a result of God's grace, if God were to

---

6. Athanasius, *On the Incarnation*, locs. 492462.

7. Macchia, *Justified in the Spirit*, 422.

stop giving, we would stop existing."[8] The converse is also true; if the believer stops giving himself, God will stop existing in that person's life.

Indeed, the quest for spiritual and moral autonomy is outright rebellion against God, but sin is more than defiance and disobedience—it is deviation. Sin is the failure to fulfill God's intent; to miss the mark. The New Testament uses various Greek words, both passive and active, to describe the character of sin. These include *adikia*, which is irreverence and unrighteousness, and *ponēria*, which is wickedness of a vicious or degenerate kind. These speak of an inward corruption or perversion of character. In addition, *parabasis* speaks of trespass or transgression, the act of stepping over a known boundary, while *anomia* describes lawlessness, or the disregard for a known law. Rebellious disobedience is captured in the terms *apeitheia*, *aphistémi*, and *apostasia*. However, the most common word used to depict sin is *hamartia*, a word that denotes a missing of the target.[9] Any would-be marksman knows that external factors can cause you to miss the target. If your sights are improperly aligned, you will miss the mark. A forceful "jerk" rather than a smooth squeeze of the trigger will cause you to miss the intended target. A gust of wind will cause the round to drift and miss the mark. At greater distances, you can miss the mark because your breathing patterns and even your heartbeat can cause sufficient deviation in the weapon's alignment.

Here's the kicker: this missing of the mark is not due to minute mistakes or the adverse effects of external forces. The Bible's description of sin indicates that we miss the mark because we are aiming at the wrong target. The disastrous consequence can be summed up in one word: alienation. Sin causes immediate alienation from God, alienation from one another, and alienation from our true selves.[10]

Alienation is not merely spatial. Indeed, our sin separates us from God, but it also places us at enmity with God.[11] The sinful nature is bitter, hostile, and antagonistic toward God. The default setting of our adamic nature drives us to hide from God. Why? Many are afraid and see God as an angry judge poised to punish any wrongdoing. Many see the almighty as an adversary, a cosmic killjoy who will zap all the fun out of life. Many prefer the dark side, where they are free to choose their own path (John 3:19).

8. Volf, *Free of Charge*, 36.

9. Erickson, *Christian Theology*, 519–24.

10. Hollinger, *Choosing the Good*, 76–77.

11. Isa 59:2; Rom 8:7–10; 1 Cor 2:14; Eph 2:15–16.

Ah, there echoes in my mind the ironic declaration of Darth Vader, "[y]ou don't know the power of the dark side. I must obey my master!" Had Anakin Skywalker truly known that power, perhaps he never would have fallen. You see, the dark side promises freedom, but it is all a ruse. By submitting to the dark lord, you become his servant—and he is a vicious master. You will forever suffer in a vain attempt to find spiritual perfection and physical satisfaction apart from God. This pursuit will control every facet of your life, and the objects of your affection will soon become your god(s). As Jedi Master Yoda rightly warned, "Once you start down the dark path, forever will it dominate your destiny; consume you it will."[12]

Such enmity is evident in our alienation from one another, as well. Mankind was meant to live in harmony; man and woman were designed to complement and complete one another. That went out the window the moment sin entered the equation. Adam and Eve immediately blamed the other for their own actions. Equality fell prey to domination and manipulation as individuals sought to fulfill their own needs and wants.[13] All of the division we see today—be it familial, gender, ethnic, political, socioeconomic—is the fruit of alienation.

And let us not forget the alienation from our true selves. Adam and Eve saw themselves differently once they had sinned, and they were ashamed. Shame is indescribably destructive because self-worth is one of our deepest needs. Whether high or low, self-worth affects every area of life. The more sin we hide, the greater our shame becomes. The greater the shame becomes, the more desperate we become for self-worth. Unfortunately, many seek self-worth in what Robert McGee calls the "satanic formula," which states Self-Worth = Performance + Others' Opinions.[14] We find our identity in what we achieve, and what (we think) people think about us. Many will (mis)shape their identities in this way.

Sin thus casts the individual into confusion, futility, and darkness.[15] From this self-alienation, many will devolve into self-deceit and self-centeredness.[16]

12. A long time ago, in a Galilee far, far away, Jesus offered the same warning. So did Paul (John 8:34; Rom 6:6; 16–20).

13. This is why the kingdom mind will use stuff to get people, while the worldly mind will use people to get stuff.

14. McGee, *Search for Significance*, 21.

15. Rom 1:21–22; Eph 4:17.

16. Jer 17:9; Matt 7:3; 1 John 1:8; cf. 2 Sam 12:1–15. The nadir of this devolution is more fully addressed in chapter 12.

This threefold alienation is why Church Father Augustine, in his revelatory doctrine of Original Sin, explained that humans are born misrelated to God, and headed in the opposite direction from the day of our birth. Every human is born with a sinful nature, an inherited depravity that inclines us toward sin. If you doubt that, allow me to ask a question: did you find it necessary to teach your child to lie, or did they exhibit that behavior on their own? Perhaps they did not lie very well at first, but from a very young age they knew when to lie, and did so to preserve their own self interests. It was natural to them.[17]

Okay, so we all have issues, but does that mean God will banish us from heaven? After all, God is all about love and forgiveness, right? And you probably aren't that bad, perhaps even better than most. Perhaps. But those people are not the measuring stick. God does not grade on a curve, he grades on a cross. He set the righteous standard, and the fact is, we fall woefully short. It is not hard to understand why. Our hearts are desperately wicked (Jer 17:9). So wicked, in fact, that we could not come to God if we wanted to—and the fact is, our sinful nature does not want anything to do with God. The darkness in which we dwell hates the light (John 1:5; 3:19–21). Sin renders us spiritually dead, worldly minded, disobedient children driven by demons and the desires of our flesh (Eph 2:1–3).

Staring into the abyss, what are we to do? In truth, there is nothing we can do. This ever-widening chasm, what existentialist philosopher Søren Kierkegaard (1813–1855) described as the "infinite gulf," can be bridged by God alone.[18] How is this accomplished? Many think our loving God should turn a blind eye to our sins. To do so would be to create God in our image. After all, we are the ones who tend to turn a blind eye to sin. We excuse our behavior with the familiar fallback, "I'm only human." This goes to show how twisted our understanding has become. Sin has never been a component of human nature—"it is a foreign element . . . and is a corruption of its purity."[19]

God is in the business of restoring, rather than ignoring. Our loving Father extended a bridge to reconcile his lost and wayward children and deliver us from sin's destructive reign. Christ is that bridge (John 14:6). If we refuse to cross (if we refuse *the* cross), God will remain hidden and will

17. This does not mean that we are void in matters of conscience. Scripture clearly teaches that we all have knowledge of right and wrong (Rom 2:15).

18. Lane, *Concise History*, 268.

19. Gause, *Living in the Spirit*, 18.

not hear our prayers.[20] As Stott observes, the cross enforces three truths: our sin must be extremely horrible, God's love must be wonderful beyond comprehension, and Christ's salvation must be a free gift that leaves us nothing to pay.[21]

The issue is really a question of who is in charge. Sure, many will throw God the occasional prayer, give him a shout-out on Sundays, and maybe even do some benevolence in the church or on the mission field. But what role does God play in your journey through life? Many will leave him at baggage claim to do all of the heavy lifting. Some will do better and invite him along for the ride. Some will shake their head and say, "oh no, Jesus is no passenger. He's my copilot!" An improvement, but you are still in the wrong seat.

If we accept the cross, Jesus will change our direction (I am the way), our understanding (I am the truth), and the manner in which we live (I am the life). This is the beginning of salvation.

20. Ps 66:18; Isa 59:2; John 9:31.
21. Stott, *Cross of Christ*, 85.

2

Many Do Not Understand God's Salvation

WHAT IS THIS THING we call salvation? Is it simply a change of our eternal address? There certainly will be a move from hell to heaven, but that is only one aspect (and not even the primary aspect). Salvation is the divine work that overcomes the threefold alienation caused by sin. This is the essence of the Great Commandment, in which love restores our alienation with God, others, and self.[1]

This is salvation, yet salvation is so much more.

God's desire is not simply to absolve the sinner, but to embrace the sinner; to draw you into the intimate communion, or *koinonia*, of divine love. Put another way, salvation is God's way of bringing you into the Trinity's embrace. It is not that you are embraced by the Trinity, mind you, but that you are part of the embrace they share together.

That does not mean that God is some lonely old soul, wandering the golden streets of glory in the hopes that someone will come talk to him. Our self-existent and self-sufficient God needs nothing outside of himself.[2] Does this render us meaningless? Quite the contrary. God created us and "determined that we would be meaningful to him. That is the final definition of genuine significance."[3] It is the love we share with God, and that God shares with us, that gives us meaning.

1. Matt 22:34–40; Mark 12:28–34.
2. John 17:5, 24; Acts 17:24–25.
3. Grudem, *Systematic Theology*, 162. Grudem expounds further on this under-

24

So, how do we enter God's loving embrace? It is here that Christianity will see two very different theologies emerge. The Reformed tradition believes that God has already elected who will be saved (and who will not). The Arminian tradition believes God desires that all would be saved, but he leaves the choice to the individual. In the interest of full disclosure, I side with the latter. Scripture requires the individual respond in faith to the work of Christ, a truth echoed in the early ecumenical councils.[4] As Gause rightly asserts, "[t]he will of the sinner is essential to repentance. Sin is a willful act; therefore, repentance must also be a willful act."[5] As such, this chapter will present salvation as a multifaceted blessing that is instantaneous, yet lifelong; one that is an exclusive result of God's grace, yet demands our participation.

To pick up the problem discussed in the previous chapter, the depraved mind cannot turn to God even if it wanted to (and it does not want to). Therefore, God must take the first step. The Reformed tradition says that first step is regeneration, which enables the lost soul to rightly respond in faith to salvation God has ordained.[6] But how can one who is not yet saved be regenerated? This is not possible according to numerous scriptures, and John Calvin would agree.[7]

Rather than regenerating elect individuals, God extends "prevenient grace" to all individuals. John Wesley, in his treatise "Predestination Calmly Considered" described this as a supernatural restoration of free will. God shines enough light to reveal our true condition.[8] This is accompanied by his offer of deliverance, and a measure of faith sufficient to enable a right response.[9] This is the critical and necessary beginning of our salvation

---

standing as he deconstructs process theology in pp. 166–67.

4. John 3:15–18, 36; 5:24; 10:27–28; Acts 16:31. Notably, Maximus the Confessor and Pope Martin I affirmed that Christ had two wills, human and divine, at the Rome Synod of 649. For more on that, see Appendix 2, "Salvation: Choice or Chosen?"

5. Gause, *Living in the Spirit*, 22.

6. Grudem, *Systematic Theology*, 700.

7. John 12:24–25; Rom 5:1; 6:8–14; Col 2:13; 2 Cor 5:7; 1 Pet 3:18. John Calvin himself affirmed this *ordo salutis* in his commentary on John 1:13, where he explains that it "may be thought that the Evangelist reverses the natural order by making regeneration to precede faith, whereas, on the contrary, it is an effect of faith, and therefore ought to be placed later" (Calvin, "John 1:6–13," para. 23).

8. Rom 2:24; 2 Cor 7:10; 2 Tim 2:25.

9. Rom 12:3; cf. John 1:1–13; 6:44; 12:32. Many will reject this gift because they love the darkness (John 3:19). Others claim they are too far gone. Too far for God to reach you? If so, why would he call to you? No, my friend, you are not disqualified by past sins.

experience. As Paul Anderson rightly notes, Jesus "does not say that no one *may* come, as a factor of God's permission; rather, it is a factor of human limitation and lack of potentiality—no one *can* come except being drawn by the Father."[10]

The Father draws us to the cross that we may be redeemed, a financial metaphor that means to purchase, or to buy back. Though salvation is a free gift, it came at great expense. The wages of sin is death, and therefore, something must die to cover that cost.[11] Adam and Eve learned this soon after they used fig leaves to cover the consequence of their sin. God instead covered them with animal skins (Gen 3:7, 21). Blood was shed when God covered the very first sin, because life is in the blood, and it is given for our atonement (Lev 17:11). Without the shedding of blood, there was and is no forgiveness of sin (Heb 9:22).

What is the price of our salvation, and to whom was it paid? This question was approached by Origen of Alexandria (185–284 AD) in his "ransom theory," which held that the fall in Eden placed mankind in bondage to Satan, and God paid the necessary price to free his creation.[12] It sounds heroic, even romantic, but this would mean Satan has some sort of authority over God, who is indebted to nothing and no one. Other theories (good and bad) were developed in the years that followed, but none had the impact of Anselm of Canterbury (1033–1109 AD). He defined salvation as "satisfaction." He rejected the ransom theory and declared that God owed nothing to the devil but punishment.[13] We are the ones in debt, and God is the one to whom payment must be made. Sin has taken what is rightfully his—namely, us. Salvation is seen as restoring the divine honor that was impugned by mankind's offense. We are obligated, but unable, to make the payment; God has the ability, but no obligation to make payment. The solution is the incarnation; Christ is a human with the obligation, and God with the ability to cover the offense.

Anselm's concept was further developed by Thomas Aquinas (1225–1274 AD). In his classic work *Summa Theologiae*, Aquinas explained that "a proper satisfaction comes about when someone offers to the person

---

These actually affirm the need for salvation. Your relationship with God is based on your response rather than your résumé.

10. Anderson, *Riddles of Fourth Gospel*, 184.

11. Rom 6:23; 1 Cor 11:30; Heb 12:9; 1 John 5:17.

12. This theory was also held by Irenaeus and Augustine, among others.

13. Anselm, *Cur Deus Homo*, 21–24.

offended something which gives him a delight greater than his hatred of the offense." Christ's "was not only sufficient but a superabundant" offering because of the greatness of his love, the worth of the life he laid down, the comprehensiveness of his passion, and the greatness of the sorrow he took upon himself.[14]

This understanding was followed by the fuller development in the Reformed tradition of the penal or forensic substitution theory, an adaptation that looked to appease God's wrath rather than God's holiness. With ample analogy from Old Testament substitutionary sacrifices, this theory sees Christ as offering himself on our behalf. One aspect is what Paul calls "propitiation," or the turning away of God's wrath.[15] When our sins were placed upon Jesus, God's wrath turned from us and onto his son. God's holiness demanded propitiation. God's love offered itself as the propitiation.

It is here that we truly begin to see the unimaginable cost of salvation. It is not in the price paid to Satan in the ransom theory, or the price paid to God in the satisfaction theory, but in the price paid by God for you. It was the Father, not the Romans or the Jewish leaders, who placed Jesus on the cross.[16] His beloved Son was betrayed and beaten, scourged and sacrificed. When our sin was placed on his spotless lamb, the incarnation enabled the Son to experience the separation from the Father that defines hell.[17] God's wrath turned to that sin, and Jesus experienced the personal hell of every man and woman who will ever live. This was the price of our reconciliation, and our loving God was pleased to cover the cost (Isa 53:10). So great is that love that salvation does not stop there.

The individual who receives this grace through faith is now justified, which is a legal term that describes a divine acquittal. And still, the work of salvation is far from complete. Sin affected everything from the physical and spiritual to the temporal and eternal, and God's solution is no different. It is here that we enter into atonement (literally, at-one-ment), and God regenerates the believer. Because the sinful nature has been removed and replaced with the divine nature, the Holy Spirit is able to take residence

---

14. Aquinas, "On the Satisfaction of Christ," 302. The selection is drawn from *Summa Theologiae* 3a.48.2.

15. Rom 3:25; Heb 2:17.

16. Isa 53:6; John 3:16.

17. For more on this, please see Appendix 5, "How Two Wills Presents the True Christ and True Victory."

within, and to pour the love of God into a newly created heart.[18] God also replaces the restrictions of sin with the righteousness of Christ.[19] This transference gives the individual standing before God, and authorizes you to confidently approach the throne of grace to receive mercy and grace in your time of need (Heb 4:16). Old things have passed away, and all things become new—the one who was dead in sin is made alive unto God. This person is "born again."

If the idea that death precedes life proves a bit puzzling, you are in good company. This befuddled Nicodemus, and that guy was one of the day's sharpest theologians. Nicodemus failed to see that Jesus was speaking in spiritual terms and immediately thought "born again" referred to physical child birth (John 3:1–12). As it turns out, the physical example does provide some clarity. Childbirth is a dying process from the infant's perspective. The womb is the only world the baby has known, but it is a world of darkness. One day, an unseen force begins to push the new creation toward an uncertain place. The newborn is constricted as it struggles forward. There is pressure on every side. Most infants fight every inch of the way until eventually (and to the joy of everyone), the baby breaks through. Everything looks and sounds different to the newborn. This new life is loud, it's exciting, it's confusing, and it's so bright! The child is totally exposed, frightened, yet exhilarated! And what is the first thing that happens? The umbilical cord, the connection to the old world, is necessarily severed, and the newborn soon feels stinging pain as someone lays a whack on the backside.

Sounds like Christianity to me.

And there in the delivery room stands the eternal Father, ready to immediately adopt this newborn as his own. This change of familial identity grants all the rights, privileges, and inheritance common to an heir. Before drawing the first breath of new life, this believer is established as a child of God.

This is but a brief overview of salvation, and our understanding is expanding with each passing day. One might think we should have this thing figured out after two thousand years, but why? Salvation is beautifully intricate, divinely orchestrated, and deeply personal event that transcends all reason. Salvation is too great to ever comprehend this side of heaven, and too great to ever stop trying.

18. Ezek 36:26–27; Rom 5:5, 8:9; Eph 4:22–24; Col 2:13–14; 2 Pet 1:4.
19. Rom 1:17, 4:5–7; 5:1–11; 1 Cor 1:30–31; 2 Cor 5:17–21; cf. Hab 2:4; Ps 32:1–2.

For example, modern theology is grappling with Anselmian satisfaction theory and the long-held Christus Victor model (the crucified Christ is victor over the powers of darkness). It is not that either theology has erred, but that they are incomplete.[20] Both see Christ's death as sufficient for our justification—the cross satisfied the debt and enabled our right standing with God. The cross provided everything you need. Many would shout an emphatic "hallelujah!" at the thought, but this theology would be problematic for the Apostle Paul. In his view, the cross is the beginning, rather than the end of our salvation experience. Paul presented salvation as an ongoing process in which the believer has been saved (Rom 8:24), is being saved (1 Cor 1:18), and will be saved (Rom 13:11).

Salvation is not only a matter of what God did for us, but what God is doing in us. As the Christus Victor model rightly asserts, the Son of God came to destroy the devil's work (1 John 3:8). Because the devil's central work was the destruction of the *imago Dei*, salvation's central work is the restoration of the *imago Dei*—the "image of God" in which mankind was created.[21]

Salvation, therefore, not only looks forward to what we will claim in heaven, but also looks back to reclaim what was lost in Eden. Such understanding was expressed by the Apostle Paul when he described "the renewing of our mind" (Rom 12:2). Though the Greek word *metamorphoō* is correctly translated as "transformed" in that familiar passage, the prefix *meta-* in Greek composite verbs also carried the meaning of reversal—much like the prefix re- in the English language.[22] This is an important distinction. To transform is to alter or change into something entirely new, something that had not existed. In one example of metamorphosis, this transformation takes us from egg to caterpillar to pupa to butterfly. The act of reform, on the other hand, returns the individual to a previous state; namely, the image of God in which mankind was originally created, but was

---

20. This is the great problem of Martin Luther's theology. With great respect for the reformer, the fact is that his unwavering commitment to Christus Victor and satisfaction theory essentially entrenched Christianity at Calvary. Luther's forensic justification brings the believer to the place of forgiveness, but not to freedom; it overcomes the penalty of sin, but not its power.

21. Such restoration enables God to set apart a holy people for intimate fellowship (Eph 5:25–27; 1 Thess 5:23; Heb 13:12). This work enables a return to communion with God (1 John 1:3–4), responsibility to God (Titus 2:13–14; cf. Gen 2:16–17), and stewardship for God (Gen 1:26–27).

22. Ladner, *Idea of Reform*, 42.

lost in the great fall. Was this not the expectation of Christ when he said we must be born again?

Salvation is not simply a matter of heaven and hell, but of renewal, restoration, and transformation. Indeed, the Greek verb translated "save" (*sōzō*) means "to rescue from danger and to restore to a former state of safety and well-being; to cause someone to become well again after having been sick; to cause someone to experience divine salvation."[23] Yet to see salvation as a continuation rather than a one-time event begs the question: If Christ has done his part to provide that salvation, who is responsible for the continuing work of salvation? The answer is twofold.

First, Christ continues to do his part. Having been justified by Christ's blood and reconciled by Christ's death, the born-again believer is saved by Christ's life (Rom 5:10). Did you see that? Salvation is a work that continues beyond justification and reconciliation, in which the work of salvation started at the old rugged cross continually works in our lives through the intercessory prayers of our high priest. In fact, Paul said that "much more, having been reconciled, we shall be saved by his life." Much more!

Imagine for a moment the grace that Jesus offered in his death on the cross. He loved us while we were swimming in sin and enemies of God. He loved us enough to lay down his life, to bear our sins, and become our propitiation (*hilasterion*). Incredible as it is, Jesus offers "much more" love and grace in his life than he did in his death. When we struggle, when we have need, when we hurt, when we are losing hope, Jesus offers a greater measure of grace than we have experienced or can imagine (Eph 3:20). And why would we expect anything less? If God saved us when we were enemies, how much more will he save us when we are his children? If the death of the Savior benefited us while we were still ungodly, how much more will his life bless those who are reconciled? If Christ's death accomplished so much, how much more will his life accomplish?[24]

We can rejoice in knowing that we are saved by Christ's life, yet Christ is not alone in the continuing work of salvation. He is joined in this effort by Cinderella. Okay, a little tongue-in-cheek there, but it is an accurate analogy. The Holy Spirit has long been treated much like the fabled heroine. While I am not willing to align the Father and Son with the two wicked

23. Louw and Nida, *Greek-English Lexicon*. With such a definition, it is no wonder that Augustine of Hippo presented the church as a hospital, and salvation the lifelong healing of wounds caused by sin.

24. For a better understanding of the magnitude of this blessing, take a look at Romans 8.

stepsisters, the fact is we are quick to invite the other members of the Trinity to our fancy galas (which take place every Sunday morning) that we may sing of our love for them, and their love for us, in the hopes that we can dance but a moment in their embrace. Meanwhile, "Cinderella" is kept behind the scenes with the expectation she will quietly clean up our messes and the dark corners of our hearts.[25]

In the Disney classic, Cinderella eventually made it to the ball, Prince Charming sought after her, the glass slipper fit, and everyone lived happily ever after. That seems to be the story of modern theology, as well. There has been much effort to better understand the implications of a pneumatological soteriology—in other words, how the Holy Spirit fits into our glass slipper of salvation. Finding that perfect fit will ensure you live happily (for) ever after, as it enables the believer to progress from imputed righteousness to imparted righteousness, a blessing that is better than any fairy tale out there.

It is "because" the Spirit leads us that we "will live" as adopted sons and daughters of God (Rom 8:12–17). That does not mean the believer's struggle with sin has ended. Far from it. While the believer dies to sin, sin does not die to the believer.[26] This is exacerbated by the orientation to self that most have carried for many years and which takes much time to uproot. This includes the tendencies and behaviors learned while led by the sinful nature—what Paul referred to as "the flesh." The flesh loves those old tendencies, but the Spirit desires transformation. This is the battle and burden of every Christian. Satan adds to the dilemma by targeting our tendencies with crafty temptations that lure us to return to the actions and attitudes that were common to our sinful nature.

The new creation in Christ will be very unhappy and uncomfortable when sin does arise because it is no longer natural, but this reaction is not enough to overcome. A primary means of spiritual growth will occur through sanctification, a partnership with the Spirit that is subsequent to,

25. Relegating the Holy Spirit to a tertiary status is nothing new. Such has been the case from the times of Justin Martyr and Origen, who presented God as a graded Trinity—the Father is greater than the Son who is greater than the Holy Spirit. This not only results in a deficient soteriology, it is heretical. In the fourth century, the popular Alexandrian presbyter Arius took the next step and declared that only the Father is God, while the Son and Holy Spirit are created and inferior. Thus was birthed the Arian Heresy, the first great challenge of Christian theology.

26. Or, as John Calvin puts it, "though it ceases to reign, [sin] does not cease to dwell" (*Institutes*, III.3.11).

yet symbiotic with salvation.[27] This work further restores the image of God as the believer grows in love, is delivered from the lure of sin, and cultivates spiritual fruit. Like repentance, this will be a lifelong endeavor.

Hopefully you can see that to be born again is not to receive a tune-up or a tweaking. The change is nothing short of a radical reorientation of thought and life.[28] What does this look like? Think of the incredible change that resulted when sin entered the creation. With it came sickness, selfishness, anger, pain, sorrow, and death. Humanity was radically altered by sin. In response, the Son of God was radically altered by the incarnation.[29] Jesus subjected himself to humanity's frailty and fragility. He willfully accepted our limitations and was subjected to our temptations. The immortal put on mortality that the creator could redeem his creation. His struggle was real and lasting, evident by the sympathy he continues to extend (Heb 4:15).

In the same way that Christ was radically transformed when he became a man, a man will be radically transformed when he becomes Christlike. The person saved by grace will be changed by grace. This new creation will not act or react as the old person did. The transformation is a lifelong endeavor, yet so immediately thorough that it will cause friends and family to pause with perplexed stares as they wonder, "Who are you, and what have you done with my loved one?"

Despite our new nature, many Christians echo the old phrase, "I am just a sinner saved by grace." While there is great worth and humility in recognizing our guilt and God's grace, the statement is not true. You were a sinner, but because you are saved by grace, that is no longer your nature or identity. You are now a saint who sometimes sins.[30]

---

27. For more on that, see Appendix 3, "The Salvation/Sanctification Symbiosis."

28. This includes a rejection of one's autonomy and control (John 12:25). Therefore, when Jesus bids his followers to lose their lives, the Greek word *apollumi* does not speak of misplacing or modifying, but rather destroying that old life. Devotion and obedience to Jesus must be so thorough that nothing else can distract or divert.

29. Phil 2:6–8; Heb 5:7–8.

30. Rom 6:4–7; Eph 4:17–24. This is further illustrated in John's first epistle. There, 1 John 2:1 speaks of helping believers not sin, while 1 John 3:9 says no one born of God will sin. Though the statements would seem contradictory, they are not. The former is in the Greek aortist tense, which presents the sin as a one-time (rather than continuing) event. In this case, the believer has an advocate with the Father, Jesus Christ. The latter verse presents sin in the Greek present tense, which would note continuing action. As Williams further explains, "it is clear that John is by no means teaching that the regenerate person never commits a sin, only that it is not natural to him" (Williams, *Renewal Theology*, 89).

God does not coexist nor dwell in union with sin.[31] Christ bore our sins in his body on the cross, that we might die to sin and live to righteousness (1 Pet 2:24). If a believer still had a sinful nature, the Spirit would not dwell within (Mark 3:25). Think about it: do you as a Christian have authority over the devil? How could you have authority over the devil if you still had a sinful nature? The sinful nature is subject to sin, and sin belongs to the devil.

It comes down to this: you can have only one nature. You are led either by sin leading to death, or the Spirit leading to life (Rom 8). How do you know which one you have? How do you know which one is the Lord of your life? The one to whom you submit is the one who rules, and the one who rules will be the one who resides. You will grow in the likeness of the god you serve (Rom 8:5–8); therefore, give careful consideration to your own character and natural tendencies to know who truly possesses your soul.[32]

Jesus is the perfect example of what the right choice will look like. Jesus shows us what we are to be, and he imparts himself that we may become. Because we are saved by his life, we are transformed into that perfect image by Christ through the Spirit, and we become "one spirit" with him.[33] Jesus took on our nature so we could partake of his nature.[34]

As a believer, I am called to live a life that is pleasing to God.[35] This is best achieved when I allow God to live his life through me. Salvation is not simply a matter of inviting Christ into my life, but Christ inviting me into his life. *He* is life, and I am saved by his life. Only by losing myself in him can I find myself in him.

This is salvation.

---

31. Augustine destroyed this argument in his many refutations of the Manicheans, most notably, *On the Nature of Good.*

32. Here is a good assessment: read Galatians 5:13–26 and conduct an honest appraisal. Which do you see growing in your life: the fruit of the Spirit, or the fruit of the flesh? The fruit produced reflects the nature of the tree (Matt 12:33–35; 15:18–19; Luke 6:43–45; Rom 7:5).

33. Rom 8:29; 1 Cor 6:17; Col 3:10.

34. Rom 6:16; 2 Cor 5:17; Gal 2:20; 2 Pet 1:4.

35. John 8:29; Rom 12:1.

3

Many Fail to Rightly Obtain Salvation

HAVING CONSIDERED THE WONDROUS blessing that is salvation, let's return
to the Bible's most important question: what must I do to be saved? "Must"
is an interesting word, so easily and often overlooked. The word appears
three times in John 3, a cornerstone text for soteriology. The Lord explained
that we must be born again (vv. 3–7), that he must be lifted up (vv. 14–15),
and John the Baptist declared that Jesus must increase while John must
decrease (v. 30).

We have addressed the first component at length. Much like a conception is necessary for physical birth, conception is necessary for spiritual
birth. Instead of seed and egg, this conception unites God's grace with your
faith. We commonly call this "belief," but the biblical definition of that word
is a little different than you might expect.

I believe there are few things as humbling as golf. I believe pizza to be
the best meal to accompany Monday Night Football. I believe all cats hate
me, and I believe chocolate is what heaven tastes like. Yes, my beliefs can be
subjective, and they can be very personal. For example, I believe the smiles
of my children to be the most beautiful thing in the world. I also have objective beliefs. I believe our planet revolves around the sun, I believe gravity
is constant, and I believe fire burns (trust me on that last one).

Biblical belief is different. It not only demands that you acquire the
truth and acknowledge it as truth, but also that you apply the truth to your
life. Biblical belief requires you to act on what you affirm, and why wouldn't
this be true? Sin and death did not come by the opinions of Adam and Eve,

but by their actions. Redemption was not achieved by Jesus' opinions, but by his actions. Your solution is no different. Biblical belief must be allowed to change you, and then use you to change the world. It is no wonder C. S. Lewis would call Jesus "a transcendental interferer."[1]

Because salvation is participatory, biblical belief requires action on your part right from the start. We must respond in faith to God's grace, and the proper response begins with repentance. Many confuse repentance with confession of sins, which is necessary, but even an admission saturated with sorrow and regret does not meet the biblical requirement.[2] To repent is to turn your back on sin; a reversal of direction that leads you into God's divine life and fellowship. Repentance is really a lordship issue. You can only serve one master: Either sin leading to death, or Spirit leading to life. This is what Paul means when he says we must "confess with your mouth Jesus as Lord" to be saved (Rom 10:9). Confession of sin is not enough. We must repent of our sins; we must eject ourselves from the throne (and whatever else we have allowed to take residence there) and ask God to take his rightful place. We will see an immediate reversal of attitude and behavior when our rebellion against becomes submission to God. While it is a catalyst of salvation, repentance is also a lifelong endeavor. Future sins will be forgiven only when they are confessed and forsaken.[3]

The great problem that has long plagued the church is the tendency to place our actions on the left side of the equal sign in the salvation equation. We believe our entrance to heaven will be based on, or at least influenced by, our good works. Many seem to have confused God with Santa Claus. He's making a list, and checking it twice, and the way to avoid the naughty list is to ensure the good outweighs the bad. Not so. Salvation is achieved by your Savior, not your behavior.

To claim that your salvation is the result of your righteous works is to deny God's grace; it is to remove God and place yourself upon his throne. This is the danger of a works doctrine, and the reason Jesus so forcefully opposed the Pharisees.

There is no doubt that Jesus hammered the legalistic Pharisees. Many Christians seem to think this means that the Law is wrong, bad, or no longer

---

1. Lewis, *Surprised by Joy*, 163.

2. The command to repent is clearly addressed fifty-three times in the New Testament. Notable examples include Matt 4:17; Luke 13:3, 5; 15:7; Acts 2:38; 3:19; 17:30; 2 Pet 3:9; Rev 2:5.

3. 1 John 1:9; 2:1–2; Prov 28:13; Ps 66:18.

necessary. Jesus never taught this. Jesus kept the Law and declared it to be good and eternal (Matt 5:17–20). However, Jesus took serious issue with rabbinic interpretation of the Law, which taught that a believer achieved righteousness through obedience and purity.

When speaking of the Law, Jesus often tagged on the phrase "and the prophets."[4] This was a subtle way of poking the Pharisees in the eye. It was Jesus' way of saying that the prophetic tradition, rather than the rabbinic, provided the proper interpretation of the Law. So, how did the prophets view the Law? The Torah is not a legal list of do's and don'ts, a religious ritual by which one could obtain righteousness. The Torah is a divine covenant of grace, a moral guide to develop godly character. The goal was not religious purity and freedom from defilement, but internal transformation leading to justice, mercy, and faithfulness.[5]

While the Pharisees focused on external observances, Jesus emphasized internal character and the root causes of behavior (Mark 7:1–23). This is what Jesus meant when he said he did not come to abolish, but to fulfill the Law and the prophets. Like the prophets, Jesus had nothing but disdain for the rabbinical system because it presented ritual and sacrifice as a substitute for moral integrity.[6] The Law was to show this lack, and drive people to God for the fix. The rabbinic tradition did the opposite, driving the people away from God. The Pharisees placed works over grace, and Jesus would have none of it.

Most Christians would agree that the "woe of the Lord" is a very bad thing. If one woe is very bad, then three woes must be incredibly bad. How bad? Consider the cataclysmic judgment that will strike the world when the seven-year tribulation nears its nadir. Hail and fire, seas of blood, pestilence, the sun and moon darkened, venomous locusts, a third of mankind wiped out by four angels—a very grim picture, to say the least. When an angel declares this divine verdict, it is spoken as a "triple woe" to the earth's inhabitants.[7]

---

4. Matt 5:17; 7:12; 11:13; 22:40; Luke 16:16; 24:44. Jesus' followers followed suit (Acts 13:15; 24:14; 28:23; Rom 3:21).

5. For example, Jeremiah affirmed the revival sparked by Josiah, but noted that their hearts had not changed along with their religious behavior. Ezekiel made a similar point (chapters 18 and 36). There also stands the rejection of routine ritual in the examples of fasting (Isa 58:6–12), festivals (Amos 5:21–24), and worship (Mal 1:6–14). Cf. Mic 6:8; Matt 23:23.

6. Stassen and Gushee, *Kingdom Ethics*, 91.

7. Rev 8:13; 9:12.

Now, if you think three woes are bad, consider the heavy sentence Jesus handed the Pharisees. Not one, not three, but eight statements of woe marked the final public statement he would make against Israel's religious leaders (Matt 23:1–35). Why such a harsh judgment? Because the Pharisees interpretation of the Law fell short. Woefully short.

In such understanding, many will push the pendulum from extreme legalism to extreme liberality. They will say works are unnecessary, even ungodly. Not so. Belief is a commitment to carry out God's commandments. We do these works not to be saved, but because we are saved.[8] The Apostle Paul called this the "obedience of faith." In the words of theologian and martyr Dietrich Bonhoeffer, "only [one] who believes is obedient, and only [one] who is obedient believes."[9] This is a topic we will tackle in a later chapter.

Suffice it to say, piling up good and righteousness works is not going to get anyone saved. Instead, Jesus must be lifted up—a reference to Numbers 21, a story with which Nicodemus would be very familiar. Fiery serpents had afflicted people who voiced unbelief. With no emergency room or WebMD in the wilderness, a bite by a poisonous snake meant a slow death with intense suffering. God told Moses to lift up a brass serpent. When the people looked upon it, they were healed.

Why would Jesus point to this example? It is a picture of our Lord and his sacrifice, a "Jesus selfie," if you will. The serpents represented sin, and one bite proved fatal. God's solution was made of brass, a material often used in the Bible to represent the judgment of God. The picture was clear: when sin is covered by God's judgment, and lifted up for all to see, the effects are negated for those who look to it in faith.

The symbolic brass serpent was not the source of God's healing and blessing, but the people soon worshipped the symbol rather than its sender.[10] They turned to religious activity instead of turning to God. Nicodemus and his fellow Pharisees had done the same. So often, so do we.

As Matt Chandler rightly asserts, "[i]dolatry that exists in man's heart always wants to lead him away from his Savior and back to self-reliance no matter how pitiful that self-reliance is or how many times it has betrayed

---

8. John 14:15; Jas 2:14–26.

9. Bonhoeffer, *Cost of Discipleship*, 63.

10. The event is captured in 2 Kings 18:1–6, in which the brass serpent is called "Nehushtan."

him. Religion is usually the tool the self-righteous man uses to exalt himself."[11]

In this second "must" statement, Jesus told Nicodemus (and us) to set aside empty, formulaic religion and look to God. It is God who brings healing. It is God who brings forgiveness. It is God who brings deliverance. Not religion. Christ must be lifted higher than any works you do, and higher than any blessing he provides you.

Still, one "must" remains for the born-again believer who has lifted Christ and is being transformed into Christlikeness. As the voice cried in the wilderness, Jesus must increase, while we must decrease.

We will discuss the teeter-totter of increase and decrease in the pages to follow. Before we do, I must share a secret: I loathe the phrase "What Would Jesus Do?" In fact, I would rather hear fingernails scratching chalkboards.

The issue of imitation has long been contested in Christian history. The approach has been embraced by people ranging from Aristotle to C. S. Lewis, who have argued that one of the best ways to acquire a virtue is to behave as if you had it already. There is value to this approach, which is why Thomas à Kempis's *Imitation of Christ* remains one of the great Christian works. Such an attitude undergirds the famous advice of Peter Bohler, who told a struggling young preacher named John Wesley to "preach faith until you have it, and then because you have it, you will preach faith." That does not mean "fake it until you make it." It means we should mirror God's grace until we assimilate God's grace.

Such an approach has also had its share of opponents, including church father Augustine and the great reformers Martin Luther and John Calvin. For them, any assertion that external imitation of Christ would result in Christian life was nothing short of Pelagian.[12] They argued that a believer should instead conform to the likeness of Christ through renewal and regeneration enabled by the Holy Spirit. Luther would categorize any self-effort toward righteousness within his "theology of glory." Augustine would deem such efforts superficial at best, and Pelagianism at worse.[13]

---

11. Chandler, *Explicit Gospel*, 14.

12. McGrath, *Christian Theology*, 250.

13. Martin Luther (1483–1546) presented a theology that can be summarized as this: everything is God's grace, and apart from God's grace there is nothing. He charged those who presume to ascend to the divine through human work and ingenuity as having a theology of glory (as opposed to a theology of the cross). In his view, the theology of glory is consistent with efforts to manipulate the divine, or the self-serving search for God's wisdom, glory, and power.

I would argue that both groups are correct. We are commanded to imitate Christ and emulate his seasoned saints.[14] But many well-meaning Christians slap this "WWJD" on bumper stickers and bracelets simply as a reminder to act and react as would Christ. While this Christianized "check it before you wreck it" has no doubt resulted in better behavior, we would do better to develop Christlike character. Such an approach echoes Jesus' endorsement of the prophetic rather than rabbinic interpretation of the Law. Genuine imitation of Christ is necessary, but it must work from the inside out. Such virtue ethic necessarily focuses on what we are to be, rather than what we are to do.[15] To neglect this is to run the risk of conforming to Christianity, rather than converting to Christianity.

Our heavenly Father gives us everything needed for life and godliness (2 Pet 1:3). The born-again believer is given a new heart, a new spirit, and a new nature. This enables the Spirit to dwell within and thus enable "you to walk in My statutes, and . . . be careful to observe My ordinances" (Ezek 36:26–27). It is beautiful when you think about it. God does not forgive your sin only to leave you in a sinful condition. God not only pulls you out of hell, he puts his Spirit in you. Salvation is the bestowment of Christ's own nature, by which we are led by the Spirit, renewed daily, and transformed into the likeness of Christ.[16]

He must increase, and we must decrease.

This is what Diane Chandler calls the "Christian legacy," *imago Dei* to *imago Christi* for *gloria Dei*.[17] A new believer is reformed in the image of God to be transformed into the image of Christ, all to the glory of God. The examples we imitate and emulate show us how to act as God's sanctifying grace forms the life of Christ in us.[18] We "put on the Lord Jesus Christ" to cover us externally while God transforms us internally.[19]

14. 1 Cor 11:1; Heb 6:12; 13:7; 3 John 1:11.

15. Hollinger, *Choosing the Good*, 45–46. For more on this, Thomas à Kempis's masterpiece *The Imitation of Christ* is a must. I also recommend Kevin J. Vanhoozer's modern approach in *Faith Speaking Understanding*.

16. For more on the dual work of sanctification, see Appendix 3, "The Salvation/Sanctification Symbiosis." In addition, the second section of this book will deal with key strategies through which the enemy of your soul will try to stop your transformation and return you to the tendencies of the old nature.

17. Chandler, *Christian Spiritual Formation*, 64.

18. 2 Pet 1:5–7; cf. 1 Cor 15:10; Col 3.

19. To "put on the Lord Jesus" also enables us to see what God is transforming us to be. Bible scholars will often address the already/not yet paradigm in the cosmic and

Hard heads and hard hearts can cause two big problems at this point. First, any imitation that is merely external (religious) rather than internal (transformative) is hypocrisy (Matt 23:1–35). Second, many new and well-meaning believers go no further than mimicry. Discipleship demands we go much further. A Christian walk that commits only to do what Jesus would do might change a situation, but it will not change the individual. We must learn not only to live for God, but to live from God.

Let us return to the statement I have come to loathe. Do you know who never had to ask the question, "What Would Jesus Do?" Jesus himself.

It was his nature to do those things. Now, do you know what the word "Christian" means? It means "Christ-like" or "little Christs." This is the heart of salvation. God's purpose is not simply to pull you from the jaws of hell. If this was the ultimate goal, Jesus would have gone straight to the cross (and we could ignore what he did and taught for the previous three-and-a-half years). No, God's purpose is to restore you to the original image and likeness in which you were created, and Jesus is the perfect(ed) example.[20]

As you are reformed in that image, Jesus will increase and you will decrease—and you will break free from that pesky question "What Would Jesus Do?" You won't have to effort such behavior. You will do such things out of your new nature. Look at it this way: I can bark like a dog, scratch like a dog, eat dog food, and sleep in the dog house (which I have on more than one occasion). None of these things make me a dog. But if God transformed me into a dog, it would be my nature to do those things.

Such reformation is the work of the Holy Spirit. His goal is not to *force* us to *do* something, but rather *form* us to *be* something. This is why grace always trumps works. Religion conforms to Christianity, grace reforms to Christ. When that happens, your actions will be natural and will flow from Christian character.

You must be born again. Christ must be lifted up. He must increase while you decrease. This is how salvation is obtained, and necessary to ensure it is maintained.

Wait, did he just say "maintained"?

Yes, salvation needs to be maintained. That's what the owner's manual says.

----

eschatological contexts, but it also carries weight within the soteriological. As Paul explains in Colossians 3:1–4, the recipient of salvation is already able to see what is not yet completed in his life.

20. Rom 12:1–3; 2 Cor 3:18. For a more detailed analysis, please see Appendix 3, "The Salvation/Sanctification Symbiosis."

4

Many Fail to Rightly Maintain Salvation

WHEN I THINK OF maintenance, my Harley Davidson immediately comes to mind. I have learned some hard lessons while trying to maintain that Wide Glide. I admit that I am no grease monkey. I am mechanically challenged, to say the least. But taking the Hawg into the shop for minor adjustments or to add chromed accessories—you just don't do that. A real biker takes care of that himself.

I am very careful when changes are complicated or comprehensive. I make sure I have all the right tools and parts. I devote sufficient time and attention. Above all, I keep the owner's manual open before me. I carefully study that manual before anything is loosened or bound. Do I have the right part in the right configuration? Have I left anything out? Thankfully, I can make a call to the maker if I make a mess of things. The maker has all the answers. I know that with the right guidance from Milwaukee, I can get back on track. So, when the time for change comes, I look a few steps ahead to make sure I am not sabotaging the next step, take a deep breath and begin.

I'm not wound quite so tight when the work order is less complicated. I still do a parts check and read over the manual, but there is far less pressure when changing a battery than when changing the exhaust. I throw on some music and may even have a spring in my step—or step on a spring, depending on how the day is going. If that happens, I probably won't bother the maker. The maker has enough stuff to do without dealing with my dilemma, right? But I will keep that hotline number nearby just in case.

Then we have those "simple fixes." These are the ones that get me in trouble. I look at these and say, "piece of cake." I may glance at the instructions. Probably not. Times-a-wastin' and I've got this! Such was the case when I installed a sissy bar (a backrest, for you non-riders). Line it up, put in the screws, easy day. Unfortunately, I didn't realize the kit had two sets of screws until I had put the front ones in the back slot. No sweat, just unscrew them, right? Nope. They come with stupid glue already applied. What is stupid glue? The kind that is so strong it is stupid. This glue could keep the wing on a 747 at thirty thousand feet. I had to drill out the steel screws, drive to the Harley shop to buy new screws (while praying the service tech didn't ask why I needed more), then start all over again.

So much for simple.

Maintenance is not merely a matter of decoration. It also affects function. My bike came with sufficient power, fresh oil, and ample light to penetrate the darkness, but these things need to be replenished from time to time. I point this out because just like a Harley, or a car, or a lawn mower, or a furnace, your salvation must be maintained after it is obtained—and it is usually the "simple" things that cause the most trouble.

Having entered salvation through biblical belief, you must maintain salvation through right relationship. God's maintenance plan is not simply to get you *in church*, but to get you *in Christ*. This is so important that Paul uses the phrase ninety-two times in his letters.[1] Being in Christ speaks not of some super-spiritual osmosis in which we are assimilated into his essence. Being in Christ is relational; in the truest sense of the Greek, it means you are in the sphere of Christ's control, and are in Christ's embrace.[2]

Where else would you rather be?

Relationship is all about proximity. It is not possible to have a good relationship with someone you don't know. You may know about them. You may run into them at work or social functions. You may know them by name and even greet them in passing. You may know them well enough to accept their friend request on social media. But such things do not constitute a relationship, at least not the kind we are talking about. This kind of relationship is not a matter of going through the motions of social norms, it is about intimate time spent together.

1. Additionally, Paul uses the phrase "in Him" twenty-nine times, and "in the Lord" forty-five times.

2. Porter, *Idioms of the Greek New Testament*, 159.

The Bible likens our saving relationship to a marriage.[3] That can be problematic, as marriage is often viewed as a temporary arrangement in this modern era, but it is true nonetheless. Biblical marriage elevates yet deepens a relationship that began with, and continues in, sacrificial love. In this relationship, joy is multiplied because it is shared between the bride and groom. Burdens are made easier for the same reason. Though at times apart, they are never alone. Though years may pass, their love is renewed time and again.

While love may have opened the marital doors, a lasting relationship requires work. Marriage is not a fifty-fifty endeavor. Divorce is fifty-fifty. Marriage requires both parties to commit 100 percent.

I once heard the story of a couple who, on their sixtieth wedding anniversary, was asked to give the secret to their success.

"Like the Bible says, we never go to bed angry," the sweet old lady said.

"Yeah," the husband added, "and that's why I haven't slept in thirty-seven years."

Not the best example of relationship, to be sure! I know quite a few couples who have been married more than half a century, and I thoroughly enjoy watching these couples converse. After all that time, you might think they would run out of things to say. Not a chance. You might think they could read each other's minds. Perhaps, but they would never silence their significant other with such assumption. No, they cherish the chit chat because it is the lifeblood that keeps their relationship strong.

Conversely, I have counseled many marriages in which communication was lost. I've seen hearts yearn to hear words of love and affirmation, only to sit in deafening silence. I've seen understanding give way to assumption, and passion give way to anger and apathy. If unaddressed, these once-beautiful and fulfilling relationships are quickly reduced to the awkward encounter between two people who barely acknowledge one another. All too often, one individual will look for satisfaction elsewhere, and the covenant of marriage is destroyed (cf. Jas 4:4).

What has this to do with my salvation? No one can come to Jesus unless the Father draws him (John 6:44). That is God's proposal; an invitation to covenant. Faith is the right response—an acceptance of the proposal, if you will.[4] Jesus, our groom, has stated his vows. We state ours by confessing

---

3. Isa 54:5; John 3:29; 2 Cor 11:2; Eph 5:25–27; Rev 19:7–9; 21:2, 9.
4. John 1:4; 5:26, 39–40; 10:10; 12:50; 2 Cor 5:21; 1 John 5:11–13.

him to be our Lord and Savior, and then submitting to him as such (Rom 10:9; Eph 5:24).

Once we are hitched, we must begin to build a lasting relationship. Jesus describes this as "abiding." There are upwards of eighty-five New Testament passages that speak to the conditions of salvation as "continuing," "abiding," "holding fast," etc.[5] To abide is to remain in an ongoing, intimate relationship. We abide in daily Bible reading, regular prayer time, committed discipleship, and the like. We spend quality time with God. Relationships require work, otherwise one party is taken for granted.

We are the bride of Christ, and we have the unmistakable command to remain in a loving, living relationship with the lover of our souls.[6] However, many spiritual marriages that start strong will not end well. What started as covenant will end in divorce court.[7] Some will challenge this idea by declaring God is faithful even when we are not. Indeed, he is (2 Tim 2:13). But God is not the one filing for divorce. We are. When we choose cheap grace, or put personal preferences over God's word and will, we have declared that Jesus is no longer our Lord, no longer our first love, and God does not settle for second place.

If you doubt that, I would invite you to consider the Bible's "warning passages."[8] There is some scary stuff in there, especially when you realize that these passages were not preached to heathen sinners residing in the wasteland. These warnings were given to believers. Disciples. Church members. Christians. Saved folk.

They were written to you and me.

If a believer can enter into a right relationship, it stands to reason that he can exit by the same door. If all the benefits of salvation belong to us only because we are in Christ (Rom 8:1), the benefits of salvation are forfeited the moment we are no longer in Christ. Such truth was expressed by Paul, who said "I discipline my body and make it my slave, so that, after I have preached to others, I myself will not be disqualified" (1 Cor 9:27). Paul was clear that he wanted to take every precaution to avoid disqualification. That word is drawn from the Greek word *adokimos*, an extremely strong

5. Shank, *Life in the Son*, 334–37.

6. John 10:27–28; Rom 1:17.

7. If you question the worth of this analogy, may I recommend you read Jeremiah 3, 9, and 23; all of Hosea; and James 4. For good measure, take a look at Hebrews 13:4. Though it speaks of a physical marriage, keep in mind that the spiritual is held to a higher standard than the physical since Jesus raised the bar of Christian ethics.

8. Hebrews 2:1–3a; 6:4–8; 10:26–29, 36.

term found in five other passages, all of which refer to rejection by God or reprobation.[9] Don't be deceived, my friend, and don't become disqualified. Though your salvation was initiated at the cross, it is not completed at the cross. On the contrary, you were told to take up your cross daily and follow Jesus.[10]

There are Christians who would disagree with the idea that salvation can be forfeited. Most who disagree fall within one of two camps. The first is the Reformed tradition, who believe that God had already picked those he will save (and those he won't). Salvation is an unconditional gift from God in their view. Once offered, you can't possibly reject it, and once received, you can't possibly lose it. What of those who later reject God? They were never really saved in the first place, according to Reformed thought.

The other camp subscribes to eternal security, a thought more commonly summed up with the familiar "once saved, always saved." It sounds enticing, but one must be careful of this false doctrine. I have found that many people who advocate eternal security have something in their life that is contrary to Scripture and would probably disqualify them from heaven. Instead of submitting to God's rule, they try to change the rules. That's not going to fly.

Doctrines that teach eternal salvation have to do some pretty fancy footwork to dance around scriptures that posit the possibility an individual can change his beliefs (and therefore change his eternity),[11] and warn against apostasy and falling away from the faith.[12] Simply put: fail to maintain your relationship, and you will forfeit the benefits that result from that relationship.

9. Rom 1:28; 2 Cor 13:5; 2 Tim 3:8; Titus 1:16; Heb 6:8.

10. Matt 16:24; Mark 8:34; Luke 9:23.

11. John 3:18; 5:24; 6:39–40; 10:27–29 (in light of 1:21–23); Gal 4:9–11; Phil 2:15–16; 1 Thess 3:5.

12. John 15:6; 1 Cor 9:27; Gal 5:4; 2 Thess 2:3; 1 Tim 4:1–2; 5:8–15; 6:10; 2 Tim 2:17–18; 3:8; Heb 2:1; 6:4–8; 10:26–29, 36; 2 Pet 2:1–22; 3:17; 2 John 1:8; Rev 3:5, 15–16; 22:19. None of the normative creeds of ecumenical Christendom (the Apostles' Creed, the Nicene Creed and the Athanasius Creed) have a statement about the perseverance of the saints, though subsequent statements of faith have included such. These include the Protestant Confession of Faith (1559), the Synod of Dort (1618) and the Westminster Confession of Faith (1646). The latter defines perseverance as "They whom God hath accepted in his Beloved, effectually called and sanctified by his Spirit, can neither totally nor finally fall away from the state of grace; but certainly persevere therein to the end, and be eternally saved" (17.1).

Salvation engages your head, heart, and hand. That is why reciting the "sinner's prayer" is not enough to save you. That may be tough to swallow, especially if your well-meaning pastor or a favorite televangelist invited you to repeat that prayer and promised this would magically make everything right. It won't.

That is not to say that such prayer is of little worth. On the contrary, the Bible requires you to verbally confess Jesus as Lord (Rom 10:9–10), but there is a huge difference between *professing* Christ and *possessing* Christ. After all, the demons acknowledge Jesus is Lord (the fact shakes them to the core), yet they are not going to heaven (Jas 2:19). What is the difference between the demons' belief and my belief? Relationship with and obedience to Christ. Words mean nothing if my actions do not affirm that to which I attest. It is not enough to *acknowledge* that Jesus is Lord. We must *allow* Jesus to be Lord, and that is a decision made day by day, from moment to moment.[13]

This symbiotic salvation (head, heart, and hand) must carry through our entire Christian walk. Take a moment to read John 15:1–11, and you will see what I mean.

Seriously, go read it. I'll wait.

What you just read is one of the most important passages in the Bible. To remain fruitful, one must remain in the love of Jesus (15:9), maintain love for fellow believers (15:12) and obey his word (15:7, 10). The vine language of John 15 also includes the unmistakably strong warning that the individual who once had rightly responded to Christ, but failed to abide in that love, will find himself cut off, thrown away, and burned. Therefore, we must continue to grow, to be, to *become*.

The key to this is obedience, as an enduring salvation will unite relationship and responsibility. We come to know God's love through his word (written and living), and we demonstrate our love by obeying his word (written and living).[14] One has not truly heard until one has obeyed; "un-

13. The present subjunctive of the Greek verb "to believe" (*pisteuō*) presents biblical belief not as a one-time act, but a continuance in belief that reverses one's natural tendencies and allows spiritual growth and transformation.

14. This is the example of God himself. God is love, and love is perfected only when it is shared. Love is shared through relational communication and covenant. The Trinity, in relational communication, made a covenant within itself to bring forth a creation with which it could share that love, "that God may be all in all" (1 Cor 15:28). The all-knowing God knew man would fall into sin, and he knew what it would take to redeem man. The second person of the Godhead agreed to cover the cost; in response, God declared, "Let there be light!" Salvation was not an afterthought. It was part of the creation covenant

less the life is changed, no salvation has occurred, and at the final judgment ultimate destruction will be the verdict."[15]

It probably comes as no shock that "obey" is not a popular word in our modern society, nor within the church. A call for obedience is usually met with a response such as "only God can judge me," or something of the like. Perhaps, then, we should listen to God on this matter. He will indeed judge all of us—and that will not be a good thing for many. To illustrate, let's return to the Lord's teaching in Matthew 7. Having dropped the theological bomb that "many on that day" would be told to depart from him, Jesus in his next breath described two storm-ravaged houses. One was built on rock, the other on sand. One had a good foundation; the other, not so good.

Foundations are everything. A foundation that uses correct materials will enable a strong structure to be built, and maintenance will be minimal. A cracked or unstable foundation will weaken the structure, perhaps to the point of it being condemned. No further growth will be possible. So, what does God use as a foundation? Righteousness and justice are the foundation of God's throne (Ps 89:14). The church was founded on Peter's confession that Jesus is the Christ and the Son of God (Matt 16:13–18). Expansion of that church was founded on Jesus.[16] But when it comes to your salvation, obedience is the foundation. Stay with me here, because we're going to build something!

Though Jesus was a carpenter, he wasn't putting his construction know-how on display in the hopes of landing a contract to build a subdivision by the sea. Jesus was talking about the building of a disciple. After all, we are God's temple (1 Cor 3:16). The two builders he described had much in common. It is apparent they received the same instructions. The houses were not in different stages of construction, so they must have been built at the same time. They were hit by the same storm, so it is reasonable to assume they were built in the same area. The foundation was the only difference noted, so they must have used the same materials.

Same word, same time, same place, same way, same materials—but only one was able to withstand the storm. What made the difference? "Therefore everyone who hears these words of Mine *and does them*, may

---

(Titus 1:2; 1 Pet 1:18–21). That covenant required action and obedience on the part of Jesus—the action was to set aside all rights as God and to take the role of a human servant; the humble obedience was the death on a cross. Our covenant is no different. It requires action and obedience.

15. Osborne, *ECNT*, 275

16. Isa 28:16; 1 Cor 3:9–11.

be compared to a wise man who built his house on the rock" (Matt 7:24, emphasis mine). Obedience was the difference.

No one builds a house with the expectation it will collapse amid a seasonal storm. That would be foolish. To build a spiritual house that lacks obedience is equally foolish. That Jesus calls them "fools" is a powerful indictment. The psalmist twice described how the fool has said in his heart, "there is no God."[17] Do you see what Jesus did? He described the disobedient and the atheist in the same way. Sure, that one may affirm that God exists, but God has no greater place in the life of the disobedient than he does in the life of the atheist. Let that sink in.

Many who disobey God still place great effort into building spiritual homes. They shed blood, sweat, and tears to overcome a lack of obedience with an abundance of good deeds, but there is a big difference between *acknowledging* Jesus as Lord and *allowing* Jesus to be Lord. Jesus affirmed this with a pointed question in Luke's treatment of this story. "Why do you call Me, 'Lord, Lord,' and do not do what I say?" (Luke 6:46). This same sentiment is echoed in a powerful engraving at a cathedral in Lübeck, Germany, which reads:

> Thus speaketh Christ our Lord to us,
> You call Me master and obey Me not,
> you call Me light and see Me not,
> you call Me the way and walk Me not,
> you call Me life and live Me not,
> you call Me wise and follow Me not,
> you call Me fair and love Me not,
> you call Me rich and ask Me not,
> you call Me eternal and seek Me not,
> if I condemn thee, blame Me not.

One can neither obtain nor maintain salvation through opinions, proclamations, and good works. Loving relationship and trusting obedience are the materials needed to build an enduring temple founded upon the Rock (John 14:15). Obedience does not produce salvation, but obedience is the product of salvation.

To fall short of what Paul called "the obedience of faith" is to lack right standing with God. As the Beloved Disciple explained,

17. Pss 14:1; 53:1.

By this we know that we have come to know Him, if we keep His commandments. The one who says, "I have come to know Him," and does not keep His commandments, is a liar, and the truth is not in him; but whoever keeps His word, in him the love of God has truly been perfected. By this we know that we are in Him: the one who says he abides in Him ought himself to walk in the same manner as He walked. (1 John 2:3–6)[18]

Many will consider John's words, and the writing on the cathedral wall, to be the controlling commands of a totalitarian deity. They are not. They serve as the loving warning to children who don't understand what disobedience really is. To disobey God is to dethrone God.

An unwillingness to obey God is a pretty good indication that either sin or self has taken priority. Remember, this is about who you choose to follow. Choose well, and you will bear the fruits of repentance. Choose poorly, and you will forfeit heaven.[19]

To obey Christ is to abide in Christ. This is why obedience is such an important and indispensable aspect of salvation, and why Paul exhorts all believers to avoid all sin. Don't obey its lusts, don't fall for its lies, and don't give it the slightest foothold. If you give sin an inch, it will become your ruler (Rom 6:12–16). Instead, be led by God. Submit to his lordship. His plan is right, and his desire is to walk with you every step of the way.

Are you ready to walk with God in such unity? Yes, me too! Let's go ahead and tell him that right now. I know you're reading a book, but we need to get in the habit of responding to God the moment he reveals truth in our lives. Through Isaiah, God declares, "Come now and let us reason together." Come now. Not later—right now. God goes on to say,

Though your sins are as scarlet, they will be as white as snow; Though they are red like crimson, they will be like wool. If you consent and obey, you will eat the best of the land; But if you refuse and rebel, you will be devoured by the sword. (Isa 1:18–20)

Let us consent and obey that we may taste and see that the Lord is good! And be sure to get your fill; in the coming sections, we will see the satanic strategies that look to steal your blessing.

---

18. Other passages to consider include John 3:20–21, 36; Acts 5:32; Rom 2:4–11; Eph 4:2–24; 2 Thess 1:8–10; Heb 5:8–10; Jas 4:17; 1 Pet 4:16–18; 1 John 1:6; 2 John 4–6, 9. In these passages, we see that obedience is a critical element of salvation.

19. 1 Cor 6:9–11; Gal 5:19–21; Eph 5:5–7; Rev 21:27.

SECTION II

When Good Seed Fails to Take Root

Others fell on the rocky places, where they did not have much soil; and immediately they sprang up, because they had no depth of soil. But when the sun had risen, they were scorched; and because they had no root, they withered away.... The one on whom seed was sown on the rocky places, this is the man who hears the word and immediately receives it with joy; yet he has no firm root in himself, but is only temporary, and when affliction or persecution arises because of the word, immediately he falls away.

—Matt 13:5-6, 20-21

It is a seed's nature to grow. It is built for growth, but internal and external factors affect germination. A seed must be planted in the right soil and be given the right amount of living water and light. That seed must not become too hot, nor too cold. Eliminate any of these factors and the seed will die. However, with the right conditions, growth will occur—and you will see *radicle* growth right from the start.

Growth is not only desired, it is necessary for survival. Seedlings soon exhaust their initial reserves, and then must be sustained from without. The radicle is the first thing to emerge. This primary root will anchor itself in the soil, which marks the beginning of "establishment." That is what we desire to be: established in the faith, firmly rooted and being built up in Christ (Col 2:7).

Countless people have progressed past our last section and are exhibiting radicle growth. They are neither hard-headed nor hard-hearted when it comes to God. They are established; they know the word, they know the word made flesh, and they obey the word. Hallelujah and glory to God!

But they are still in danger of missing heaven.

Wait, what?

That's right. The time of radicle growth is critical because the young plant is very vulnerable to injury and disease. New believers planted in God's garden are much the same. Unlike those whom Jesus will reject because they were never truly saved (and thus he never knew them), there is another group that will fail to bear fruit and therefore miss out on heaven—and Jesus knew them quite well.

This bleak reality is captured in Jesus' description of the church's latter days. Many believers will fall away, betray one another, and hate one another. Many false prophets will arise and mislead many. Amid this increasing lawlessness, the love of many will grow cold. But the one who endures to the end will be saved (Matt 24:10–13). This means salvation requires endurance. The Bible teaches that such endurance requires growth.

The Apostle Paul relayed a similar warning: Many will buy into deceitful spirits and doctrines of demons and fall away from the faith (1 Tim 4:1). Instead of accepting sound doctrine, they will choose preachers and teachers who tell them what they want to hear. They will trade the truth for a lie, and they will pay an eternal price (2 Tim 4:3–5).

Peter also gave ample warning. While the Lord is able to rescue the godly from destruction (Peter offered Noah and Lot as examples), salvation rests on the response of each individual. Many will forsake the right way and go astray. Though a right relationship with Jesus delivered them from sin and death, many will return to their old ways and become entangled in a web of deceit. Worse than a rejection of Christ's initial invitation, this is a betrayal of grace. When God's judgment is rendered, it would have been better had they never known the way of righteousness (2 Pet 2).

Those are just a few examples, and each are downright scary. Thus, the rest of our discussion will not center on the many Jesus never knew, but the many he knew only for a while. This will begin with a look at people who know, love, and obey God . . . for a season. Many will fall away when they hit stony ground—a hard situation they can't get over, or a hard individual they can't go around. If the problem and believer are not handled well, the growth that started strong will come to a quick halt. If the hindrance is not removed, that Christian will wither and die.

Growth is necessary to sustain life even after that good seed of God's word has been planted in our hearts. The Christian must be rooted downward and bearing fruit upward (cf. Isa 37:31). In this section, we will look at the stones that so often stop spiritual growth: offense and unforgiveness, fear and shame, solitude and temptation, comfort and complacency. In Section III, we will look at the weeds that choke out the fruit that results from spiritual life and growth.

This may challenge you a bit, especially if you have bought into the idea that Christianity is sugar and spice, and everything nice. It's not. As the great C. S. Lewis rightly noted, "I didn't go to religion to make me happy. I always knew a bottle of Port would do that. If you want a religion to make you feel really comfortable, I certainly don't recommend Christianity."[1]

Suffice it to say, Christianity ain't for wimps. It requires you to take up your cross daily. To love your enemies. Bless them who curse you. Do good for them who hate you. Pray for those who spitefully use you. Show mercy to those who offer none. To give, and to forgive. To love unconditionally. To extend grace without agenda or expectation. If you think those things are easy, you haven't done them.

Christianity requires you to be like Christ, and that means you can expect to face the same trials and troubles he faced.[2] There will come a day when you are betrayed by a very close friend, perhaps even betrayed with a kiss. At some point, you will be abandoned by many you hold dear. You will be wrongly accused and openly slandered. Beaten down and left for dead. There may even be times you feel forsaken by God. Such "stones" are hard situations that can bring spiritual growth to a sudden stop. This is of critical importance; in God's garden, that which is not growing is dying (John 15:1–11).

Sounds kind of depressing, huh? It may even sound like I've been possessed by the spirit of Eeyore. Not at all. Nothing has brought more blessing and joy than my life with Christ. Believe me, I've tried just about everything the world has to offer (and even came up with a few concoctions of my own), but nothing has come near the satisfaction. Not even close. But I am well aware of the fact there are serpents slithering around in my garden, just

1. Lewis, *God in the Dock*, 48.

2. Matt 5:11–12; John 15:18–20; 16:33; 17:14–19; Jas 1:2–4; 1 Pet 4:12–19; 1 John 3:13.

waiting for the chance to strike. I know there are wolves in sheep's clothing. I know there are tares among the wheat. Though it may sound strange, I am okay with that. As long as I am rooted in God, they can't bring me down. They only build me up.

Still, hitting a hard time is never fun. It can drain the life right out of you, and that is Satan's goal. But Satan is not the only one who makes use of our trials and tribulations. In fact, these often serve as the best indicators of where you need (and God desires) spiritual growth. You see, we are much like sponges, and if you ever want to know what is in a sponge, all you have to do is squeeze it. Every time I am squeezed, the pressure reveals what is in me—the good, the bad, and the ugly. Are there times I am squeezed unjustly? Of course. The same thing happened to Jesus and the apostles, so why should I expect anything different? What they did to Christ, they do to Christians. What matters is what comes out.

You have a few choices when you are squeezed. You can quit. Many do. Or you can succumb to Eeyore's moody blue melancholy, cast your eyes downward, and wallow in self-pity. Many do. Or you can look up. You can look up with the knowledge that God will make all things work together for your good. Yeah, being squeezed may reveal some things that were buried deep within; things you didn't want to see, or that you didn't know were in there. It may leave you feeling empty inside. Take heart: God answers your emptiness with his fullness! What they did to Jesus, they do to us—but what Jesus revealed in response, he now pours into us. The great thing about a squeezed sponge is that it is ready to be refilled. That is one of the great ways God makes all things work together for your good.

We are going to talk about hitting some hard times in the coming pages. Whether you continue to grow in the faith will be largely determined by whether you see these stones as obstacles or opportunities. Fair warning: even the right choice does not mean these stones won't hurt when you hit them. I've certainly taken my share of lumps along the way (many of which were self-inflicted). Have I hit hard times? It's more like I am hit by hard times. Like a freight train. I often feel like Wile E. Coyote taking another anvil to the face. Perhaps you know the feeling.

Amid the anvil impacts, I have come to learn four important truths. First, Christianity is a battleground, not a playground, and it is necessary that we approach it as such. Second, because the battle is the Lord's, the victory is already won! That was certainly the attitude of a young fellow named David in 1 Samuel 17:45–47. He did not let stones stop him, but instead used them to his advantage and—well, you know the story. Third, God is not caught unaware by the stones we hit (or that hit us). In fact, he uses them to prepare us for future fights.[3] Fourth, we should never fight alone. Though David picked up five stones, it was his friends who took out Goliath's four angry family members.[4]

We will elaborate in the coming pages. First, allow me to illustrate the point with one of my more whimsical revelations. It started when I put a work shed in the backyard. Rather than Eeyore, my wife thought I had the spirit of Tigger come over me, as I bounced from spot to spot. This shed would be a man haven for all my tools; a place where I could fix things, build things, and waste a lot of time doing a bunch of nothing. There was only one problem: the backyard was as dark as the devil's heart. I could not see well enough to differentiate the shed key from a piano key. Even if I did, I could not see well enough to get the key into the key hole. I'm not saying it was scary or anything (don't be ridick-erous), but the dilemma did stiffen my bounce a bit.

I soon had a solution (hoo-hoo-hoo-hoo!). I would erect a light pole outside the shed. I found a good one at a good price. Having invested some money, I invested some time and energy. I grabbed my shovel and started to dig. I knew this job would not be easy since the shed sat on Virginia clay, but I had pumped myself up and was convinced the effort would pay off. Light would overcome the darkness!

At the cavernous depth of fifteen inches I heard the unmistakable sound of steel hitting stone. Not *a* stone, mind you. Solid stone. I spent extra time and energy digging sideways in an effort to determine how big and bad my new adversary really was. He was pretty big and bad. I could be sitting on Gibraltar for all I knew. A little unlikely for Virginia, I will grant you, but it was evident Eeyore was smothering Tigger right before my eyes. My motivation and desperation for light began to wane. Maybe I could just bring a flashlight from now on. How often do I come out here at night, anyway? This really isn't worth the effort.

---

3. In allowing him to square off against a lion and a bear, God was preparing the young shepherd David for the giant he would face in the future (1 Sam 17:34–37). When David realized this, his next step was to refuse Saul's armor. He didn't need it. There is no reason to fight with man's attitudes and attributes when our weapons are mighty in God (cf. 2 Cor 10:3–5, Eph 6:10–18).

4. These giants were taken out by Abishai, Elhanan, Jonathan (David's nephew, not Saul's son), and Sibbechai (2 Sam 21:16–22).

The outcome may have been different if I knew how to overcome the obstacle, if I had the right tools to dig deep, or a few people to help me break through. I had none of these. I gave up on going deeper, and that shed was shrouded in darkness for many seasons to come.

It may sound like Eeyore had triumphed. Not at all. The wonderful thing about Tiggers, is Tiggers are wonderful things. The top is made out of rubber, and the bottom made out of springs. Put another way, I tend to bounce back. What follows are some lessons learned as I have contended with hard people and hard problems. God always provides the right tools and the right friends that I may persevere. He will do the same for you.

So come on, Rabbit, we've gotta lotta bouncin' to do!

5

Many Hit Stones of Offense and Unforgiveness

WHEN WE TALK ABOUT stones that stop Christian growth, there is no better place to start than offense. Few things hit us harder, and boy, is it easy to be offended these days. From public protests to road rage, the daily news cycle is inundated with people who are offended, and pretty vocal about it. The issue is so bad that many people get offended at hearing the word "offended" because the word is usually followed by the (often unwarranted) demand to be heard, to be compensated, or to be accommodated. As noted by Köstenberger, "[t]olerance has become such a god in our culture that not to have it is heresy. The effect is that tolerance swallows up truth, negating any need to search for things that might offend or challenge our preferences."[1]

The church is certainly not immune. Offense is a primary reason people give when leaving a church. Noted author and church analyst Thom Rainer once shared top reasons people gave for quitting their church. You may want to sit down for this.

- "The worship leader refused to listen to me about the songs and music I wanted."

- "The pastor did not feed me."

- "No one from my church visited me."

1. Köstenberger et. al., *Truth Matters*, 8.

- "I was not about to support the building program they wanted."

- "I was out two weeks and no one called me."

- "They moved the times of the worship services and it messed up my schedule."

- "I told my pastor to go visit my cousin and he never did."[2]

Biblical offense is very real, very crippling, and very soon to be addressed. Before we tackle the topic, we need to define biblical offense. I am not speaking of people who get mad when they don't get what they want. I am not speaking of Christians who will not receive biblical correction or reconcile differences in a biblical way. I am not talking about people who come into the house of God singing his praises and seeking his blessings, but get mad because someone didn't say hello, or didn't shake their hand, or sat in their seat. That is not biblical offense, that is a lack of biblical maturity. I don't mean that in a critical or harsh way. You cannot expect a toddler to have the maturity of a young adult, or that young adult to have the maturity of a senior adult. Still, many Christians are neither taught nor expected to grow up, and this is a deadly deficiency that demands full attention (which we will give later in this section). But this is not biblical offense.

A right definition of biblical offense also disqualifies those who manipulate a situation in order to gain leverage or control. That person is not offended, he is ungodly. This behavior is most common in churches that give priority to entitlement over empowerment, and rights over responsibilities. In these, church membership more closely resembles club membership. Patrons pay their "dues," and expect the staff to meet their demands and expectations. If not, they will leave the church, often under the banner of offense.

The Bible's definition of offense does not speak of someone who is puffed up, but rather one who is torn apart. The offended individual is dealing with a situation (be it real or perceived) that has ripped a heart out. The injury may have been caused by a family member, by a church member, maybe even be a member of the pastoral staff.[3] Such matters must be addressed, and there is a biblical way to address them.

The word translated "offense" is drawn from the Greek word *skandalon*. It is from this we get the English word "scandal." Therefore, biblical

2. Rainer, "Main Reason People Leave a Church," para. 5.

3. Notice in Galatians 5:7 that Paul does not ask *what* has hindered you, but rather *who* has hindered you from obeying the truth.

offense is not a matter of posturing or pouting. Something scandalous has taken place. That root word is used throughout the New Testament to describe a trap or snare used to entice one to sin, an obstacle used to make one stumble, or behavior that causes one to fall away.[4] It is evident that offense is a preferred tactic of the enemy. Treat it as such.

The Apostolic Fathers knew the power of offense all too well. This second generation of church leaders was centered on three men: Clement, Ignatius, and Polycarp. The trio led a young and dispersed church through unimaginable difficulties. The apostles had been martyred, persecution was rampant, and false doctrine was trying to creep in. The Fathers knew success required unity with God and fellow believers. Now, they had different opinions on how this godly unity was best achieved. The answer, for Clement, was humility. For Ignatius, it was leadership, and for Polycarp, it was discipleship. Despite the different approaches, the trio knew that unity was non-negotiable. That much has not changed.

Please know that unity and proximity are not synonymous. Tie two tomcats by their tails and they will be united, but they will not be in unity. Therefore, unity is not achieved when we learn to deal with someone, or simply bite our tongues. True communion (*koinonia*) is centered on godly love and selfless service. Godly unity demands a great commitment to the Great Commandment; it demands participants have the same purposes and perspectives; that they be of one heart. This unity of heart (upward and outward) is the work of the Spirit through sanctification, and it is the desire of God.

Many parents and grandparents know the frustrations of dealing with children who are not in unity. Multiply that by the size of your church, and you will get a taste of what Sundays can be like for God. Indeed, he loves it when his children play well together, yet God's call for unity runs deeper than the lack of infighting. To be in unity with God and each other is to reside within the Trinity's embrace. This is the goal of salvation, and the reason disunity is a key satanic strategy.

External opposition will never destroy a body of believers (Exod 1:8–12). Internal strife, on the other hand, will tear those believers apart. A house divided cannot stand. Remember, the main consequence of sin is alienation from God, from one another, and from your true self. Offense will widen the chasm of all three. Conversely, believers who stand in unity

---

4. Cf. Matt 13:41; 16:23; 18:7; Luke 17:1; Rom 11:9; 14:13; 16:17; 1 Cor 8:9–13; Gal 5:11; 1 John 2:10; Rev 2:14.

will be saturated in great power and great grace, the kind needed to fulfill your hopes and calling (Acts 4:32–33). So powerful is this unity that God's word likens it to the precious oil that is poured on Aaron's head, and runs down his beard (Ps 133:1–3). It is said that Aaron's beard reached to the ground—ZZ Top had nothing on that guy! Here is the beauty of that analogy: when brethren are united, the anointing poured on the head (which is Christ) covers the whole body (which is the church). Our love for God and each other are the threads that unite. If these come unraveled, God's grace and power will slip through the seams.

Offense thus remains a preferred tactic of our enemy. We are not ignorant of a solution; there is a wealth of material that addresses how we are to handle offensive people, offended people, and personal offense. Countless books, articles, and sermons tell us what makes people tick, and what ticks people off. These resources tell us how to cope, how to confront, and how to overcome offense. No, that's not the problem. The problem is, we don't really understand its deadly effects. If we did, overcoming offense would be a priority in every church and Christian home. Instead, we shrug our shoulders, walk on egg shells around certain people, cave in to their demands, and offer unbiblical concessions in the name of compassion and patience.

That is why *skandalon* remains one of Satan's favorite stones. Satan hit Judas with one of these stones. The disciple was offended by Mary's extravagant worship, and it contributed to his betrayal of Christ. Satan even tried to take out Jesus with this stone (Matt 16:23). Satan continues to use the festering pain and resentment that results from harmful actions and words to halt the growth of many Christians, and to convince many to give up the fight. This should not happen, but it should come as no surprise. When asked to describe the last days, Jesus said that many will be offended and fall away. This will lead to betrayal and hatred among believers. The bitter infighting that follows is an invitation to ungodly counsel leading to lawlessness (Matt 24:10–13). I can think of no better example than Job.

Satan had been given permission to afflict Job. You probably know what happens in the first three chapters—Job loses his wealth, his health, and his children. His wife also seems to lose her faith. Just when you think it can't get any worse, Job's friends come knocking at his door. I submit to you that their counsel is Satan's most lethal snare. The demonic intent is to bring offense that will drive Job to curse God. The demonic influence is evident in Job 4:12–21, when Eliphaz described a creepy vision that came to him one night and instilled a fear that shook him to the very core. He could sense a spirit in the room but could not see it. Then came a whisper: can mortals be righteous before God?[5]

The "godly counsel" Job's friends provided was quite pointed. They argued that Job was unable or unwilling to see that he had fallen short. Can you imagine? Job's children are dead. His business is destroyed. His life's work has vanished. He is in failing health, and his wife has given up hope. Now his friends show up and inform Job that he is not right with God and not hearing from God. There must be sin in his life, and that is why God must be angry with him. At this moment, a bad seed had been planted, and it only needed the right conditions to grow.

This attack was far more effective than all the previous attempts. Job was adamant that he had done nothing to deserve such punishment, and thus demanded explanation from God. Amid the three debates that comprise much of the book, Job came to realize that Eliphaz has been deceived and directed by the accuser rather than God (Job 26:1–4). Ultimately, God gave Job double for his trouble—the Lord gave Job twice as much as he had before. How Job came to receive this double blessing is telling. The favor didn't flow when he stood on God's word, even as his wife urged him to curse God and die. Job didn't get this double blessing when he worshiped God, even though his health was deteriorating. Job didn't get this double blessing when he proclaimed his intent to serve God no matter what. The Bible says the Lord restored Job's fortunes once he prayed for his friends (Job 42:10). The self-righteous ones. The ones who were quick to accuse him. The ones who demanded to be right. The ones who said they had a word from God but did not. Why did Job's blessing depend on his prayer of forgiveness? Because "many will be offended, will betray one another, and will hate one another. Then many false prophets will rise up and deceive many. Because lawlessness will abound, the love of many will grow cold. But he who endures to the end shall be saved." The only way to endure until the end is to forgive. This breaks the power of offense and silences the false prophecy that would lead you to reject God's word and will.[6]

When offense occurs, you can expect false prophets to arise. Many are much like Job's friends. False prophets are not satanic priests with hooded robes and black hearts. A false prophet is one who speaks in God's name

---

5. Not only does Satan repeat the question-strategy employed in Eden, but the Hebrew language conveyed in Genesis 3 and Job 4 suggests his dialogue with Adam and Eve was in much the same whisper.

6. This Bible does not record the words of Job's prayer, but I imagine it might have sounded something like "Please forgive them, for they know not what they do."

what God has not said.[7] Most often, these are well-meaning Christians, ministers, and pastors who are simply trying to help, trying to keep the peace—and some are simply trying to keep people from leaving their church.[8] Pastors and church leaders have become masters at negotiating cease fires in this era of offense. This is a good and necessary skill, but if not careful, we can set Satan's snares. We do this by succumbing to societal standards that prioritize personal preference and rights. To keep the peace, many pastors and church leaders simply placate and accommodate; they address the visible symptoms, but not the root cause. The results are catastrophic, because the deception that occurs (even if unintended) leads straight to lawlessness.

Striking a peace treaty may bring peace for a season, but not for a soul.[9] The failure to bring biblical direction (and possibly correction) only deceives people into believing their conduct and condition are acceptable. They are not. As Jesus warned, an offense that remains rooted deep within will grow into outright lawlessness. Such a believer now shares the same fate as those whom Jesus never knew and cast out.

This scenario reminds me of that creepy little creature in the movie *Alien*. Offense will continue to grow and feed off of a person until they are destroyed from within. In the movie, the chest-busting slug soon becomes a full-grown alien with a really bad attitude. It is happy to chew you up, bones and all, and leave nothing that resembles what once had been. As scary as this sounds, you know the bad guy in the movie. He looks nothing like you; his appearance gives him away. Christians are not as fortunate. On our battlefield, the enemy often looks like everyone else. Christians, much like Job's friends, can quickly turn carnivorous. Personally, meat-eating sheep scare me more than that alien.[10] Because their offense is allowed to grow into lawlessness, they quickly devour through gossip, accusation, hatred, and outright attack. General Joab is a good example.

---

7. Deut 18:20; Jer 23:18–32; Ezek 13:1–2.

8. Good counsel is not always God counsel, and even a *skandalon* can seem to make sense. Therefore, test all spirits to see whether they are from God (1 John 4:1; cf. 2 Cor 11:13–15; 1 Thess 5:21).

9. That is the difference between a peacekeeper and a peacemaker, and Jesus only blesses the latter.

10. I know that sheep are not meat eaters, but some in God's flock tend to cannibalize from time to time. There is nothing quite as frightening as a little old lady who goes for the jugular. That kind of stuff sticks with you.

The valiant warrior won many battles and destroyed the enemies of the Lord time and again. His devotion placed him in close proximity to the king, but Joab also had a tendency to disobey the king. One time, David showed mercy to Absalom, his son, and ordered the boy be spared. Joab defied the king's direction. He thought the rebel deserved to die and took matters into his own hands. He even berated David for weeping over the death of Absalom.[11]

Soon after, David promoted Amasa to commander of the army. Though Joab deserved a demotion (or worse), and Amasa was the better choice, Joab was deeply offended when he came to see his new boss. That Joab's sword fell out of its sheath as he drew near is very telling. As Christian soldiers, we put on the whole armor of God. One component is the sword of the Spirit, which is the word of God (Eph 6:10–18). Beware of offended believers who have dropped their sword. They are the ones most likely to attack the king's anointed, and that is exactly what happened. Joab called Amasa "friend," and leaned in to give him a kiss of fellowship. This was no doubt a moment of great honor and excitement for Amasa, to be recognized by such a great man of God! It was then that the unsuspecting Amasa felt the sting of Joab's blade. The mighty man of God feigned friendship only to get close enough to destroy Amasa, and thus protect his own position (2 Sam 20:4–13).[12]

Joab's example is one of offense growing into lawlessness. If offense is left unaddressed, or addressed with ungodly counsel, the individual's focus will turn inward rather than outward; the demand to be heard, compensated, and accommodated will dictate actions and attitudes. Then, the offended will go on the offensive. It is here, Jesus warned, that the love of many will grow cold.

Now we are really in trouble.

As discussed in the last section, salvation is dependent on our love for God and one another. Without love, you are without God (1 John 4:7–21), and how can one be in right standing with God when God is nowhere to be found? God takes this love thing pretty seriously—yet, many Christians

---

11. 2 Sam 18:1–18; 19:1–7. This is a bit of reaping and sowing for King David. When he needed to get rid of Uriah after his adulterous affair with the man's wife, Bathsheba, David told Joab to take care of it (2 Sam 11:14–17). You can't use this spirit to silence your adversaries and not expect it to come back and bite you.

12. It is worth noting that, despite all of his great victories, Joab is not included when 2 Samuel 23 lists the heroes and valiant men of Israel during David's reign.

commonly say things such as "we have to love people, but we don't have to like them."

Really? Really?!

Such attitude is nothing but ungodly counsel that leads to lawlessness. As Christians, we must have a great commitment to the Great Commandment. A young scholar of Scripture learned this the hard way when, in an attempt to put Jesus to the test, asked, "What is the greatest commandment of all?"[13] Jesus had 613 commandments from which to choose.[14] Without a moment's hesitation, he said, "Love the Lord your God with all your heart, soul, mind, and strength. The second is like it. Love your neighbor as yourself. Upon these rests all of the Law and prophets."

The young theologian was blown away. He commended Jesus, and agreed, "there is one God, and besides him there is no other." It would seem he had our first section covered well. He went on to agree that the love Jesus described is better than any religious activity. This guy is two-for-two. The young man had acknowledged the truth of God, and the truth of love. Now, don't miss this: Jesus saw the answers were genuine and heartfelt, and told the scholar, "You are not far from the kingdom of God."

To know you are not far from the kingdom of God may seem comforting, but "not far" is "not there." This man knew who God is, and he knew what the scriptures said about love, but he had still come up short because he had done nothing about it. Close, but not quite.

Knowledge of God is the right starting point, but a terrible stopping point. Once we come to know the greatness of God, we express it through the Great Commandment. Make no mistake, love is a verb in God's vocabulary. The Apostle Paul put it this way:

> Love is patient, love is kind and is not jealous; love does not brag and is not arrogant, does not act unbecomingly; it does not seek its own, is not provoked, does not take into account a wrong suffered, does not rejoice in unrighteousness, but rejoices with the truth; bears all things, believes all things, hopes all things, endures all things. Love never fails." (1 Cor 13:4–8a)

That stands in stark contrast to the offense we have discussed, does it not? That is why the stone of offense is a favorite weapon in the adversary's

13. Matt 22:34–40; Mark 12:28–34.

14. That's right, there are a few more than the Ten Commandments that hang on your grandma's wall. The Jewish Talmud identifies 248 positive commandments (do this), and 365 negative commandments (don't do this) in the Torah.

arsenal. Growth in God's love will come to a quick halt when it hits the stone of offense. If that stone is not handled properly, infighting will invite false prophecy. Without the truth of God, people fall into outright lawlessness and handle the matter in worldly ways. Because they operate contrary to God's word and will, godly love grows cold. When this happens, bitterness and unforgiveness will take root, and many will be lost (Heb 12:15).

Jesus discussed the need to overcome such bitterness and unforgiveness in Luke 17:1–10. He opened with a warning: it is inevitable that offenses/stumbling blocks will come. Be on your guard! If your brother sins, correct him; if he repents, forgive him. Every time.[15]

Of course, repeated forgiveness is easier said than done. Seeing the difficulty, the disciples asked Jesus to increase their faith. That was a nice way of saying they would need a whole lot of faith and love to deal with some people. Jesus' answer was profound: you don't need an increase of faith to overcome offense, you just need to exercise what faith you have. Fail to do this, and the results will be disastrous. Jesus pointed to the sycamine tree to illustrate.

The sycamine, or black mulberry, is very similar to the sycamore, or white mulberry. Their fruits are identical in appearance, but unlike the delicious sycamore fig, the fruit of the sycamine is revoltingly bitter. That bitter fruit grows courtesy of a root structure that delves as much as thirty feet in depth to feed off of unseen things hidden well below the surface. Because those roots reach so deep, the sycamine is difficult to kill. You can cut away what you see on the surface in an effort to keep things in check (a Christianity of concession), but the bad fruit will return if the root is not removed.

Here is another fun fact: the wood of a sycamine tree was a favorite for crafting caskets. How poetic. Let unforgiveness and bitterness take root, and they will bury you, spiritually and physically.

On the other hand, he who endures to the end shall be saved.

Okay, so how do we endure?

We just have to uproot the unforgiveness and remove the stones of offense.

Okay, so how do we do that?

All you need is love.

God is love, and love is all you need. John the Beloved was onto this long before John Lennon. As the apostle explained, God is love. The one who abides in love abides in God, and God abides in him. This is how love

---

15. Cf. Eph 4:30–32; Col 3:13; 2 Pet 1:9.

is perfected in us, and by this we can have confidence on the day of judgment; "as he is, so are we in this world" (1 John 4:16b–17). That pretty much sums up everything we have read thus far. Only nine words, each one syllable, yet profound beyond our understanding.

As he is. God is total love. We are not talking about an emotion or fondness. God's love is defined as divine self-giving. He made himself totally vulnerable to bring us into a greater and deeper relationship than we could ever imagine. God does not simply accept us, he embraces us. This love is our example. In the same way that Jesus loves us, we are to love one another (John 15:8–12). As he is, so we are in this world.

That kind of love is an action and a choice. How, then, do we love our enemies? We bless those who curse us, do good to those who hate us, and pray for those who spitefully use and persecute us (Matt 5:44). Because the fruit of the Spirit is love, then we share that fruit by instilling joy and peace in everyone we meet. We extend goodness, kindness, and gentleness, and we demonstrate patience, faithfulness, and self-control toward all and at all times.[16] Why is this? Because salvation is not a demonstration of power, but a demonstration of love.

We live in a church age in which many are interested only in God's power and provision. Now, I love to see the power of God at work, but I am always mindful of Paul's insight captured in 1 Corinthians 13. He said you can speak with the tongues of men and of angels, but without love, you are just making a bunch of noise. You can prophecy and understand all mysteries and knowledge, and have the faith to remove mountains, but without love, you are nothing. You can give all your goods to the poor, and give your body to be burned, but if you don't have love, it is of no value. Love is what matters most.

Granted, love can be difficult sometimes. After all, stones are hard. But loving those who make it so hard to love is the way of Christ. God demonstrated his own love toward us by sending Christ to the cross, even while we were still sinning (Rom 5:8). We were not sinking in sin, mind you. We were swimming in sin. We were having a good 'ol time, just splashing around. Yet God loved us and was ready to forgive us.

Forgiveness is one of the greatest ways we demonstrate the love we have received. Have you ever heard the phrase "forgiveness is not for them, it is for you"? Though well-intentioned, such sentiment is biblically inaccurate. God calls on believers to forgive others for the sake of all involved.

16. 1 Cor 13:4–8; Gal 5:22–23.

Was this not the example of Christ? Jesus had the authority to forgive sins.[17] Yet even as the wounds of crucifixion sent unimaginable pain shooting through his body, Jesus cried out "Father, forgive them, they don't know what they are doing" (Luke 23:34). He cried out on their behalf.

For whom was Jesus praying? The Roman soldiers? Yes. The Jewish leaders? Yes. Anyone else? Sure. Pontius Pilate, and the people who falsely accused him. Maybe the ones who chose Barabbas over Jesus. Yeah, them too. How about the disciples? You know, the one who had denied Christ, and the ones who had abandoned Jesus in his darkest hour. The ones he loved so dearly yet hurt him so deeply. Yes Father, please forgive *them*. They don't know. They don't really realize the damage offense and bitterness can cause. But Jesus knows. He would not allow bitterness to take root, and his love never grew cold (and never will).

The forgiveness you offer is not only expected, it is effective. When Jesus declared that "whatever you bind on earth shall have been bound in heaven; and whatever you loose on earth shall have been loosed in heaven," he was not talking about engagement with demons (though that passage is often used in such context). Jesus was talking about biblical correction, and he made clear that the forgiveness you extend is honored by heaven.[18]

Thus, your forgiveness manifests the Great Commandment in the work of overcoming the alienation from God, others, and self that results from sin. Your willingness to forgive first overcomes the alienation between you and God. He cannot and will not forgive you unless you have forgiven all others.[19] Why? Because forgiveness overcomes the alienation between you and the other party. In forgiving them, you place the offender into God's hands in the hope of God's blessing and the understanding that their behavior is the result of a fallen condition. There are few things more Christlike than this.

Forgiveness not only restores unity with God and others, but it enables God to restore your broken heart and set you free from the emotional prisons that alienate (Isa 61:1). Thus, your willingness to forgive has thwarted alienation on all levels! Conversely, a failure to forgive will cause further alienation on all levels.

Whether the offense is between you and God, or you and someone else, biblical forgiveness requires the offense be made known and repentance be

17. Matt 9:6; Mark 2:10; Luke 5:24; 7:47.

18. Matt 18:15–19; John 20:23.

19. Matt 6:12–15; 18:35; Mark 11:25–26; Luke 11:4.

offered (Luke 17:1–4). These are challenging commands. It is far easier to sweep the matter under the rug, act as if it never happened, and let bygones be bygones. But without repentance, there can be no forgiveness.[20] Consider the insights of John Stott on this issue:

> Does this startle you? It is what Jesus taught. Oh, we must "forgive" him in the sense that our thoughts towards him are free of all animosity and full of love. But this is not Christian forgiveness. "Forgiveness" means more than that; it includes restoration to fellowship. If we can restore to full and intimate fellowship with ourselves a sinning and unrepentant brother, we reveal not the depth of our love but its shallowness, for we are doing what is not for his highest good. A forgiveness which bypasses the need for repentance issues not from love but from sentimentality."[21]

A forgiveness that does not require repentance demonstrates preservation of self rather than love for God and others. It allows the offended to carry on without reliving or confronting the acts that have alienated, and thus, the root remains. God desires to uproot that problem so no more bad fruit may grow. The biblical model therefore necessitates repentance, received with forgiveness and restoration of fellowship.[22] By this, alienation is averted at every level.

There is no question that such forgiveness can be difficult. It can be painful, and downright sacrificial. But remember, Jesus' ultimate demonstration of love was not in what he said on the cross, but what he gave on the cross. It was his death, more than all the good things Jesus did during his life, that fully demonstrated his love. This is the ultimate expression of love; in his death, Jesus gave all that he had to save us. He held nothing back.

As he is, so are we in this world.

Take a moment to think of someone who has wounded you deeply. It may be a friend, a family member, or perhaps it was one of those carnivorous Christians. I'm not asking you to dwell on the way they attacked you, or the scars that remain. Instead of focusing on what they did *to you*, I want you to consider what they did *for you*. You see, to be carnivorous means you are a flesh eater. If we allow the carnivorous Christian to devour our flesh, our carnal nature, all that remains is the Spirit of God who dwells in us!

---

20. Luke 13:3, 5; Rev 2:5.

21. Stott, *Confess Your Sins*, 28–29.

22. Matt 7:1–5; 18:15–18; Luke 17:1–4; Gal 6:1–2; Jas 5:19–20.

Those carnivorous Christians may have hit you like an Acme anvil to the face. They may have adversely affected your Christian growth. They may have left you offended. I encourage you to not focus on who's right or wrong. Focus instead on the goal of offense—to make you stumble and fall away; to evict love and invite lawlessness. But when you forgive, the offense no longer has power over you. The love of God has power over you, and over them! In that understanding, consider the words of Psalm 27:2: "When evildoers came upon me to devour my flesh, my adversaries and my enemies, they stumbled and fell."

Your true enemy is not the one who offended (they know not what they do). Your true enemy is the one who inspired the offense. But when you walk in godly love, the evildoers who came upon you to devour shall stumble and fall! Don't you just love it when the devil gets a taste of his own medicine!?

Let love give you victory over the vicious, but know this: if Satan can't cause your love to grow cold, he will look to make your faith fall flat.

6

Many Hit Stones of Fear and Shame

AS WE CONTINUE TO remove these stifling stones from our spiritual gardens, let's return for a moment to our discussion of Adam and Eve. Their great failure and sin was to act on the desire to be God, rather than be godly. When things went terribly wrong, they made another great mistake: the dynamic duo tried to hide from the only one who could help them. The reason for this? They were naked and afraid (Gen 3:10).

Mankind has been playing hide-and-seek with God ever since that fateful day, and we will continue to play this game to the very end. Take a peek at Revelation 6 and you will see that many on the day of God's judgment will beg the mountains and rocks to hide them. Why? Because their guilt will be evident and will evoke much fear. But you don't have to wait until the end of days to see this game played out. People all around you see their own nakedness and try to hide their shortfalls and shame in prosperity, popularity, and personal achievement. Many try to hide in a bottle or a needle. Many try to hide in solitude. Many try to hide within their own intellect, good deeds, or flawed logic.

Many hide, as did my son when he was a toddler. He would sit upright in the middle of my bed and throw a blanket over his head. A child's logic believes that if he can't see me, then I must not be able to see him. But his father knew exactly where he was the whole time, even though the boy was allowed to remain under his inadequate covering for a little while.

Adam and Eve took a similar approach, but theirs was no game. They went into hiding because they didn't want to face God. Guilt has a way of doing that. Don't judge them too harshly; deep down inside, we often hide for the same reason. In the words of Isaiah, every one of us have gone on our own wayward path (we choose to be God rather than be godly). Jesus is despised and rejected because his goodness only illuminates our lack of goodness, and humans don't do well with such realization. Isaiah went on to say that many hide their faces from Jesus. As a result, they are unable to see that Jesus is heartbroken and grieved, that he lovingly offers to carry our griefs and sorrows, and that he endured the crushing death of the cross to free us from the penalty of death (Isa 53:3–6).

Yet we hide. We hide because we don't want to face our failures. We hide because we don't want to face the consequences of our sins. We hide because we don't want to face God. If your Christian walk has been halted by the fear of what God may say or do, by what God thinks of you, consider the question God asked Adam.

"Where are you?"

God is not seeking information when he asks a question. God knew exactly where they were. Yet, there was great purpose in this question. It represented the distance that sin had caused between God and man.[1]

Satan's query made them question God. God's query made them question themselves. Where are you? Where has this disobedience brought you? Has that forbidden fruit provided all the pleasure it promised? Where are you? Are you unable to walk with God because you're busy trying to hide sin from him? Have you found true peace and joy apart from him?

Where are you?

We have discussed what Satan is all about—he wants you to be your own God, rather than be godly. Then, when you realize the error of your ways, Satan stands ready to beat you down with criticism and condemnation. But in this story, we also see what God is all about. Notice that it is God who comes looking for Adam, even while Adam is hiding. Thankfully, he continues to seek and save those who are lost.[2] God knows where you are, and why you are hiding. Don't run from the only one who can help you. Instead, consider the question God asked when Adam and Eve came out of hiding: "Who told you that you are naked?" God wasn't the one who had hit

---

1. There is no hiding from God (Jer 23:24). But what if God decided to hide from you? What hope would you have? The reality is, sin causes this very scenario (Isa 59:2; 64:7; Ezek 39:23–24; Mic 3:4).

2. As discussed in Section I, our salvation is not the result of us "coming to God." We are not saved because we "found Jesus." Jesus wasn't the one who was lost! Jesus found us while we were hiding in our sins. Aren't you glad to know he is looking for you today?

them with that knowledge. God was not the one who triggered that shame. That was Satan's handiwork. In this, we see that Satan uses shame and fear to keep us in hiding. If you are in hiding, you are not abiding. If you are not abiding, you are not growing. If you are not growing, you are withering. If you are withering, you are dying.

Shame will keep you from walking with God. Fear will keep you from fulfilling God's purpose for your life. These are spiritual stones that will keep you from going forth, and from growing forth.

My friend, you have nothing of which to be ashamed. That little voice may be saying, "yes, but you don't know what I've done." No, I don't know what you have done. But God does. You are no more hiding from the Father than my son was hiding from me. You may think you are, but God knows right where you are at, and exactly what you have done. And do you know what? He still loves you. He knows you are damaged goods, yet he still accepts delivery. It is time to come out of hiding.

A great example is the healing of a man with a withered hand.[3] This condition was reason for great shame in Jesus' day. Most people believed someone so afflicted must be cursed of God. They would avoid him for fear of becoming unclean. His handicap would inhibit, if not prohibit, his ability to earn a living. Such deformity would disqualify him from the priestly service and proximity to God (Lev 21:16–23). Imagine the shock when Jesus told the man to stretch forth his hand, to expose the deep shame that had been hidden for years! In this command, Jesus let the man know that he knew all about his condition, and there was no reason to be ashamed. It also shows us that God will not undo what we won't uncover.

Many seek to overcome shame with the approval and acceptance of others. This can be an addiction as strong as any drug, lust, or greed. In an effort to satisfy the constant cravings, many will work tirelessly to gain accomplishments and affirmations of a spouse, boss, friend, or family member. Inevitably, your desires and dreams will take a back seat to their expectations, only to find (time and again) that you've come up short. Even when you net achievements and affirmations, they prove as unsatisfying as the pig pods eaten by the prodigal (Luke 15:11).

We are often left feeling like we've fallen short and are nothing more than a failure. Feelings of shame and inadequacy are barriers that keep you from going where God wants you to go, doing what God wants you to do, and being who God wants you to be. This is not God's plan for our lives. We

3. Matt 12:9–14; Mark 3:1–5; Luke 6:6–11.

are to be content in him (Phil 4:10–13) and to find our identity in Christ (Eph 2:10).

Stop sacrificing your true self to become something others want you to be. This is detrimental, and potentially disastrous to your ability to grow and abide in Christ. The pursuit of plaudits and popularity will enslave you, and you cannot serve two masters. The one who seeks the affirmation of man cannot be a servant of Christ.[4] Are you a slave to the expectations of man, or a servant to the exaltations of God?

For those with people-pleasing tendencies, allow me to give you two revelations: first, you will never meet their expectations. Second, you never had to. God's opinion is the only one that matters. That doesn't mean you turn your back on people. We are still servants to all, but we are no longer slaves to their expectations. We learn *who* we are by learning *whose* we are, and then we grow in and from that understanding.

Sadly, many believers will never grow into their divine destiny because shame has shackled them to the opinions of others. Many are paralyzed by the past, and many others are frozen in fear of what the future might hold.

Fear controls more of our lives than we realize. Some of it is good. My fear of higher insurance premiums keeps my vehicles at a reasonable speed (in this area, my beautiful wife is fearless). Out of a healthy fear of alligators, I have left many golf balls in the water hazards that decorate Myrtle Beach courses.

Still, I don't need to tell you that much of the fear we carry is not healthy. Anxiety is a major contributor to several chronic physical illnesses such as heart disease, migraine headaches, chronic respiratory disorders, and gastrointestinal conditions. Women with the highest levels of phobic anxiety are 59 percent more likely to have a heart attack, and 31 percent more likely to die from it. Full-blown panic attacks in postmenopausal women tripled the risk of a coronary event or stroke.[5] Fear can cause significant spiritual effects, as well. That's why Satan buries these stones throughout your spiritual garden. Hitting those fears can cause your fears to materialize (Job 3:25). Your fears can trap you (Prov 29:25). Your fears can ruin you (Prov 10:24). Your fears can rob you (Matt 25:24–29). Your fears can destroy you (Luke 21:26).

Here's the kicker: you're worrying over nothing.

4. Matt 6:24; Luke 16:13; Gal 1:10.
5. Harvard Health School, "Anxiety and Physical Illness," para. 10.

Roughly 85 percent of what you worry about never comes to pass. When something you fear does happen, studies have found that you will handle it far better than expected 79 percent of the time. That means that upwards of 97 percent of all things you worry about are untrue or exaggerated.[6] But how often do those untrue or exaggerated worries stop you in your tracks?

Fear is a favorite stone that Satan loves to bury in your spiritual garden. He will cause you to worry about your family, your finances, your body, your job security, your sobriety, your emotions—he will attack anything and everything in your life, but these attacks are only a means to an end. Satan isn't trying to take your money, or your health, or your job. What he really wants is your faith, and fear is one of the greatest ways to rob you of faith.

Why is Satan after your faith? Because you are saved by grace through faith (Eph 2:8). Without faith, it is impossible to please God (Heb 11:6). With faith, you have the ability to overcome everything that would hinder your Christian growth (1 John 5:4).

Many will lose heaven because they lack or have lost their faith in God. They still have faith—even atheists have faith, they simply have placed that faith in something other than God. And that is Satan's goal. He wants you to put your faith in anything but God, because your eternity is founded on faith.

I cannot and must not move quickly past this point: biblical faith does not simply declare *that* God is, it declares *who* God is. When the beloved disciple looked at Jesus, faith enabled John to see something far more than a great preacher or great prophet. John saw the word become flesh; he saw divine glory comprised of grace and truth (John 1:14). John gave testimony to what he heard, seen, and touched—not a man of God, but the life of God (1 John 1:1–4). Similarly, through faith, we see not only who Jesus was, but who Jesus is; not only what Jesus has done, but what Jesus is doing. This is critical to our right standing with God.

As we discussed in Section I, salvation is all about relationship. Jesus defined eternal life as knowing the Father (John 17:3), and Paul's greatest desire was "to know him and the power of his resurrection" (Phil 3:7–11). We can only know of God what he chooses to reveal, and revelation can be seen only through faith. The revelatory knowledge we obtain through faith enables deeper relationship and reformation, a communal life with and

---

6. Leahy, *Worry Cure*, 18, 109.

mutual fellowship in God.[7] Without faith, it is impossible to see and thus proceed. Without faith, it is impossible to please him, for he who comes to God must believe that God is, and that God is a rewarder of those who seek him.

Perhaps now you can better understand why Satan has placed his crosshairs squarely on your faith. Paul certainly understood this well. Consider his teaching in 2 Cor 4:1–4:

> Therefore, since we have this ministry, as we received mercy, we do not lose heart, but we have renounced the things hidden because of shame, not walking in craftiness or adulterating the word of God, but by the manifestation of truth commending ourselves to every man's conscience in the sight of God. And even if our gospel is veiled, it is veiled to those who are perishing, in whose case the god of this world has blinded the minds of the unbelieving so that they might not see the light of the gospel of the glory of Christ, who is the image of God.

Grace and faith are indispensable partners when it comes to obtaining and maintaining right standing with God. Satan knows he cannot eliminate God's grace from the equation, but if he can steal your faith, he will shut the door through which God's grace pours into your life. If this happens, you are in the danger zone. You are no greater than what you believe in.[8] Therefore, Satan uses stones of fear to stop a growing faith. The Apostle Peter is a great example.

Though Peter grew to become a powerful man of God, the man we meet in the gospels was less impressive. In fact, the dude had issues. Peter tended to speak before he considered his words—ironic, considering his given name "Simon" meant "heard." Listening certainly was not one of Peter's strong points. He had an apparent taste for shoe leather, based on the number of times he put his foot in his mouth. Peter also wrestled with prejudice.[9] As a result, the burly fisherman often found himself on the receiving end of a spiritual spanking. No disciple was so strongly reproved as was Peter. It is of little wonder, as no disciple was so bold as to rebuke Jesus, either (Matt 16:21–23).

---

7. For more insight, I recommend Augustine's classic book *The City of God.*

8. Consider God's servant, Job. Satan hit Job's family, finances, and health. But Satan's stated goal was to force Job to give up on his faith in God.

9. See Acts 10 and Galatians 2.

Yet Peter's greatest flaw was his inability to see himself for who he truly was. This is no more evident than on the last night of Jesus' life.[10] As the suffering servant wrestled with his impending betrayal and execution, Peter and the disciples argued about who was top dog among the disciples. Peter never doubted his right-standing with God. In fact, Peter thought he was in better standing than all the others. When Jesus dropped the bombshell of his impending betrayal, Peter was quick to declare it would never be him: "Even if all are made to stumble because of you, I will never be made to stumble!"

It is evident that Peter had a lot of confidence in himself, and little confidence in his fellow disciples. Of course, we know Peter's eternal loyalty would last about an hour. Oblivious to the fate that awaited him, the disciple charged ahead.

"I am ready to go with you, both to prison and to death!"

To his credit, there had been no place Jesus traveled that Peter did not follow. The disciple had stood at Jesus' side as Israel's religious leaders took up stones to kill him. Peter had ventured up the Mount of Transfiguration, where he beheld Jesus in his glory. Even when eleven others sat in the boat, Peter had stepped out and walked with his master in the miraculous. Peter had walked beside Jesus when no other man could or would. There was no way he was going to stop now!

Jesus' response was not what Peter expected. The Lord did not throw an arm around his friend's shoulder and offer affirmation or appreciation for such loyalty. Instead, Jesus let him in on a little secret: Peter was not in better standing than the others. Worse yet, he was ignorant of the fact that his standing with God was in jeopardy. Amid his arrogance and assurance, Peter was oblivious to the satanic strategy meant to destroy him.

"Simon, Simon!" Jesus said, having reverted back to Peter's old name because the disciple had reverted back to his old ways. "You need to see that Satan has demanded permission to sift you like wheat, but also know that I have prayed for you, that your faith would not fail. When once you have come through this, strengthen your brothers."

Jesus' words must have hit with the force of a full-speed locomotive, and left Peter's befuddled face strewn among the wreckage. No doubt that face contorted in pain and confusion as Peter wrestled with the reality of what just hit him.

---

10. Matt 26:31–36; Mark 14:26–31; Luke 22:31–34; John 13:36–38.

Have you ever sifted wheat? Not many have, especially not in the way they did it in Jesus' day. To sift was to agitate and harass. This vigorous shaking was meant to separate worthless chaff from the grain. When both were subsequently thrown into the air, the wind would blow the chaff away. In this understanding, it is not difficult to see the rich meaning conveyed in Jesus' warning. Satan viewed the disciples as worthless. A forthcoming forceful attack aimed to separate them from the seed, that they would fade away in the winds of adversity.

Chances are, you know exactly how that feels. When the doctor opens the conversation by saying "I'm sorry," you're going to be sifted. When you get a call from police that your child is behind bars, you're going to be sifted. When the pregnancy test says your baby is having a baby, when you leave your workplace unemployed, when you come home to find fire has destroyed everything, when you are betrayed by your spouse, when the bill collector takes what's left, you're going to be sifted. Satan may not have caused those events, but he will certainly use them to his advantage.

As you are tossed into the winds, that timeless temptation will tickle your ear: "Did God really say?" If Satan can convince you that God doesn't care or isn't fair, that God doesn't exist, or that you are unworthy, he will halt your growing faith, and will soon strip your spiritual garden of the good seed God had planted. If Satan takes your faith, he takes everything faith has provided—or ever will provide. Faith is the assurance of things hoped for, and the evidence of things not seen (Heb 11:1). Satan can't steal your hope, but he knows that hope cannot be realized without faith. This includes your hope in heaven (Col 1:13–23). Simply put, if you lose your faith, you lose your fight. The best way to ensure you don't lose your faith is to place it in God. When you turn to God in faith, you place in his hands the substance of those hopes. When you give God what you have, he will give when you have not.

Faith is the key that unlocks all of your blessings, in this life and the next, and that is why Peter's faith was Satan's true target. How do we know this? Consider the content of Jesus' prayer. He didn't pray for Peter's deliverance. He didn't pray that the battle would be averted. He didn't pray that angels would encamp about. Jesus prayed that Peter's faith would not fail.[11]

Your faith is full of power and promise. Satan knows it, he wants it, and he will use the same stones he used to stop Peter's faith. Peter denied Jesus three times because he was afraid of what people would think, what

---

11. It is a good prayer to echo in our time of testing: faith, don't fail me now!

people would say, and what people would do. Peter was afraid that he would suffer a similar same fate.

Fear is a very real foe, even among Christ's closest disciples. It is little wonder that more than nineteen million Americans are classified as chronic worriers, which means they worry almost every day six months or longer. Eighty percent will become depressed and stay depressed for years. Many are Christians who are in a faith crisis this very moment. How can they overcome such fear?

The first thing you should do when fear rears its ugly head is roll your eyes and say "whatever!" For the record, the Apostle Paul had that attitude long before any teenager. His direction was simple: don't worry about anything, give God all your fears, let the peace of God guard your hearts and minds—and *whatever* things are true, noble, just, pure, lovely, and of a good report, focus on those things (Phil 4:6–8). When the devil tells you everything that can go wrong, tell him, "Whatever God said, that's what I choose to believe!"[12]

As you progress in faith, hold close the credible counsel of the late, great comedienne Gracie Allen. Her advice was to never put a comma where God put a period. They are words to live by! A period follows every promise of God. A period brings the thought to a halt because the matter is finished. When worry sets in, however, we often insert a comma. The comma creates a pause that prolongs the situation. The comma, the dastardly deviant that it is, also opens a door to the dreaded question mark, which is a faith killer.

Allow me to pause here and ask a question: what do you think Satan looks like? Many might envision him as a large, muscular beast with horns on his head, lifeless black eyes, and fiery breath spewed through razor-sharp teeth. That's not how I see Satan. I think he is more like the Riddler from the Batman series and movies. He is nothing but a thief covered in question marks.

Where God placed a period, Satan looks to insert a comma leading to a question mark. Jesus declared "It is finished!" Satan wants you to worry whether it really is. Satan is the agent of all fear and doubt that tells you that you're not good enough, it's not going to work out, and there's no way to beat this. Your hopes and dreams are not possible, and your prayer won't be

---

12. If you find that to be a difficult, or even childish approach, let me ask you this: has God ever lied to you? Has Satan? Who told you that you were naked? Who planted those stones of fear in your spiritual garden?

answered, so just accept your circumstances, learn to live with it, and make the best of the situation.

Whatever.

All those scriptures that you post on Facebook and Instagram, that you quote from heart and sing about on Sundays, do you really believe them? That all things will work together for good. That greater is he who is in you than he who is in the world. That God calls those things that are not as though they were. That no weapon formed against you shall prosper. Do you believe this? Then don't put a comma where God put a period!

When Satan asks if God really said that, then your correct answer is "Yes. God really did say that. And God is not a man that he should lie (Num 23:19). His word will not return to him empty, without successfully accomplishing what he desires (Isa 55:11), so I will now take that promise back to God in full faith." And if you like, stick out your tongue and give the Riddler a fat raspberry as a parting gift.

As we wrap up this chapter, I would be remiss if I did not point out an important part of Jesus' prayer. He used this phrase when speaking to Peter: "when you have returned to Me." That meant Jesus would not be beside Peter in his time of trial, at least not in a tangible way. As it was in our school days, the teacher provides all the information we need for success, but remains quiet during the test. Peter could only pass this test through faith. Your test is no different. In times of sifting and testing, when you can't seem to hear from God or feel his presence, just remember: we walk by faith, not by sight. Your victory is not based on how you feel or what you see. What matters is *what* you believe, which is based on *who* you believe.

7

Many Hit Stones of Solitude
and Stunted Growth

IF SATAN FAILS TO steal your faith, his next strategy is to sever you from fellowship. If you are going to stand in faith, he wants you to do it alone, because solitude provides ample opportunity to destroy any Christian, even one who is rooted and growing.

Consider the example of Elijah. Soon after he sparked an awesome revival, the mighty prophet received some hate mail from Jezebel, and it sent him into a spiritual spiral (1 Kgs 19). Instead of standing firm in faith, Elijah sought safety in solitude. He traveled more than one hundred miles to Mount Horeb, the mountain of God. He was offended and afraid, and not handling either very well. As his depression deepened, Elijah asked God to take his life.[1] Instead, God asked Elijah a penetrating question. Twice. He asked, "What are you doing here?" Remember what we said earlier: when God asks a question, he is not looking for information. God was offering Elijah some much needed perspective. Do you not realize who God is? Do you not realize who you are? Who is this Jezebel, and why have you let her run you off? It was at this moment that God told Elijah to go find some specific brothers in the faith. God was not done with Elijah, but the prophet could not go it alone. Nor can we.

As Dietrich Bonhoeffer rightly noted,

---

1. Don't quickly dismiss this battle with depression. As James 5:17 tells us, Elijah was a man with a nature like ours. If you have never been there, you will be one day.

[s]in demands to have a man by himself. It withdraws him from the community. The more isolated a person is, the more destructive will be the power of sin over him, and the more deeply he becomes involved in it, the more disastrous is his isolation. Sin wants to remain unknown. It shuns the light. In the darkness of the unexpressed it poisons the whole being of a person. This can happen even in the midst of a pious community.[2]

To better understand Satan's strategy of solitude, we must know our enemy. Peter knew him well, and rightly described Satan as a roaring lion on the hunt and ready to devour (1 Pet 5:8–9). Much has changed since Peter wrote these words approximately sixty years after Christ's crucifixion, but the way in which the lion hunts has not.

I have never been on a safari, and my experience with lions is limited to the safe confines of the regional zoo. I am a bit of an Animal Planet junkie, so I have learned a little about lions. Spoiler alert: they do not frolic to the tune of "Hakuna Matata" and are not the originators of trapeze americano.[3] On the contrary, the lion is a finely tuned eating machine. Typical lions can grow to seven feet in length and weigh in at five hundred pounds. Its five-inch teeth can bite through any bone in the human body. One lion can consume seventy-five pounds of meat in a single sitting.

Despite such awesome attributes, you can scrap any idea of the lion jumping in the middle of the herd to pick a fight with the biggest and baddest opponent. Most prey are faster than the lion, and some are stronger. Isolation is the name of his game (and her game, as well, since female lions do much of the hunting). These skilled hunters carefully select their target, and they have an eye for the ones out on the fringe—the weak and wounded who can't keep up, the ones who wander because they believe themselves too strong to fall prey, and the young who are oblivious to the danger that stalks them. These are the easiest pickings; their solitude makes them susceptible.

We discussed the weak and wounded in the previous chapters. We saw that unforgiveness and offense, as well as fear and shame, can quickly halt spiritual growth and lead to spiritual death. Destruction is far more likely if we try to face these things alone. The same is true for Christians who are strong in God's word and anointing but lured away by temptation. We must take note of the many Christians who are legitimately wounded by life, bad

---

2. Bonhoeffer, *Life Together*, 112.

3. I say this with great respect for the joy brought by Simba and Alex, of course.

choices, and even by the church, because Satan certainly has them in his sights. That roaring lion can sense the slightest weakness, injury, or ailment, and he will take every advantage.

If I may speak for a moment to those who are weak or wounded: I know it is easy to turn your back on the herd when the church has let you down. That is exactly what the roaring lion wants you to do. No Christian should struggle alone, and no Christian can overcome alone. Even Jesus needed help carrying his cross. I was once challenged on this and told, "I appreciate the church, but Jesus is all I need." Well, Jesus said you need a church family that will help you bear your burden.[4] If you don't have one, find one. Your victory depends on it.

I find no better or more beautiful picture of unity than the giant sequoia tree. They grow upwards of three hundred feet, weigh millions of pounds, live thousands of years, and do this with a root structure that runs only twelve to fourteen feet deep. Such growth and life is possible because the roots intertwine. Simply put, the giant sequoias hold each other up. That is the power of unity, and it is an example we would do well to follow. When believers stand united, Satan doesn't stand a chance![5]

Satan is no match for unified believers who are growing in the presence and power of God. That would be like pitting a lion against a herd of cape buffalo. Sure, that lion carries the title of "king of the beasts," but he is no match for the might of these creatures. Any lion that picks this fight will end up in a world of hurt, hurled through the air like a rag doll or quickly trampled underfoot. The bovines are just too powerful—they know it, and the lion knows it. That is why cape buffalo barely acknowledge the angry glare of lions that walk within spitting distance. Cape buffalo are simply unimpressed.

Yet there are times in which lions will separate a cape buffalo from the herd and bring down this massive and mighty adversary. How could this happen? Lions don't fight fair. They are the only big cats to live in family units, ironically called a "pride," and the pride is very skilled at setting up traps.[6] Many times, the cape buffalo is ignorant of the lion's tactics (cf. 2 Cor 2:11). Therefore, we would do well to identify Satan's common schemes.

4. Ps 133; Eccl 4:9–12; 2 Cor 13:14; Eph 4:1–3; Heb 10:24–25; 1 Pet 3:8–9; etc.

5. The mathematical equation is found in Deuteronomy 32:30, which says one can chase a thousand, and two will put ten thousand to flight. Every time you stand united with one more believer, God adds a zero to the equation. That means seven Spirit-filled and unified believers can withstand one billion roaring lions!

6. Remember our talk of *skandalon* back in chapter 5?

Contrary to popular legend, most prey is faster, stronger, or more agile than the lion. Because the beast tires easily, he won't charge until he is within one hundred feet. That means the cunning carnivore has to get up close and personal. He does this by studying and stalking his prey. Your adversary is no different. Satan has been studying you; he knows your tendencies, and how best to lure you away through temptation.[7] It's just a step or two at first, but the distance grows greater as the temptation grows stronger. As Jerusalem's first pastor rightly noted, each believer "is carried away and enticed by his own lust. Then when lust has conceived, it gives birth to sin; and when sin is accomplished, it brings forth death" (Jas 1:14–15). Similarly, Psalm 17:12 tells us the hungry lion lurks in secret places—the places that no one knows about, the places where you are all alone, the places where you ought not be—and there he waits for the opportune moment, patient and unseen. Christians who wander into these dark recesses often believe themselves strong or wise enough to overcome, and impervious to any attack. Indeed, pride goes before destruction. When the attack comes, the prey is hit with breathtaking ferocity, and you better believe the vultures and scavengers will be quick to pick apart the mighty one who has fallen. They feed off of it. They love it.

A second strategy of the lion is to simply wear down a cape buffalo. A common tactic finds smaller lions driving the unsuspecting prey away from the herd and toward an ambush site. Their attacks are little more than a nuisance at first. Some lions may sustain injury as the attack unfolds, but it is all part of the strategy to entice and ultimately exhaust the big, bold buffalo. Inevitably, the lions will back down and feign defeat. As the cape buffalo stands tired but victorious, he will be blindsided by the largest lion, which lay in wait. The predator will slash its retractable claws across the buffalo's eyes to blind it (cf. 2 Cor 4:4). Having lost its perspective, the cape buffalo will then feel the lion's razor-sharp teeth sink into its jugular. As the life-giving blood is drained away, the lion will pull down its powerful prey. It happens in churches every day, as cape buffalos grow susceptible while defending and strengthening others. This should never be done alone.

Along with the wandering and the wounded, the lion's third target of opportunity is the young yearling too naïve to remain in the protection of the pack. I once saw a powerful video in which a young cape buffalo was

---

7. Look at the example of Job. God asked Satan, "Have you considered my servant?" He most certainly had. Satan knew quite a bit about Job, and he knew how to hit him where it hurt the most.

hit hard by lions lying in wait. The force of the attack knocked the young buffalo into the water, and into the jaws of a hungry crocodile. Talk about a bad day. A tug-of-war ensued between the lions and the croc, with the lions winning out. The lions gathered to feast on the motionless prize, only to be met by a herd of angry cape buffalo. One by one, the carnivores were conquered—and to the shock of the spectators, the young buffalo began to show signs of life. It soon got back on its feet and continued with the herd on its life journey.[8]

Young believers are much the same. They are unaware of the dangers all around them, and desperately need seasoned, battle-scarred buffalo to protect them from and teach them about the roaring lions that lurk nearby. Growth is the key to overcoming the lion's tactics and temptations. The problem is, some believers don't want to grow up. This is a huge stone that halts the spiritual growth and life of countless Christians.

Many have said their "sinner's prayer," been baptized, and even attended church for decades, but have not grown in the faith. In my military days, we often noted the difference between an individual who retired with twenty years of experience, and one who retired with one year of experience relived twenty times. There are many in the Christian army with the same credentials as the latter, and this is catastrophic for a number of reasons.

In God's garden, that which is not growing is dying. That is why believers are given the non-negotiable command to grow continually in the grace and knowledge of Jesus Christ.[9] A refusal to grow up is a refusal to accept responsibility. This tends to lead to selfish decisions that put others in jeopardy or leave others to pick up the pieces. When an adult exhibits such behavior, we often say "you need to grow up!" or "you need to act your age!" Christians are not exempt. We are all going to hit (or be hit by) the stones mentioned in previous chapters. We will not respond well if we have failed to grow in the faith and likeness of Christ. This will lead to solitude from God and fellow Christians, and solitude is Satan's hunting grounds.

While a refusal to grow up may have worth on a playground, it is deadly on a battleground.[10] Yet there remain many Christians who prefer to follow the example of Peter Pan, the little boy who didn't want to

8. The video, called "Battle of Kruger," can be viewed on YouTube. Fair warning: there is a word or two that some will find offensive, so you may want to hit the mute button.

9. John 15:1–8; 1 Cor 3:1–3; 14:20; Eph 4:11–16; Heb 2:10–15; 5:12–14; 6:1–2; 1 Pet 2:2; 2 Pet 1:5–11; 3:18; 1 John 3:2–22.

10. That is why we are to train up a child in the way he should go. That command, found in Proverbs 22:6, has spiritual as well as physical implications.

grow up. Pan and his crew of Lost Boys lived on the adventurous island of Neverland. There, the carefree children could live without the confines of responsibility.

Many churches are filled with lost boys who want the blessings of God without the battles or burdens of Christianity. Their "Neverland" is aptly named. The childish believer will never have what God said he can have. He will never do what God called him to do. He will never be who God called him to be. He will never feel true joy, know true love, walk in true forgiveness, experience true victory, rest in true peace, or find true strength. This is because he refuses to grow up and take responsibility for himself, and his church.

While lions love to feast on those who have not grown strong enough to withstand, a strong walk with God will shut the mouth of every roaring lion (just ask the prophet Daniel). To have that strong walk means you are no longer carried or crawling. The one who progresses from crawling to walking will eventually run—a category we will discuss in the next chapter. As it is in our physical life, to be carried, crawling, or walking are all important parts of our spiritual progression, but none should become permanent. To understand that spiritual growth, I invite you to consider John Wesley's "Christian Perfection," a doctrine anchored in 1 John 2:12–14:

> I am writing to you, little children, because your sins have been forgiven you for His name's sake. I am writing to you, Fathers, because you know Him who has been from the beginning. I am writing to you, young men, because you have overcome the evil one. I have written to you, children, because you know the Father. I have written to you, Fathers, because you know Him who has been from the beginning. I have written to you, young men, because you are strong, and the word of God abides in you, and you have overcome the evil one.

When the Bible speaks of being "perfect," it does not mean absent of error or flaws. To be perfect is to be fit for one's purpose; to grow and mature into what God intends each human to be. Jesus is the prototype of human perfection; that we are conformed to his likeness has been God's plan from the start.[11] Jesus is what humanity was supposed to be. As Thiselton rightly notes, many have questioned whether Jesus was actually human. The better question is, are we?[12]

---

11. Rom 8:29; 1 John 3:2.

12. Thiselton, *Living Paul*, loc. 1122.

We are commanded to grow into such perfection.[13] To recover the image of God is the "glorious privilege of every Christian," in Wesley's view.[14] Such growth renders one free from evil thoughts and tendencies, and it allows the love of God to guide all actions and attitudes. The mature believer is "purified from pride; for Christ was lowly of heart. He is pure from self-will or desire; for Christ desired only to do the will of his Father, and to finish his work. And he is pure from anger, in the common sense of the word; for Christ was meek and gentle, patient and long-suffering."[15]

Christian growth starts with babes in Christ, or those who have been born again (see chapter 2). They have overcome the world and are protected by the power of God through faith (1 John 5:4–5). But they are, of course, still babies. They always need someone to feed them and clean up the messes they make. They whine and cry (a lot), but that is to be expected. In fact, it is a good thing. Newborns cry when they don't know what to do, when they are afraid or need help, and when they need protection or provision. A good parent always responds to those cries. Such response builds and strengthens neural connections, and aids in the child's development.[16] The father's voice not only brings comfort, but also enables growth and development. So it is with babes in Christ.

Still, a new believer is not accustomed to the word of righteousness (Heb 5:13). Like any tot, they don't like to be told what they should or should not do. While holiness and perfection are a delicacy to the mature believer, the babe in Christ finds it is hard to swallow. That's why they need pure milk early on.[17] Back in my day, a toddler who wanted to be like Popeye was told he must eat his spinach. Well, to be like Christ, the spiritual toddler (regardless of physical age) must progress from the milk to the meat. This transition marks the beginning of Christian perfection as babes in Christ become "little children."

The Bible describes a little child as one who has chosen to leave behind the former lusts in pursuit of holiness and righteous behavior.[18] They are encouraged to follow the example of Christ by laying down their lives for and meeting the needs of fellow believers (1 John 3:16, 18). In other words,

---

13. Matt 5:48; 2 Cor 7:1; Phil 1:6; 3:12; Jas 1:4.

14. Wesley, "Plain Account of Christian Perfection," loc. 656.

15. Wesley, "Sermons of John Wesley," para. 26.

16. Harvard University, "Serve and Return," paras. 1–3.

17. 1 Pet 2:2; 2 Pet 3:18.

18. 1 Pet 1:14–16; 1 John 3:10.

they are taught to play nice and treat others well. Every parent knows this does not happen without its challenges. Toddlers tend to throw tantrums when they don't get their way. So do little children of God.[19] It is tempting to just give them what they want to keep everybody happy. To do so would produce spoiled Christians rather than suffering servants. When children don't get their way, they tend to take their toys and go home. Sometimes it is tempting to let them go, but don't give up without a fight. As we have seen, solitude is Satan's killing field.

We must remember that they are only children. Granted, as adults they should know better, but they are still developing in the spiritual sense. As Jesus said from the cross, they don't really know what they are doing, and they don't know there is a lion lying in wait. We must help them mature, and this is the time it must happen. There is a powerful parallel in the physical development of children. A two-year-old's brain is as active as an adult brain. Within a year, it is twice as active, and will stay that way for a decade. Ninety percent of a child's brain development happens before age five. These are formative years; if proper development is lacking, it will take a lot of time and tears to overcome the damage done.[20]

The tyrannical toddler needs discipline, and the Peter Pan Christian needs discipleship.[21] The bulk of correction and direction offered in 1 John is addressed to this group, and understandably so. Parents expend most of their effort and energy on children of this age (they are called the "terrible twos" for a reason). It is a time of challenge, but also one to be cherished. This is when a child's unique personality is put on display. Much of their identity is developed through communication. That is why a little child will ask you one thousand questions in the span of two stoplights. Spiritual children are much the same, and well they should be. This is how they come to know the Father (1 John 2:13) and learn to follow the leading of his voice

19. Spiritual babies are a lot like physical babies. I've had four of these (physical babies, that is), so I have a little experience here. I've had a lot more than four spiritual babies, and I am happy to say that most have grown up quite well.

20. Harvard University, "Serve and Return," para. 3. Responsive relationships are essential to a child's development. The lack of stable and caring communication can impair physical, mental, and emotional health, and flood the developing brain with potentially harmful stress hormones. Conversely, children who receive warm, responsive nurture in their early years are less likely to respond to poorly to stress later in life.

21. Job 5:17; Prov 3:11; 12:1; 13:24; 19:20; Matt 18:15; Eph 6:4; 1 Tim 4:6–7; Heb 2:10–15; 12:4–11; Rev 3:19.

(John 10:27). Little children are taught to obey the Father (1 John 3:24), and soon learn that reward follows obedience (1 John 2:28).

Of course, little children don't always follow a father's instructions. Sometimes they act like they didn't hear the father. Other times, they make excuses or try to talk their way out of it. There are times they will flat-out ignore the father, or even cop an attitude and argue their case. Even in stubborn refusal, little children are learning truth (1 John 2:18–21). This relational dialogue is critical as it will train their senses to discern good and evil (Heb 5:14).

Despite this growth, little children still struggle with sin and are susceptible to deception.[22] They can easily be lured away, so more growth is needed. If the conditions for growth are favorable, little children will become young men and women of God.

While babes in Christ have overcome the world, and little children have overcome the spirit of antichrist (anything that would take the place of Christ), young men and women of God have overcome the evil one (1 John 2:13–14).[23] This is an important distinction. Spiritual growth has focused on overcoming alienation with God, others, and self to this point. Now, the believers are taking the fight to the enemy, and well they should. When Jesus first described his church, he said the gates of hell would not overpower (Matt 16:18). Gates are a defensive mechanism, meant to keep others out. Such a description conveys a clear intent: believers are not to simply avoid the roaring lion, but to grow strong enough to storm the lion's den.

This is only possible because these believers have graduated from the elementary teachings—repentance from dead works, faith toward God, instruction about washings and laying on of hands, and the resurrection of the dead and eternal judgment—and look to press further into maturity (Heb 6:1–2). The word of God abides in them (1 John 2:14), and they have put away childish things (1 Cor 13:11). Still, young men and women of God have not reached full stature. Peter therefore charges these growing believers to be subject to elders (1 Pet 5:5). In protecting them from the lion's snares and temptations, he urges they be clothed with humility (5:6) and overcome the fear and worry we discussed in chapter 5 by casting all anxieties on Jesus (5:7).

---

22. 1 John 2:1; 3:7–8; 5:21.

23. The use of the perfect tense in the original Greek indicates that, though the victory has been won, the battle rages.

Eventually, young men and women of God will grow into spiritual fathers and mothers. To be a parent (be it physical or spiritual) is to birth someone to new life and/or raise that child into adulthood. To do this, good parents offer plenty of love and freely give themselves to their children—and they are not afraid to speak a hard truth when needed.[24] They are the ones who take responsibility for all of that toddler development we talked about a moment ago.

Spiritual fathers and mothers are able to do this because they know him who has been from the beginning (1 John 2:13–14). This intimate knowledge, combined with spiritual maturity, gives them remarkable insight.[25] They are uniquely qualified to offer direction as well as correction, yet these are not the greatest tools at their disposal. What really sets them apart is the Christian character they have developed, which now stands as an example to the flock. This is of immeasurable worth, and severely lacking in the modern church.[26]

There is one more thing spiritual mothers and fathers do very well: they do not hesitate to deal a world of hurt to a roaring lion who has threatened one of their babies.

24. For more on this, just do a good study on Paul's writings to the Corinthian church.

25. In Acts 2, Peter quotes from Joel 2, in which God speaks of a time when the Spirit will enable sons and daughters (little children) to prophesy, or to preach about what is happening in the spiritual realm. The young men and women will see visions, which means they will see what is happening in the spiritual realm, and the old (spiritual fathers and mothers) will dream, which means they will see what is being planned in the spiritual realm.

26. Even Paul struggled with the lack of spiritual fathers in his day (1 Cor 4:14–16). But for the modern context, I recommend you read Lyons, *Next Christians*.

8

Many Hit Stones of Comfort and Complacency

THOUGH I DO NOT fancy myself a wordsmith, writing has been a prominent part of my professional life. In that time, the oxymoron has often brought a smile to my face, or a shake to my head. There is one oxymoron to which I aspire: living sacrifice. But the bitter sweet reality is that most oxymorons evoke little more than deafening silence.

The concepts of comfort and stones may seem to carry similar contradiction, but it is often the problems with the softest touch that are hardest to overcome. When is your bed softest, warmest, and most comfortable—when you crawl in at night, or when your alarm clock starts ringing? Mm-hmm.[1] That warm, comfortable bed keeps many people out of church. It keeps many out of the gym. It leaves many chores undone. It makes many late for work.

If you are not careful, that kind of comfort will creep into every corner of your life. Perhaps you are comfortable in a relationship. It is not all you hoped for, but it is better than nothing. Many feel they are too old to go looking for Prince Charming, let alone Prince At-Least-Pick-Up-After-Yourself, so you settle with what you have. You learn to live with it. You

---

1. For the record, I love my bed. I bought into that old sales pitch, "the one-third of your life spent on that mattress greatly affects the other two-thirds." You know what? It's true. We bought an exceptional mattress, but as a result, I must formulate a daring escape from my posturepedic prison every morning.

make the best of the situation. God has picked out Mrs. Right, but you are comfortable with Mrs. Right-Now.

How about work—have you ever grown comfortable there? You know your job, and you do your job. Yeah, there's a better position open, and it is the one you always dreamed of, but you don't feel like putting in all the extra hours. Plus, you will have to contend with Suzy Bucketmouth and Willy Whatsinitforme. It would be easier to herd cats across Texas. So, you just stay in your comfortable cubicle that is ironically adorned with motivational posters.

We grow comfortable where we are, comfortable with who we are, comfortable with what we are doing. Sometimes, we even grow comfortable in our relationship with God. Such was the case for Eutychus (Acts 20:7–12). Paul had been preaching for six to ten hours (and people complain when I go over thirty minutes). Lamps were lit, and they emitted more than light. The room would become rather hot and uncomfortable as smoke grew thick. Eutychus was wise enough to find an advantageous spot on the window sill, where the air would be fresh and cool. In this comfort, the young believer sank into a deep sleep. Soon after, he fell three stories to his death.[2]

This just goes to show that we can grow comfortable, even if it is the Apostle Paul himself pouring into our lives. Comfort can quickly lead to spiritual slumber, and that can lead to a catastrophic fall. It is time we wake up![3] It is time we consider whether we have grown comfortable in our relationship with God. Do we simply pay him weekend visits and spend the big holidays at his house? Have you grown comfortable with God? More important, do you think God is comfortable with you? I mean no offense, but as we said in the introduction, it is important to ask whether we may be wrong about being right with God. He doesn't want weekend visitation, he wants full custody. While God invites us to find our rest in him, he does not advocate a comfortable Christianity. Quite the opposite. God thinks we should break out in a happy dance when our faith comes under attack. Why be joyous in such times of trial? Because the testing of our faith produces endurance, and if we allow endurance to do its work, we will be perfect and complete, lacking in nothing (Jas 1:2–4).

Endurance—place that word in a holding pattern. We will return to that concept in a few pages. In the meantime, please know that God will

---

2. Let this be a lesson to you: it is never a good idea to fall asleep in church.

3. Cf. Rom 13:11–12; Eph 5:14; 1 Thess 5:6.

consistently push you to new levels and take you to new heights. God is always looking to get you out of your comfort zone, and with good reason. What you call comfort, God calls confinement. In fact, comfort makes Christ sick (Rev 3:14–22).

The church at Laodicea was satisfied with self-sufficiency. It was comfortable. Jesus likened this to the mixture of water that resulted when the city built an aqueduct to bring water from the hot springs of Hierapolis, six miles to the north, which poured into the cold water that flowed from Colossae, which lay ten miles to the east. While the hot waters provided physical restoration, and the cold waters provided refreshment, the lukewarm liquid of Laodicea was not able to restore or refresh. The church was much the same, as its indifference led to idleness. Jesus was nauseated by the bad taste this left in his mouth. His attitude has not changed.

Now, I understand the very real threat of burnout, and I am the first to caution against anyone growing weary in welldoing. Everyone needs to take a break from time to time, but many allow their break to become a permanent vacation. Comfort will keep Christians from God's purpose and promise. When you grow comfortable with God, you take up residence right where you are.[4] You will progress no further, and a Christianity that is not progressing is digressing. That is why the Apostle Paul, unwilling to settle for the satisfactory, pressed forward in the upward call of Christ (Phil 3:12–16).

Having admitted that my bed can be a posturepedic prison, I must confess to another creature comfort I have embraced in these middle ages: comfortable shoes. My priority is no longer style nor savings, it is comfort. I like the microfiber that allows my shoes to breathe, and whoever invented memory foam should win the Nobel Prize. I most appreciate my comfortable shoes when I take my wife to an ocean getaway (remember, everyone needs a break from time to time). I was once so determined to get to our personal sea of tranquility that I set out barefoot, and quickly found Dante's nine levels of hell awaiting me. I tripped through the luggage landmines to emerge upon a splintering wood deck that led to abrasive asphalt. I don't know why I was careful to avoid any broken glass, as the gravel walkway that followed had the same effect. I negotiated the sand dunes' slippery slopes, only to stop on sand that was roughly the temperature of fresh lava.

---

4. Many of you are called to be Sunday School teachers, but you are comfortable right where you are at. Many are called to preach the gospel, but you are comfortable right where you are at. Many are called to the mission field, or to start a new business, or coordinate community benevolence . . .

Having left a trail of towels and sunblock in a vain effort to lighten the load, my soft-stepping trot had intensified into a mad dash for the refreshing water that beckoned. I finally submerged my irritated feet, only to be painfully reminded that there was salt in that water. Such was the journey until one fine day, when my wife offered a remarkable solution.

"Why don't you just wear your sandals down to the beach?"

It was as if the heavens parted and the wisdom of God spoke into my soul. I think I even heard an angelic choir singing in the background. It came as little surprise. I have found that the voice of God has remarkable similarity to that of my wife.

The next day started with a nice stroll to the beach. More like a strut. I think I even heard the Bee Gees's "Stayin' Alive" playing in the background. "Got the wings of heaven on my shoes, I'm a dancin' man and I just can't lose."[5] I cracked open my Bible and was soon reading about the burning bush in Exodus 3. I openly laughed when my eyes read how God told Moses (who was in a sandy stroll of his own) to remove his sandals, because he was standing on holy ground. Oh, the irony. But it was at that moment when the Spirit of God blindsided me with an unexpected revelation: Moses was to remove anything that came between him and the holiness of God, even the things that brought much comfort. Wow, the steps of the righteous really are ordered of the Lord!

As we have discussed, all Christians hit hard times in our walks with God. Like my journey to the beach, we often put barriers (in this example, shoes) between us and the uncomfortable stones. But it is God's plan to remove those stones before they stunt your growth. The trick is, you will never know they are there unless you can feel them. Don't let comfort come between you and God's will for your life. Such comfort leads to complacency.[6]

Since we are on the topic of shoes, let me ask: how do you feel about running? You wouldn't know it by looking at me now, but I loved running as a kid. This zeal resulted from a Forest Gump-like episode that happened shortly before my fourth birthday. Many details are long forgotten, but I distinctly remember being struck with paralysis while eating Cheetos and

---

5. Bee Gees, "Stayin' Alive," 1977.

6. When we grow comfortable with Christ and fail to see what he is trying to remove from our path, we can quickly become what I call a "garden-variety Christian." We meet this sort in a garden called Gethsemane, where the disciples prayed too little, boasted too loudly, and slept too much. All of these are serious stones that caused each disciple to stumble.

watching Captain Kangaroo (some things never change). I remember the tears on my mother's face—their warmth stood in stark contrast to the cold, bare hospital room when she struggled to explain why her only son would never run and play like before. I remember a bright green plant surrounded by four rolls of Lifesavers candy brought by my Uncle Sonny, a surrogate father. Better than the candy was the motorcycle vase in which it came. Even then I loved motorcycles, but this one meant far more. It maintains a place of honor on the desk in my home office. Other memories are not as tangible, but no less life changing. This includes the visit of a godly cousin named Johnny, who made the three-hour journey to pray for me. As the doctors talked of muscular dystrophy, he poured what I thought to be cologne in his hands and placed them on my back, then he started talking in a language I did not understand. An episode of Sesame Street taught me to count to three in Spanish earlier that day. I assumed he had learned some Spanish, as well. My last memory of this ordeal, a nurse's shriek, came the next day when I climbed out of my puke-green toddler hospital bed and slowly shuffled down the hospital hall. Partial paralysis, it turns out, could not overcome my thirst for Mountain Dew.

Magic legs.

Unfortunately, my adult years have shown that a twenty-nine-inch inseam and flat feet can carry a runner only so far, but such shortfalls mattered little to a boy who was told he would never run again. I had no qualms walking to school as a boy—five miles, uphill both ways, in two feet of snow while carrying twenty pounds of books.[7] On the baseball diamond, I loved to stretch a single into extra bases, and was even known to steal home a time or two. I rode a bicycle to work in my Marine Corps days, fifteen miles each way. It is fair to say that what I lacked in design was gained in vigor. These days—well, I must admit, I ain't as good as I once was. My get-up-and-go has got up and went. But there is one race I still run with that same vigor, and I run it to win. It is the race of faith.

I have heard many say the race of faith is not a sprint, it's a marathon. I see it more like a relay race. We must stay in our straight and narrow lane, take the baton from those who have run the race before us, be sure to pass it to the next generation, then step aside and cheer them on. Still, there are elements of a marathon that provide valuable insight.

---

7. That journey gets longer and more arduous every time I tell it to my kids, who have been privileged to ride in a comfortable bus or family car since the first day of kindergarten.

A sprint requires a quick burst of energy that soon dissipates. A marathon speaks of endurance. It covers a great distance, and often requires the participant be able to traverse treacherous hills and valleys at one stage, only to pound city streets later on. The runner must contend with stormy weather and be able to push through when things heat up. To compete is to push oneself; to continue forward in times of pain, when every fiber within begs you to quit.

Such discipline is gained not in the race, but during preparation for the race—and that is why the Apostle Paul uses Olympians to illustrate our race of faith. Champions train for years just to qualify to compete. Comfort is given no quarter. Countless hours are spent building endurance and strength (mental and physical). Scientific schedules detail when they sleep, wake, work out, recover, and eat. Only that which contributes to the cause is consumed. Paul noted that "everyone who competes for the prize is temperate in all things" (1 Cor 9:25). That means the athlete abstains from anything that will cause him to lose his edge or fall behind. Every champion (spiritual or physical) forms, not follows, his body; he lays aside anything and everything that would hold him back (cf. Heb 11:1–3).

It is often said that championships are won on the practice field, not on the playing field. There is great value in the sentiment, yet training is not enough to ensure victory. If you desire to win the race, you must finish the race, and you can't finish the race if you don't run the race. Christianity is not a spectator sport.

Much like the race of faith, the start of a marathon is a wonderful thing. Runners feel strong and energetic. They cross the starting line with remarkable potential, focused determination, and palpable hope. Years of training are about to pay off. Such attitudes change about eighteen miles in. That's when runners often "hit a wall," also known as "bonking." This does not describe a bleeding blister or deep muscle cramp, but a physical depletion so intense it will affect mental cognition (hallucinations are common). The race is neither won nor lost at the finish line, but at this difficult point.

Runners in the race of faith know this challenge all too well. While much of our pain is mental and emotional, it can be overwhelming—and much like the marathon runner, the mental will affect the physical. Many Christians, especially those who have not fully matured, believe such pain is a sure sign that God is not in it. More experienced Christians know that pain does not mean you have strayed off the path, or out of God's will.

There will be times of pain. God is looking for someone who will press through. God has plenty of good starters; what he desires is a great finisher!

An example can be seen in footage from the Mexico City Olympics Stadium on October 20, 1968. Many spectators had already exited when a commotion was heard in the distance. Mamo Waldi of Ethiopia had claimed gold in the twenty-six-mile marathon. The race had long since concluded for most, but not for everyone. John Stephen Akhwari, wearing the colors of Tanzania, limped through the stadium entrance late that evening.[8]

Akhwari had no way to properly prepare for the high altitude and its remarkably thin air. Painful cramps slowed his progress early in the race, and the runner soon found himself swallowed by a large group of competitors. Unable to see his path or the way ahead, Akhwari became entangled as athletes jockeyed for position. He stumbled and fell. His knee was split open, and his shoulder was dislocated when it smashed against the pavement. Race organizers prepared to transport him to the hospital. He had no chance for winning, and his injuries would only get worse without proper treatment. There would be no shame in quitting. After all, eighteen of seventy-five starters had already pulled out. Yet Akhwari pressed on. He received what medical attention he could, then continued his race. It was not a pretty sight. Bandaged and bloodied, Akhwari would jog a short distance, then limp for a time.[9]

When he finally entered the stadium, the crowd stood to its feet and cheered him on. On the other side of the finish line, the Olympian was asked why, in the reception of such injury, didn't he just quit? With quiet dignity Akhwari said, "My country did not send me five thousand miles to start this race. They sent me five thousand miles to finish this race."[10]

God didn't call you to start the race. He called you to finish the race, and to finish strong. In fact, you are called to win.[11] You may be tired. You may have been knocked down and wounded along the way. You may have made some mistakes or taken a wrong turn. Maybe temptation has diverted you from your destiny. Maybe you were crippled by compromise. Maybe Satan has used discouragement to keep you down. Do you know the proper response?

8. "Marathon Man Akhwari." The link, included in the bibliography, includes video of the event.

9. Ibid., paras. 3–4.

10. Ibid., para. 5.

11. 1 Cor 9:24–27; 2 Tim 4:6–8.

Whatever![12]

You are more than a conqueror. You are not disqualified, so don't let the difficulties bring your race to an end. Don't let the lure of comfort keep you from victory. The crown described by the Apostle Paul is only given to those who finish the race, so get back up and keep moving forward! Though afflicted in every way, you are not crushed; perplexed, but not despairing; persecuted, but not forsaken; struck down, but not destroyed (2 Cor 4:8–9). And when it seems the race that remains is too difficult, when you are too wounded, when you are too winded, you have a Father who will come to your side and see to it that the good work started in you is completed (Phil 1:6).

Derek Redmond had such a father. The date was August 3, 1992, and Redmond was in Barcelona, Spain with an eye on Olympic gold. It was borderline miraculous to see the British sprinter on the track. An injury to his Achilles tendon four years earlier had ended his Olympic dreams mere minutes before he was to run. Redmond battled back through five surgeries and an agonizing recovery. Against all odds, he won at the World Championships, set a British record, and qualified once more to compete in the Olympics. There, he was better than ever. Redmond not only won his quarterfinal heat, he recorded the fastest time of the first round.[13]

Redmond was not halfway through the 400-meter semifinals when he crumpled to the track with a torn right hamstring. His deafening cry could be heard over the crowd's cheers. What started as a vocal response to intense physical pain soon gave way to a different sound, the unspeakable pain caused by shattered dreams. Redmond waved off the medical attendants who rushed to his side. Despite the physical and emotional pain, he struggled to his feet and began to hop down the track in a desperate effort to finish his race.

The race had ended, as had his career and dreams, yet Redmond pressed on. When it seemed that the pain would be too much to bear, that Redmond would be unable (though not unwilling) to continue on, a man pushed aside the security guards and medical personnel to come alongside Redmond.

It was Jim Redmond, Derek's father.

---

12. If you find my attitude offensive, you may have skipped over chapter 6. Go back and take a look, and you will better understand.

13. "Heroic Redmond Defies the Pain."

The father whispered words of encouragement in his son's ear. The father fought off all who urged his son to give up. The father put his arm around his son's waist as the son leaned on his father's shoulders. They finished the race, together. The great crowd of witnesses gave him a standing ovation, yet Derek seemed oblivious as he rested in his father's arms.[14]

In this race of faith, there will be times that your pain is great, seemingly unbearable. There will be times when there's nothing left inside you, and you will question whether it is worth it to keep pressing forward. It will seem your race is over, and all hope is lost. Determine in your heart that you are going to finish this race, and you will soon hear a familiar voice in your ear. It will be your Father. He will push through the people to be at your side. He will uphold you with his mighty arm, and together you will cross the finish line. "Even to your graying years I will bear you," he said. "I have done it, and I will carry you; and I will bear you and I will deliver you" (see Isa 46:3–4).

Those who walk in comfortable Christianity will never know such victory.

---

14. Please, I beg you, watch the moving video of this event. It can be accessed from the Olympic.org article on Redmond. The link is included in the bibliography.

SECTION III

When Good Fruit Is Choked Out

"Others fell among the thorns, and the thorns came up and choked them out. . . . And the one on whom seed was sown among the thorns, this is the man who hears the word, and the worry of the world and the deceitfulness of wealth choke the word, and it becomes unfruitful."

—Matt 13:7, 22

IT HAS BEEN SAID that a mighty oak tree was once a little nut that refused to give up. Perhaps you are a little nut who has refused to let hard circumstances stop your spiritual growth. For this I offer commendation; a relationship that grows despite the obstacles will become beautiful and fruitful. I also offer a word of warning: do not think for one moment that it is easy street from here. If your adversary can't stop your growth, he will try to choke you out.

This will happen to even the most beautiful and fruitful relationships if one party is lured into apathy or adultery. With such understanding, I invite you to imagine a marriage filled with quality time and conversation. Imagine a wife absolutely enamored with her husband. Her car has a radio station that sings his praises, and this beautiful bride sings right along each and every day, with each and every song. It almost feels like she wrote them herself! She squeezes the many ways her husband has blessed her into every conversation. She tirelessly professes her adoration on social media. This love is proclaimed on her car's bumper and back window. She has T-shirts declaring how great he is. She sacrificially takes care of his house and his family. She has got it bad for this guy.

But each day she also ventures off to bed an old boyfriend. No harm here; her heart belongs to her husband, and this is just a little coping mechanism. Though she adorns him with plaudits and praise, her loving husband is worried that the relationship is becoming routine, even taken for granted. She is oblivious to the fact that some things said and done are breaking his heart. She is quick to bring him her needs, but she doesn't seem to hear his needs the way she once did. Communication is becoming a one-way street. The ambitious wife has disregarded warnings that recent career choices are out of character. She hears little of his concern as she heads to the mall, where she buys things she does not need with money she does not have. The debt is destructive, but the husband is grieved for greater reasons. He is happy to see her in a new wardrobe and with new jewelry, but he is devastated that such things are the source of her pleasure and self-worth. Soon, she is off to another old lover. Perhaps it is a bottle of wine. Perhaps it is a gossip party at the beauty salon. Perhaps it is a risqué conversation with a coworker. *Don't read anything into it*, she says. Her heart belongs to her husband. After all, she is singing his praises in the car ride to her next endeavor.

How strong is this relationship? How deep is this relationship? How long do you think this relationship will last?

God is not interested in such a relationship. God's plan makes each believer a participant in the salvation process, as well as the Christian growth and transformation that follows. Relationships are built on commitment to and communication with one another, as well as mutual trust to action. The Bible calls this "covenant." The Hebrew *běrit* and the Greek *diathēkē* appear a combined three hundred and eighteen times to signify an oath-bound relationship given by promise, assured by a seal, and kept by obligation. God establishes his kingdom through covenant; our role is to trust in the Lord with all our heart, and to follow his lead in everything (Prov 3:5–6).

A relationship without commitment is a relationship of convenience. It is a relationship in which one party looks to get a maximum benefit with a minimum effort. This is how the thorns of this world are able to infiltrate your spiritual garden and choke out the blessings of God.

Four key points must be made from the onset. First, realize that the culprit is not exclusive to money and material, but includes the worry (cares) of the world. Second, remember that thorns are of earthly origin and a product of the adamic curse (Gen 3:18). Third, notice that this believer *becomes* unfruitful, which indicates he had grown and was bearing fruit. Fourth, keep in mind that even a fruit-bearing field that is consumed by thorns will end up in the fire.[1]

I do not have a green thumb, but this much I do know: fruit takes time to grow. If you plant an apple seed today, you will not be eating apples tomorrow. In fact, it takes the standard apple tree anywhere from six to ten years to produce its first fruit. The tree uses that time to build a solid root structure and to ensure a healthy flow of life-giving nutrients. When that tree matures, it will produce fruit—but that fruit is not for that tree.

The same can be said of Christians. When the good seed takes root, a good tree will grow and will bear good fruit. Indeed, we are known by our fruit (Matt 7:16). The growing believer can expect to see continual increase in the fruit of the Spirit described by Paul (Gal 5:22–23), but a good tree will produce many other good fruits. These include holiness (Rom 6:22), repentance (Matt 3:8; Luke 3:8), worship (Heb 13:15), good works (Col 1:10), evangelism (Rom 1:13), and benevolence (Rom 15:25–28). But this fruit is not for us. It is intended to nourish others, and to perpetuate the blessings God has planted in our lives.

That kind of fruit turns Satan's stomach. Because this individual is already rooted, the adversary must intercept the living water and life-giving light from above. This is how thorns strangle the good seed in spiritual and physical gardens alike.

Jesus identified two thorns that look to infiltrate: the deceitfulness of riches and the cares of this world. The first is somewhat straightforward, and we will give it deeper consideration in coming pages. The second is far subtler.

First, we must define "world." This is an important distinction, as God's kingdom is not of this world.[2] I like Scot McKnight's definition of "world" as the unredeemed realm of human affairs into which Jesus is sent, and out of which he saves his own.[3] The "world" describes the human system that stands in opposition to or in place of Christ. What, then, does this world care about? Dethroning God. How is this achieved? Allow me to "enlighten" you.

---

1. John 15:6; Heb 6:7–8.

2. John 8:23; 15:19; 17:16; 18:36.

3. McKnight, *Kingdom Conspiracy*, 17–18.

Western civilization is a postmodern, post-Christian society, built almost exclusively upon principles that emerged from the Enlightenment—an eighteenth-century intellectual awakening that affected everything from governance and economics to religion and science. While countless benefits have resulted, the severity of consequences cannot be ignored. Enlightenment thought is anthropocentric (centered on the human). It holds that proper understanding of man is man himself, an understanding captured in Rene Descartes's great philosophical discovery, "I think, therefore I am." Though Descartes, a committed Christian, did not think this opposed church doctrine, his work solidified a shift from revelation to reason as final authority in all truth.[4]

To make man central is to place him on God's throne as the arbiter of truth. It is a coup d'état that was centuries in the making. To understand, let us consider an interesting claim made in the third of Jesus' seven church letters. There, he identified Pergamum as Satan's throne, or dwelling place (Rev 2:13). Not Babylon, which is the seat of rebellion. Not New York City, which is the world's economic capitol. Not the Islamic holy cities of Mecca or Medina. Not cities of excess such as Las Vegas, New Orleans, or San Francisco. No, Satan is enthroned in Pergamum, and with good reason.

The city was a center of pagan worship, and home to the healing cult of Asclepius, which was symbolized by a serpent. The massive throne-like altar of *Zeus Soter* ("Zeus the Savior") was also adorned with serpent sculptures.[5] Its pagan affections notwithstanding, Pergamum was also the seat of science and medicine in Asia Minor. The city's library of two hundred thousand books rivaled that of Alexandria, an achievement recognized by everyone from the Greek writer Plutarch to the Roman writer Pliny the Elder. Shortly before Christ's birth, Marc Antony supposedly gave those works to Cleopatra as a wedding present to restore the Library at Alexandria, which was burned to the ground during Julius Caesar's siege.[6]

Would it surprise you that Satan's throne might be located in a library? Remember, this was no ordinary library. It was a bastion of Greek science and philosophy, a culture centered on idealism—an ethic that asserts one who lives up to ideal standards will be rewarded. While Pelagianism asserted your ability to not sin (and thus negated the need for God's grace), idealism asserts your ability to thrive (and thus negates the need for God's

4. Gonzalez, *History of Christian Thought*, 321–22.

5. Keener, *NIVAC*, 122.

6. Bivens-Tatum, *Libraries and the Enlightenment*, 144.

grace). As the individual increases, the need for God decreases; divine grace and presence is sought "only in situations that extend beyond our control or where our knowledge does not reach . . . [and thus] God becomes 'the God of the gaps,' the *Deus ex machina*, present only where we have not yet learned how to cope."[7] The heart of such thought is well-captured in the closing words of B. F. Skinner's book *Beyond Freedom and Dignity*: "we have not yet seen what man can make of man."[8]

The Renaissance (French for "rebirth") occurred roughly from 1300–1700 and marked a rediscovery of this "wisdom." The subsequent shift in perspective centralized man rather than God. Combine that with a meteoric rise in scientific method and understanding, and you have the makings of modernity—the intellectual rejection of revelation as authority, the recognition of reason as the only means to understanding, and the requirement for rational, scientific proof on any claim of truth. From this point forward, the Bible was no longer the answer, but the question.

German philosopher Immanuel Kant described this as "mankind's coming of age," but this era proved disastrous for religion and deficient for moral development as the creation continued to distance itself from its creator. There arose nihilism, which places no worth on traditional morals, ideas, or beliefs. Religion saw the rise of deism, which presents God as "the great watchmaker in the sky" who set things in motion, then stepped aside to let everything run its course.[9] Rarely does he intervene in our day-to-day activities.

Christendom did not respond well to such assertions, and often stood on blind faith rather than reasoned faith.[10] It certainly didn't get off to a good start when, in 1616, the church declared Galileo a heretic for teaching that the earth revolves around the sun. The church failed to acknowledge other scientific advancements and discoveries in the subsequent centuries, and it was ill-equipped to counter bad theories with sound science (looking your way, Darwin). Thankfully, this is no longer the case, but the consequences are undeniable. The intellectual world grew increasingly hostile toward Christianity, which was viewed as irrational. It is little wonder that atheism and agnosticism began a steady growth amid this implosion.

7. Stassen and Gushee, *Kingdom Ethics*, 33.

8. Skinner, *Beyond Freedom and Dignity*, 215.

9. Gonzalez, *History of Christian Thought*, 335–39.

10. Faith need not be anti-intellectual, but rather able to ask hard questions and find credible answers. See Köstenberger, et. al., *Truth Matters*, 12–13.

Nearly one-in-five Americans (23 percent) now identify themselves as such.[11] Statistics show that half were once people of faith but changed their belief when they learned evolution, became fed up with the hypocrisy in the church, came to believe that rational thought and religion are incompatible, or lacked scientific evidence for a creator.[12]

Of course, modernity failed to provide the stronger individual, familial, and societal structures it promised. To be better off, we sure are worse off. The self-oriented solutions caused more problems than they solved, and modernity's failures are too many to address in this work. Worse yet, the course correction is proving far more cataclysmic. As Swenson rightly observed, "progress" that has gained autonomous strength "does not depend on us to push it along. The trouble is, it no longer responds to us either."[13]

Autonomy's momentum has delivered man to the age of postmodernity, which is centered on the belief that objective truth cannot be accessed by reason. Universal truth and rationality are illusions. All understanding is value-dependent, and it is relative to individual preference and perspective. Moral relativism rules the day and insists that what is true for me may not be true for you; whatever works to satisfy my need is truth, and that truth can change as my circumstances change. Therefore, there is no eternal truth or moral absolutes.[14]

The effect of this philosophy on theological standing is hard to grasp, and likely to be worse than we can imagine. As noted in Section I, the great consequence of sin is alienation from God, each other, and self. The preeminence of personal preference further alienates from all three. One example is the current "moral revolution" that has seen society (and many within the church) accept the divorce culture, openness to divergent sexuality, the prevalence of heterosexual cohabitation, and normalization of homosexuality.[15] In addition, 91 percent of adults and more than three-fourths of practicing Christians believe that "the best way to find yourself is to look inside yourself" rather than looks to God.[16] Indeed, postmodernity epitomizes the disunity and dissolution that results when we fail to recognize

11. Lipka, "Closer Look," para. 2.

12. Lipka, "Why 'Nones' Left Religion," chart "Half of 'Nones' Left Childhood Faith."

13. Swenson, *Margin*, 23.

14. Newbigin, *Proper Confidence*, 26.

15. See Mohler, *We Cannot Be Silent*.

16. Kinnaman and Lyons, *Good Faith*, 251.

and properly respond to sin and Savior. To eat from its tree of knowledge "occasions a new 'fall' and loss of innocence."[17]

These thorns are able to choke the church because society is saturated in postmodern thought. God declares his word to be truth.[18] The majority of American adults do not agree. Christian researcher George Barna found that 57 percent believe that knowing right and wrong is a matter of personal experience, while slightly more than one-third believe moral truth is absolute. Three-quarters of millennials agree strongly or somewhat that "whatever is right for your life or works best for you is the only truth you can know." In addition, 41 percent of practicing Christians believe the only truth one can know is whatever is right for one's own life (a belief held by two-thirds of atheist adults).[19] This conundrum is compounded by the secularization that has further alienated religion from social context and made religion a private individual matter.[20]

But there is a catch. No matter how hard these thorns try to choke out the truth, the truth is we need a savior—and we know it. We were created with a genetic predisposition for spiritual belief. In 2004, molecular geneticist Dean Hamer located what is often called the "God gene" (or scientifically, VMAT2). Hamer said his finding indicates our inclination toward religious faith is no accident.[21] I would agree. Deep within, we know we are not right with God, and not what he intended us to be. How has Western society responded? Not well.

Atheists place their faith in science or self.[22] Humanists aspire to express the highest human values in the context of community—what James Croft and Greg Epstein call "the godless congregation."[23] A growing number seek spirituality under the New Age mantra, "I am spiritual but not religious." As columnist Terry Mattingly has noted, "the emerging consensus seems to be that vague, comforting spirituality is healthy . . . but that doctrinal, authoritative religion may even be dangerous."[24] To seek inner

17. Vanhoozer, "Challenge of Postmodernity," 60.

18. 2 Sam 7:28; Ps 119:160; John 17:17; 2 Cor 6:7; Col 1:5; 2 Tim 2:15; Jas 1:18.

19. Barna Group, "End of Absolutes," paras. 3–4, 7.

20. For more on this "secular/sacred split," I recommend Pearcey, *Total Truth*.

21. Kluger et al., "Religion." See also Hamer, *God Gene*.

22. Yes, atheists have faith; it is simply misplaced. I would argue that it takes greater faith to believe the evolutionary model than divine creation.

23. Vanhoozer, *Faith Speaking Understanding*, 152–53.

24. As quoted in Pearcey, *Total Truth*, 118.

peace and growth apart from God and others will exacerbate, rather than satisfy the alienation caused by sin. While Christianity helps you come to know God, spirituality merely emphasizes how you feel about God.

The influence of such thorns is hard to distinguish unless one has a biblical worldview. Your worldview is the beliefs and practices that shape your priorities and your relationship to God and others, assesses the meaning of events, and justifies your actions.[25] It is the way in which you answer life's key questions. Who am I? Where did I come from? What is my purpose? Worldview is aptly named, because it is the lens through which we view our world and how we live our life in response. Having the right lens is critical because, in the words of Pope Benedict XVI,

> [t]he tempter is not so crude as to suggest to us directly that we should worship the devil. He merely suggests that we opt for the reasonable decision, that we choose to give priority to a planned and thoroughly organized world, where God may have his place as a private concern, but must not interfere in our essential purposes.[26]

The following chapters represent key ways these worldly thorns infiltrate godly gardens and choke out spiritual life. Biblical illiteracy has rendered the church unable to withstand deficient and outright devilish theologies. Materialism has caused many to seek God's hand rather than God's heart. Self-orientation has removed God from his rightful place as the center of our being.

God, help us.

25. Palmer, *Elements of a Christian Worldview*, 22–23.
26. Ratzinger, *Jesus of Nazareth*, 44–45.

9

Many Are Famished Amid the Feast

GOD'S DESIRE IS THAT you live a stress-free life, saturated with health and wealth, and when problems arise, he will never put more on you than you are able to handle, right?

Actually, the Bible says none of this.[1] There are many well-meaning ministers out there (and not a few snake oil salesmen) who preach this as truth. Such messages bring plaudits and popularity. They fill pews and even pad some pockets, but they also leave many hearers angry and empty. When God doesn't come through as expected, he bears the blame—and when something else comes along that promises maximum blessing with minimal effort, the hungry hearers are soon in hot pursuit.

You can almost hear the thorns tightening around them.

Let me first apologize to all who have been hurt by thin theologies. I also know that pain, and I am sorry that you do, as well. Hurt and disillusioned, I failed to bear fruit for many years. God eventually replanted my withered soul, and I learned some important lessons in that time of restoration. First, I came to realize that God and his church are not synonymous, and he was not to blame. I must admit that there was no rush on my part to return to church, despite this revelation. After all, church folk were the

---

1. The fact is, God gets credited with a whole bunch of things he never said. Cleanliness is not next to godliness. Perseverance and brotherly kindness are (2 Pet 1:6–7). God never said "moderation in all things." That was Aristotle. God never said he would help those who help themselves. That was Ben Franklin. God never said "to thine own self be true." This can be credited to William Shakespeare. If you are a bit overwhelmed by this, no worries. This too shall pass. But God didn't say that, either.

problem! Perhaps. But the real issue was that the cares of the world had their grip on me, and I didn't want to give them up. What the church had done was a convenient excuse to stay away. Which brought me to my second lesson: if something said or done at church keeps you from God, then your faith was in church rather than God.

It was the Berean church identified in Acts 17 that helped me come to grips with this. The Apostle Paul commended this church because it fact-checked everything he taught and preached. Most preachers I knew would have been offended if a little peon such as me had the audacity to ask him to elaborate or explain (dare we say "defend"?). Soon after learning the Berean blessing, I came across 2 Timothy 2:14–15, in which Paul charged his protégé to not wrangle about words, "which is useless and leads to the ruin of the hearers. Be diligent to present yourself approved to God as a workman who does not need to be ashamed, accurately handling the word of truth."

Do you know what that means? Your spiritual growth is your responsibility. Yes, God has given apostles, prophets, evangelists, pastors and teachers to aid and equip (Eph 4:11–16), and the church is an irreplaceable part of that plan (Heb 10:25). The church is a gift from God, and much like every Christmas gift I received as a child, assembly is required. Still, we must remember that there are wolves among the sheep (Matt 7:15–20), and deceitful workers can appear as apostles of Christ—Satan himself can appear as an angel of light (2 Cor 11:13–14). Even absent of all this trickery, there are times when God-fearing shepherds will simply lose their way.

Sometimes (oftentimes) it is a fine line that separates revelation from speculation; those who are prophesying from those who are prophe-lying. Jesus warned against these before telling many to depart from him. The false doctrines of these false prophets left many with a false assurance of salvation. How do we not fall prey to these ravenous wolves? How do we guard against false prophets? Become a good fruit inspector. Jesus said a bad tree cannot produce good fruit. Do the people who pour into your life bear fruits of repentance and fruits of righteousness? Are they rightly dividing and rightly aligning with God's word? To make such inspection means we must know and apply what the Bible says. Most American Christians fail at one or both of these requirements. As a result, they are dying on the vine.

Have you ever heard of battlefield triage? It is a process in which a limited medical staff or facility assigns degrees of urgency to young men and women bearing the worst wounds imaginable. This approach helps medical officials determine who has priority, it starts necessary treatment for all of the wounded, and has been shown to vastly increase the number of survivors. But it is all for naught if the diagnosis is wrong, or too late.

Most who are wounded don't have the kind of time it takes to get to a medical center, especially in the treacherous terrain of Afghanistan, for example. All combat troops are trained in first aid, but they are equipped to fight, not to fix. Combat care is the job of remarkable young men and women called combat medics in the Army and Air Force and corpsmen in the Navy and Marine Corps. They are literal lifesavers who thrive in that precious "golden hour." These selfless and heroic troops are very limited in number and can be responsible for treating dozens of warriors as bullets and bombs threaten their every step.

They didn't become proficient by accident or chance, and they never stop improving. In such effort, the Army in 2012 found it could cut one-third of its battlefield deaths by addressing three very treatable injuries or conditions. These "primary causes of preventable death" were airway obstruction, which accounted for 6 percent of preventable deaths; tension pneumothorax (when air escapes into the chest cavity from a punctured lung), which accounted for 33 percent of preventable deaths; and hemorrhage from extremity wounds, which accounted for 60 percent of preventable deaths.[2] Regarding the latter, the Army Surgeon General's report noted that uncontrolled hemorrhage was the largest single cause of combat deaths, accounting for more than 80 percent of combat deaths.[3] Had someone been there to rightly assess the wound and rightly apply a tourniquet, many of those lives would have been saved.

Why point this out? Because we are in a battle, and many are bleeding out right before our eyes. The United States had a population of 326 million at the end of 2017. As we discussed in the introduction, polls show that roughly 75 percent (245 million) believe they are going to heaven, but the actual number will be far lower. Our worst-case (but very possible) scenario held that one-in-four will step into glory. That would mean 164 million who believe themselves bound for heaven are wrong. Eternally wrong.

Many.

But what if, like the Army, we could save one-third of those who are perishing by rightly assessing their wounds and applying the right treatment? Think about it: fifty-four million souls dying on the battlefield, but

2. Savitsky and Eastridge, *Combat Casualty Care*, 88.

3. Savitsky and Eastridge, *Combat Casualty Care*, 95.

able to be saved if we simply address the things that choke the breath of life or drain the precious blood.

The good news is there are great combat medics already assessing the body of Christ. These include organizations such as the American Bible Society and the Barna Group (a research institute that keeps its finger on the pulse of faith and culture through in-depth statistical surveys and analyses). Their triage has shown that the body of Christ is in pretty bad shape, but the major issues have been identified and deaths are preventable. So, what is the miracle cure? "He sent his word and healed them, and delivered them from their destructions" (Ps 107:20).

The problem is that few take the time to find out what God says about issues of life and eternity, and that is why the thorns will choke the life out of many. Though the Bible is the all-time best seller, it has become a dust-covered cure that sits idle on many shelves. The American Bible Society teams with the Barna Group annually to measure this dilemma. Their latest report at the time of this writing, "State of the Bible 2017," included nationwide interviews of more than two thousand adults. Researchers found that only 16 percent of adults read the Bible daily, and another 14 percent read it several times a week. In comparison, 45 percent of American adults read the Bible at least once a week in 1991. In addition, nearly one-third of today's adults never read, listen to, or pray with the Bible (a five-percentage point increase over the previous year). Ten percent of adults read the Bible less than once a year and 8 percent read it only once or twice a year. The number of people who are skeptical of or hostile toward the Bible has increased from 10 percent to 19 percent in the past six years.[4]

Another survey found that no major US city had a majority of residents who are "Bible-minded," defined as those who read the Bible weekly *and* strongly assert the Bible is accurate in the principles it teaches. Chattanooga, Tennessee topped the list at 50 percent in the rating. Only 25 percent of the nation is considered Bible-minded.[5] Cities below the Mason-Dixon line show a greater openness to the Bible. The Northeast showed the greatest resistance, especially in New York and New England, where barely one-in-ten residents qualify as Bible-minded.

---

4. ABS, "State of the Bible 2017," 3–8.

5. Barna Group, "2017 Bible-Minded Cities," para. 2. To calculate each city's ranking, Barna analyzed the Bible reading habits and beliefs of 76,505 nationwide adult respondents over a ten-year period.

Here's the irony: numerous national polls have found that most Americans (including a majority of young adults) believe the Bible has been more influential on humanity than any other text, and that the Bible contains everything a person needs to know in order to live a meaningful life. Nearly three in five Americans believe the Bible is the actual, inspired word of God.[6] Though many revere the Bible, few read it. That is a dangerous reality when one understands that God's people have always been destroyed by lack of knowledge (Hos 4:1, 6).

It is no secret that our country has little knowledge of biblical teachings and truths. We are reminded of this sad fact every time a new survey shows that most Americans can't name five of the Ten Commandments or any of the four Gospels. I am saddened to say that atheists, agnostics, Jews, and Mormons know as much or more than Christians when it comes to the Bible.[7] I have seen polls that make light of the fact that many Americans think Moses was one of Jesus' twelve disciples, Billy Graham preached the Sermon on the Mount, the epistles are the wives of the apostles, and Joan of Arc was Noah's wife. But this is no laughing matter. The American church is in trouble—and the greatest problem in the American church is the American pastor.

Yes, I can back up this statement. Only half of Protestant pastors possess a biblical worldview, according to the findings of Christian researcher George Barna.[8] He defined a Christian worldview as a belief in absolute moral truth as defined by Scripture, and acceptance of six core biblical beliefs: the accuracy of biblical teaching, the sinless nature of Jesus, the literal existence of Satan, the omnipotence and omniscience of God, salvation by grace alone, and the personal responsibility to evangelize.

Take a moment to let that sink in. Only half of protestant pastors agree with and live their lives according to those six statements. No wonder only one-in-ten Christians say the same.[9] Why so few? Worldview. Neither God's word nor his will have primacy because half of our pastors and 90 percent of Christians place their trust, belief, hope, dreams and desires in something other than God, whether or not they are aware of this tendency.

---

6. ABS, *State of the Bible 2017*, 5.

7. Pew Research Center, "U.S. Religious Knowledge Survey," para. 1–3, assorted charts.

8. Barna Group, "Changes in Worldview," para. 2.

9. Barna Group, "Changes in Worldview," para. 4.

This is the Enlightenment effect, and it stands as evidence that many Christians who have been raised in church have not been raised in Christ.

As the thorns tighten, our grip on God loosens. If the church does not know God's commandments, how can it expect to keep those commandments? If the church does not understand God's covenant, how can it expect to remain in covenant? If the church does not know the Bible, how can it know its author?

"I never knew you; depart from Me, you who practice lawlessness."

This battle for truth has seen many casualties. Many are gasping for the breath of life. Many are fading into darkness as the precious blood is lost. God sent his word to heal them, but most Americans are more interested in hearing what they want to hear rather than hearing what God wants to say. And if one preacher won't tell them what they want to hear, there are four or five others just down the road who are happy to oblige.

We have entered a time of famine much like one described by the prophet Amos; not a famine of bread, nor a thirst for water, but of hearing the word of the Lord (Amos 8:11). A comprehensive 2016 study by the US Census Bureau explains why: the average American spends less than ten minutes in prayer and Bible reading daily.[10]

We need God's word more than the food we eat, yet countless congregations are spiritually starving.[11] Many get a bit of bread and maybe some beef broth on Sunday morning, and little to nothing throughout the week. If the amount of food you received daily was equivalent to the amount of God's word you had received, could you survive? Many would not. Many will not. Many will walk out of church this Sunday spiritually dead or dying. Talk about a zombie apocalypse!

Many churches volunteer to feed the homeless and hungry, and well they should. But what of those who are spiritually starving? Of those who regularly engage Scripture, only half are part of a group Bible study.[12] Most are going it alone, and this should not be. As the great C. S. Lewis rightly noted, "[t]he Church exists for nothing else but to draw all men into Christ, to make them little Christs. If they are not doing that, all the cathedrals,

10. Bureau of Labor Statistics, "Economic News Release," 3. See especially the "Religious and Spiritual Activities" row. Keep in mind that this is an average of all Americans. The 7 percent who claim daily participation averaged ninety minutes on weekdays. The 16 percent who claim weekend participation averaged two hours on weekends and holidays, to include church attendance.

11. Job 23:12; Luke 4:4.

12. ABS, "State of the Bible 2017," 61.

clergy, missions, sermons, even the Bible itself, are simply a waste of time."[13] Amen! We have an obligation to help believers grow in the likeness of Christ, or they will not survive. The modern church does not do a very good job at this, and I'm sure this is no great revelation to you. As a result, many churches are filled with what I call "swamp Christians." A swamp is essentially a river that may be miles wide but is only a few inches deep. A swamp may look mighty, but it is shallow, and it stinks from stagnation. The reason a swamp is shallow and stagnant is that it lacks the structure (banks) that would provide direction and depth.

Let me tell you about a swamp Christian I met a few years back. We'll call him Oswald. Now, Oswald was an enthusiastic fellow. An usher who had just celebrated one year at the church, he rushed out to greet me as I entered the church foyer one fine Sunday morning. Oswald was a talker, and he made sure to keep me entertained through the obligatory meet-and-greet. As I scrolled through my sermon notes one last time, he told me about all of the great things the church was doing: an onsite carnival, an out-of-town trip, a big Christmas dinner, and the softball team was second to none. The more I listened, the more I noticed what I did not hear: his oration of activities never mentioned basic things such as Jesus, the Bible, or discipleship.

"Tell me about your salvation experience, Oswald."

The proverbial deer in the headlights was staring back at me.

"I'm not sure what you're asking me," he said.

"Oh, well, how did you come to learn about the love of Jesus and accept him as the Lord of your life?"

"I dunno, I've always been spiritual and believed in God. The pastor invited me to church and I figured it was time that I go, you know, and do the right thing."

Many people like Oswald fill our sanctuaries. They want to be in right relationship with God. They want to be a better spouse or parent, child or friend. They want to overcome their demons. They want peace and purpose. They come to church, throw some jingle in the plate, and lend a helping hand, but deep down inside, they know this engine isn't firing on all cylinders. Something very important is missing, but they don't know what it is.

How did Oswald and those like him get in such a swampy mess? Many churches equate size with success, and attendance with anointing. As a

13. Lewis, *Mere Christianity*, 199.

result, church growth often drives preaching and priorities. Under pressure to increase nickels and noses, cookie-cutter Christianity works to maximize capacity and contributions. This approach has utterly failed, evident in the fact that America is now a post-Christian nation.

The modern ministry model looks for the latest gimmick to build that bigger and better church. When the "saints" come marching in, we petition God to fix those people and their pesky problems. This is completely backwards! Numeric growth is not the church's job. Jesus said, "I will build my church" (Matt 16:18). That is his job. Our job is to "[g]o therefore and make disciples of all the nations, baptizing them in the name of the Father and the Son and the Holy Spirit, teaching them to observe all that I commanded you" (Matt 28:19–20a).[14] We are to build up one another (1 Thess 5:11); we make disciples, and Christ uses the fruit of those disciples to build the church (1 Cor 3:6–7). Spiritual growth must precede physical growth, or we will succumb to the thorn of teleological ethics, which tells us that the right thing to do is that which will bring the most good.[15] The right thing to do is that which will bring the most God!

This does not relieve us of the need to evangelize the lost. Nor should we consider "church growth" to be a dirty term or relegated to a secondary status. We all want to see our churches grow. More people means more souls saved and more laborers to reap the awaiting harvest. But many well-meaning pastors have followed secular principles and placed priority on building a larger congregation, often at the expense of building a better and biblical congregation.[16]

I am reminded of an email advertisement sent by a national church growth consultant. His pitch was simply this: "[t]he Book of Acts church saw incredibly quick growth—sometimes thousands joining in one day. That is the biblical model, and God wants nothing less for you!" Hogwash. The growth we see in Scripture is but a snapshot of the early church. The gospels and epistles were written in a fifty-year span, from roughly 45 to 95 AD. The three centuries that followed saw the church expand to thirty-one

---

14. Does that rattle your understanding of pastoral priorities? Take a gander at Ps 127:1. Then look at 1 Cor 12:3b. Check out John 6:44 and 15:16, while you're at it. And Acts 2:42–47.

15. The failure in accepting this common ethic is that if fails to recognize God as the greatest good, and that he alone determines what is good for us.

16. Once you read beyond the gospels, you will find that Scripture uses the word "grow" in only two contexts: Grow (mature) as an individual believer, and do not grow weary.

million, more than half of the Roman Empire's population. But the path from a persecuted minority to the dominant world religion was marked by an annual growth rate as little as 3.42 percent.[17]

The world promises maximum benefit with minimum effort; the promises of God are obtained through faith and patience (Heb 6:12). Plant the good seed. Remove the obstacles that prevent growth. Cut away the thorns to maximize God's light and living water. Yes, many Christians are spiritually dying within our churches, but God has sent his word to heal them. Be the combat medic who will brave the enemy's onslaught and stop the bleeding. End this famine by teaching believers to consume God's word daily—not as a snack or appetizer, but as the main course. Discipleship classes and mentoring are a must. Church members and ministers must teach people how to dig into the Bible and hold one another accountable to those truths. There can be no other way.

Daily engagement supplemented by a group Bible study will give you all the answers you need. Though Enlightenment principles and post-modernity have done everything imaginable to silence the Scripture, its truth stands as strong as ever.[18] A good knowledge of God's word will get you through anything life throws at you; it will enable you to live your life with certainty.[19] A good relationship with God's word will make an eternal difference.

The lack of such understanding will lead you down a far different path.

---

17. Olson, *American Church in Crisis*, 88.

18. For more on this, see Appendix 1, "Truth You Can Trust."

19. God's word will bring God's blessing (Luke 11:28; Mic 2:7), God's mercy (Ps 119:58), and God's healing (Ps 107:20). God's word will bring you joy (Jer 15:16), strength (Ps 119:28), comfort (Ps 119:50), and revival (Ps 119:25, 107, 154). God's word will cleanse you (Ps 119:9; Eph 5:25–27), sanctify you (John 17:17), deliver you (Ps 119:170), keep you from sinning (Ps 119:11), and perfect you (1 John 2:5). God's word will give you hope (Ps 119:81, 147), give you understanding (Ps 119:169; Prov 1:23), uphold you (Ps 119:116), equip you for every good work (John 8:31; 2 Tim 3:16–17), and keep you on the right path (Ps 119:67, 105, 133). God's word will answer your prayers (John 15:7) and accomplish what God pleases (Isa 55:11). That is because God's word is pure (Ps 12:6; Prov 30:5), powerful (1 Thess 1:5), true (Pss 33:4, 119:160; 1 Thess 2:13), proven (Ps 18:30), settled (Ps 119:89), unchained (2 Tim 2:9), divine (2 Tim 3:16–17; 2 Pet 1:20–21), living and powerful (Heb 4:12), and eternal (Isa 40:8; Mark 13:31).

10

Many Are Strangled by Strange Fire

BIBLICAL ILLITERACY REMOVES JESUS from the equation. That is especially bad when one realizes that Jesus is the answer! Such removal is not uncommon. I see an analogous warning in the Babel building program. The people were trying to work their way to heaven, and thus reach God on their own terms. As if that were not bad enough, they "substituted brick for stone," a dangerous omission in the spiritual sense.[1]

Many Babel-esque towers have been built in the Enlightenment's shadow, and all have substituted brick for stone; they have substituted religion for relationship in an effort to reach heaven. They attend Christian churches, do Christian ministry, and live lives of Christian devotion, but never really come to know the Christ they serve. Such Christianity typically results in an empty adherence to orthodoxy, or a preference for pop theology that evokes superficial emotions. Neither demonstrate faithfulness to God's word—and such faithfulness matters. As Keener rightly notes, "Paul warns that God will judge those who never embraced love for the truth of his gospel (2 Thess 2:10, 12); more generally, this principle shows how God values loving truth and expects us to value it also."[2]

Many fail to maintain right relationship with God through his word—living and inspired, written and spoken. Failure to do so often results in strange fires ignited on the altar of God. For this analogy, I use the example of Nadab and Abihu in Leviticus 10:1–7. The fire of God consumed them

1. Gen 11:3; cf. Isa 28:16 and Acts 4:11–12.
2. Keener, *Spirit Hermeneutics*, 188.

when they offered "strange fire," which likely originated from a source other than the fire authorized and ignited by God himself (this is an important matter, so I must ask you to hold this thought).[3]

The brothers were Aaron's eldest sons, and Moses' nephews, so they were not unfamiliar with God's presence and power. Their ministry on the day in question followed seven days of consecration, so we see religious commitment. Why did they violate God's word and profane his glory? We may never know this side of heaven. Perhaps they felt they had good reason. Perhaps they had the best of intentions. Perhaps they saw no problem with their actions. Still, they offered strange fire that God was unwilling to accept. On this, Cyprian of Carthage (200–258 AD) provided timeless wisdom:

> the sons of Aaron also, who set upon the altar a strange fire not commanded by the Lord, were at once blotted out in the sight of the avenging Lord. These examples, you will see, are being followed wherever the tradition which comes from God is despised by lovers of strange doctrine and replaced by teaching of merely human authority.[4]

Strange fire chokes out spiritual life because it presents unbiblical worship as acceptable worship. Such fire swept through the first-century church in Corinth, where religious activity bore greater likeness to their Greek culture than their Christian faith. Theirs was a city steeped in art, trade, and political power, and its people were sinking into an abyss of individualism and self-glorification. Poverty was regarded as disgrace and dishonor; the projection of wealth and status was paramount. As Plutarch observed: "to be deprived of the chance to display wealth is to be deprived of the wealth itself."[5] The display of wealth would come at great cost, as citizens would amass overwhelming debt to find temporal pleasures and an admiring public.

Corinth was consumed by an explosion in religious interest, but it was superficial and naïve.[6] People wanted contact with the supernatural, but for the purposes of health, wealth, protection, and sustenance. According

---

3. Gane, *NIVAC*. Cf. Lev 16:12; Num 16:46.

4. Lienhard, *ACCS/OT*, 174. The selection is drawn from Greenslade, *Early Latin Theology Selections*, 137.

5. Savage, *Power Through Weakness*, 22.

6. Savage, *Power Through Weakness*, 25–27

to Savage, "what mattered was the service the gods rendered to people, not people to the gods."[7]

Religious fervor climaxed in religious banquets, parades, and festivals. Religious message centered on oratory skills; delivery trumped content, as "truth and knowledge were sacrificed on the altar of popular acclaim."[8] The scene strongly resembled the modern church age, in which many are drawn to theatrics, professional praise, and charisma. Many ministries have adopted the consumer culture that controls society. The "attractional church" likes to invest and invite to get people to pick them. Less popular, but arguably far more biblical, is the "incarnational church," which seeks to transform believers and send them into the community, workplace, and world where they can project the love and life of Christ.[9]

If you do not see the influence of consumer culture in the church, I invite you to visit a local Christian bookstore and take a look at the best-sellers. Many are little more than self-help books that tell you how to do, how to get, how to have, how to achieve. Five Ways to Get God's Grace Now, Six Steps to Empowerment, Seven Keys to Fulfilling Your Destiny, Eight Habits to Having the Life You Deserve! These titles are an exaggeration, I'll grant you, but not much of one. As Olson rightly asserts, "American evangelicalism has often reduced the message of Jesus to practical tips about living life. The Bible then becomes a how-to guide for a successful and happy life."[10]

Next, I invite you to frolic through the classics section. You may not be able to frolic, since this less-popular section is usually pretty small, but what you will find are books replete with the search for transformation through prayer and holiness. Revival was a necessity, and the importance of seeking God was indisputable. The contrast captures a shift in focus from worshiping and glorifying God to worshiping and glorifying self. The disciplined development that drove the early church now serves to decorate our social media posts. While early believers lived life in light of Christ's resurrection,

---

7. Savage, *Power Through Weakness*, 28

8. Savage, *Power Through Weakness*, 30.

9. Frost and Hirsch, *Shaping of Things to Come*, 58–60. The authors go so far as to say that "Jesus himself would likely have been deeply alienated from the [attractional] church as it generally expresses itself in the United States, the United Kingdom, and Australia."

10. Olson, *American Church in Crisis*, 399.

we celebrate this as an annual holiday. Indeed, the "fully surrendered life is glamorized and popularized, but it is rarely realized."[11]

What can we do? Sometimes, you have to be a firefighter before you can be a fire starter. Such was the example of Paul. He extinguished Corinth's strange fire with talk of comfort through suffering (chapter 1), glory through shame (chapter 3), life working through death (chapter 4), riches through poverty (chapter 6), and power through weakness (chapters 12 and 13).[12]

Indeed, Paul's example is the key to stopping the strange fire of secular influence. Unfortunately, the church has not always responded as well. Perhaps nowhere is this more evident than in the emergence of liberal theology, whose influence continues to dominate much of Western Christianity.

Matters of faith were quickly consumed in the eighteenth century as the fires of the Enlightenment burned with increasing intensity. Talk of the supernatural and miraculous did not coalesce with the scientific understanding of the day. Anything that could not be replicated by the scientific method, or measured by empirical analysis, could not be true. The subsequent rejection of religion meant that theologians would no longer have a seat at the table of academia, and this when mankind was making his greatest intellectual strides. To reconcile faith and science (and to make religion more palatable to the "enlightened"), some theologians willfully eliminated divine revelation and miraculous activity from Scripture. Instead of quenching the strange fire, they ignited a strange fire within the tabernacle.

The first sparks flew when Friedrich Schleiermacher, the father of liberal theology, argued that the Bible is "a record of human religious experience rather than a revelation from God or a record of God's acts in history."[13] This meant the Bible is neither infallible nor inspired, but simply serves as a model for good living. Miracles never really happened; they were merely stories told by early Christians to externalize spiritual experience. Such assertion pleased the natural man, but at the expense of the supernatural God.

This approach soon gave rise to "selective literalism," the tendency to pick and choose the scriptures one is willing or able to accept, and to

11. Tozer, *Crucified Life*, 141.

12. For more on Paul's confrontation and correction, see Appendix 4, "Power Through Weakness."

13. Lane, *Concise History*, 239.

discard the rest. Jeremiah faced this strange fire in 605 BC. The judgment of God was knocking on the door of a disobedient nation, and the weeping prophet responded with God's word of warning. The prophecies were not what King Jehoiakim wanted to hear. Instead of declaring God's favor and blessing, Jeremiah warned of God's wrath and judgment. Instead of affirming Jehoiakim and the people, God charged them with disobedience. Other "prophets" told the king a different tale. God was happy, all was well, and blessings are on their way, they said. The king liked what they had to say, so as each sentence or two was read from Jeremiah's scroll, Jehoiakim would cut that portion out and throw it into the fire. He did this until nothing of the scroll remained (Jer 36).

Of course, Jeremiah had the true word of God. It was not the word the king *wanted* to hear, but it was the word the king *needed* to hear. He chose not to listen.[14] The failure to repent had a disastrous effect on the nation's relationship with God. The Almighty removed his hand of protection, and Nebuchadnezzar soon swept through the land. Tens of thousands of God's people were exiled out of their promise, forced to walk the fifteen hundred-mile Fertile Crescent trade route to Babylon. The conquering king in 586 BC completely destroyed Jerusalem. He carried the holy articles from God's temple back to his kingdom, just as Isaiah had prophesied one hundred and fifteen years earlier (2 Kgs 20:17). The everlasting kingdom promised to David lay in waste.

Many have failed to learn the lessons of that fateful day. Many fail to obey God's word when it runs contrary to their will. Many won't listen to truth, but instead seek out teachers and preachers who will tell them what they want to hear. Many believe false promises and prophecies, though the words counter what is written in Scripture. Many are tearing the scroll apart piece by piece; they destroy the parts they are unable to believe or unwilling to follow. Many allow God's word to become ash as it is subjected to their strange fire.

We could give plenty of big picture examples; for example, the denial of the charismata (and the declaration by some that Pentecostals and Charismatics are apostates), the acceptance of homosexuality in ministry and marriage, the refusal to preach on sin and sacrificial atonement, or the declaration that hell doesn't exist. Instead, let's get a little more personal.

---

14. Consider, in contrast, the response of King Josiah when God's word was revealed to him (2 Kgs 22). Even Ahab, the wicked husband of the more wicked Jezebel, responded to God's word better than Jehoiakim (1 Kgs 21:5–29).

What kind of truth trimming takes place in your life? Do you ever cut out the parts with which you're not comfortable? Ignore the parts with which you don't agree? What is the strange fire that allows you to easily discard the difficult parts of Scripture? I say this not in condemnation, but invitation. Consider yourself, whether you are in the faith! You and I can no more destroy the word of God than Jehoiakim. God's word is indestructible.[15] The fires of hell itself can do nothing to erase the everlasting truth. Though indestructible, God's word can be ignored, cast indifferently into a strange fire. When you hear God's word, listen closely to the sounds that follow. You will either hear the snipping of scissors as the scroll is sliced, or the spinning of shoes as the believer turns to follow God.

In the example of liberal theology, significant scriptures were cut away to accommodate secular reasoning. The theology denied the Trinity's existence, and many adherents follow the lead of Albrecht Ritschl in his denial of Jesus' divinity. Ritschl, the most influential nineteenth-century liberal theologian, instead defined Jesus' deity as perfect humanity and said, "he was God in the sense that he had a perfect knowledge of God and was united to him in moral obedience."[16] This is nothing but a resurgence of Gnosticism and Pelagianism, a position made worse by the fact that Ritschl also denied the doctrine of original sin, and with it the wrath of God against sin. What, then, was the purpose of the cross? The reconciliation facilitated by Jesus enabled a change in our attitude toward God, rather than a change in his attitude about us. Adolf von Harnack further diluted the holiness of God and the severity of sin by presenting Jesus as one who preached a simple message of the brotherhood of man and fatherhood of God.[17] In this view, Jesus was a great teacher, a great prophet, and a great example, but not the great I Am. Such devaluation facilitates religious pluralism, omnism, and universalism—beliefs that insist all religions are equal, all paths lead to the same God, and Jesus is only one of those paths. While adherents celebrate the ability to "coexist" that is afforded (according to the popular bumper sticker, at least), this approach fails to adequately address the

---

15. Isa 40:8; Matt 24:35.

16. Lane, *Concise History,* 241.

17. Albert Schweitzer eviscerated this view in his work *The Quest of the Historical Jesus,* and used contradictions inherent to liberal theology to strip this effort of credibility. It is also worth noting that von Harnack's liberal theology would fall out of favor with his two greatest students: Rudolf Bultmann, one of the most influential New Testament scholars of the twentieth century, and Karl Barth, whose insights would launch the neo-orthodox movement.

central problem of sin and salvation. It leaves the individual to bridge the chasms of alienation through his own works and wisdom. This is another Babel tower that has traded stone for brick; it promises a path to heaven that will fall woefully short.

This great shortfall was well noted by H. Richard Niebuhr, who rightly described liberal theology this way: "A God without wrath brought men without sin into a kingdom without judgment through the ministrations of a Christ without a cross."[18] In doing so, liberal theology provided exactly what the alienated soul seeks: the ability to be religious without all the trappings of religion.[19]

There are other strange fires sweeping through Christendom. Biblical illiteracy has given rise to materialistic hyper-faith movements and deficient hyper-grace theologies that seek blessing without growth, or growth without struggle. The latter promises the power of Pentecost to believers who have neither taken up their cross nor been resurrected with Christ. Please don't misunderstand; I certainly am not opposed to experiencing God's presence and power. I believe both are needed now more than ever, and I agree with Pinnock's assertion that "[s]peaking about God is meaningful only if there is an encounter with God back of it."[20] Dynamic experience always precedes understanding—after all, the church was born at Pentecost because a question was asked: "What does this mean?" (Acts 2:12). I also agree with Kärkkäinen's view that (often swift) charismatic experience must precede (often slow) theological understanding.[21]

---

18. Niebuhr, *Kingdom of God in America*, 193.

19. Before anyone calls down hellfire and brimstone, we would do well to realize that self-sufficiency has long been a problem in Christian congregations. This was the problem Paul tackled in Galatia, where believers tried to complete in the flesh what God started in the Spirit (Gal 3:1–5). This was also the great error of Pelagius (354–c. 428 AD), a theologian who elevated human effort over divine grace. He denied Augustine's doctrine of original sin and asserted that, because man is commanded to not sin, he must have the ability in himself to not sin, and thus the power to reform himself through commitment to Scripture and by following the example of Christ (and without the need of God's grace). Of course, the record of human history stands against Pelagius in this, as did Church Father Augustine.

20. Pinnock, *Flame of Love*, 18.

21. Kärkkäinen, *Pneumatology*, 15. He powerfully notes that such understanding was evident in the writings of Augustine, who argued that talk of the Spirit must touch an experienced reality that is tested and discerned by the church, which is guided by the same Spirit.

However, there is an increasing tendency to emphasize experience and the obtaining of "blessings" over discipleship and growth in holiness. Fueled by biblical illiteracy, this strange fire has spread like wildfire, and the results are disastrous.

With such "charismania" amid the charismata, many churches and denominations have taken a conservative approach and emphasized teaching and understanding the charismata before embracing (even allowing) an empowered experience. Many want no experience that they cannot explain or control. For them, understanding invites (or even enables) experience done decently and in order. While the message is biblical (1 Cor 14:40), the method is not. Experience precedes understanding. If you only allow the experiences you understand, you will only experience a drop from the ocean of God's greatness.

Adding to the dilemma is the fact that many will project the power of Pentecost in Christ's name, though they are not in Christ. Many workers of lawlessness will prophesy, cast out demons, and do mighty works (Matt 7:22). Many will project charismatic grace, but not possess saving grace. Why would God allow this? Because God will use whomever and whatever to accomplish his purpose.[22] In the passage on which this book is founded, it is evident that these people believed miraculous activity was evidence that they were in right standing with God. They prophesied, cast out demons, and performed miracles, so did they go wrong? They replaced relationship with religious fervor. Though allowed by God to participate in the "powers of the coming age" (Heb 6:5), their failure to live for God denied their entrance into his life.[23] Indeed, those who disregard God's direction "are not genuine disciples no matter how many spectacular deeds they perform."[24]

In light of such strange fire, there echoes in my mind the impassioned plea of Paul:

> I solemnly charge you in the presence of God and of Christ Jesus, who is to judge the living and the dead, and by His appearing and His kingdom: preach the word; be ready in season and out of season; reprove, rebuke, exhort, with great patience and instruction.

22. God used unclean ravens to feed Elijah the prophet amid a famine (1 Kings 17:1–6). God used an unclean donkey to stop Balaam from cursing God's people (Num 22; 2 Pet 2:15–16). An unclean donkey also delivered Jesus to Jerusalem for his Passion (Matt 21:1–7; John 1:14–15).

23. Osborne, *ECNT*, 275.

24. Turner, *BECNT*, 220.

> For the time will come when they will not endure sound doctrine;
> but wanting to have their ears tickled, they will accumulate for
> themselves teachers in accordance to their own desires, and will
> turn away their ears from the truth and will turn aside to myths.
> But you, be sober in all things, endure hardship, do the work of an
> evangelist, fulfill your ministry. (2 Tim 4:1–5)

We must commit ourselves to uproot these thorns; to quench the
strange fire and fan the flames of divine fire. How can we know the difference? Put every spirit to the test. If a message is filled with the world's
wisdom and is accepted by those who are worldly, it is strange fire. If a
message is confirmed by Scripture, accepted by the godly, and resisted by
the worldly, it is divine fire.[25] As Tozer rightly asserts, "[y]ou can always
test the quality of religious teaching by the enthusiastic reception it receives
from unsaved men. If the natural man receives it enthusiastically, it is not
of the Spirit of God."[26] Indeed, many Christians are afraid of being rejected
by society. We need to be afraid of being accepted by society.

But not only are we firefighters, we are also fire starters. There is a
necessary and authentic divine fire that consumes the sacrifice of flesh.[27]
This fire empowers for ministry.[28] This fire refines and purifies.[29] That latter description is especially nice. The prophet Malachi described God as
a refiner's fire and a purifier of silver. To purify silver, the precious metal
is positioned over the hottest flames to burn away impurities that would
otherwise reduce its value and strength. The silversmith has to carefully
monitor the process; silver will be destroyed if left in the flames one moment too long. How does the craftsman know the right time to pull his
precious possession from the furnace? When the silver is fully refined, he
is able to see his reflection—his own image will be looking back at him.[30]

---

25. 1 John 4:1–6; 1 Cor 2:14.

26. Tozer, *Crucified Life*, 61.

27. Lev 6:7–13; 9:24; Judg 6:21; 1 Kgs 18:38; 2 Chr 7:1; cf. Rom 12:1–2.

28. Exod 3–4; Acts 2:1–4; Heb 1:7. For those who like to sit and listen, but not share
or declare God's word, please notice in the example of Pentecost that it was tongues of
fire, not ears of fire, that sat upon each of them. It was tongues of fire because they were
expected to speak.

29. Zech 13:9; Mal 3:2–3; 1 Pet 4:12–13; cf. Jas 1:2–4.

30. Lockyer, *All the Parables*, 121. This description is especially beautiful when seen
in the context of Psalm 17:15, which states, "As for me, I will see Your face in righteousness; I shall be satisfied when I awake in Your likeness."

In closing, I return to the example of Nadab and Abihu, whose profane fire likely originated from a source other than the authorized fire ignited by God himself. The fire on the altar of sacrifice was to burn perpetually; priests carried the divine fire into the Holy Place to light the menorah and the altar of incense. This stands as an eternal truth: once the flesh is consumed by fire, God lets you carry the fire. It is no wonder that Christ came to baptize with Holy Spirit and fire![31]

31. Matt 3:11; Luke 3:16.

11

Many Asphyxiate on Their Appetites

THE SURRENDER OF OUR rich Scripture is not the only mark of poverty in the modern church. The pursuit of earthly riches has rendered many spiritually bankrupt. It is not hard to understand why. Ours is a culture that equates happiness with success, and measures success by what you have accomplished and acquired. As Idleman rightly observes, "the gods of success give us very convenient ways to keep score: the title after our name, the sum on our paycheck, the square footage of the new house."[1]

I am well aware of the dozens of passages that speak of God's willingness to bless and prosper his children. Indeed, our God is gracious, generous, and benevolent. However, in the context of salvation, the question is not what you possess, but what possesses you. It is with good reason that Jesus declared that no one can serve two masters, God and wealth; we are enslaved by what we are overcome.[2]

This was Paul's heart when he warned of materialism's thorny embrace. He said bluntly that "those who want to get rich fall into temptation and a snare and many foolish and harmful desires which plunge men into ruin and destruction. For the love of money is a root of all sorts of evil, and some by longing for it have wandered away from the faith and pierced themselves with many griefs" (1 Tim 6:9–10). A great example is Marin County, California, which boasts the nation's highest median home value, highest level of household expenditures, and highest income per capita in

1. Idleman, *Gods at War*, 133.
2. Matt 6:24, 2 Pet 2:19.

the nation. And its weekly church attendance is the nation's lowest, less than half that of the typical American county.[3]

The love of money stifles, and then strangles the love of God. Rather than become possessed by their possessions, many would do well to replace the Prayer of Jabez with the prayer of Proverbs 30:8–9: "Keep deception and lies far from me, give me neither poverty nor riches; Feed me with the food that is my portion, that I not be full and deny You and say, 'Who is the Lord?' Or that I not be in want and steal, and profane the name of my God."

Indeed, there are many Christians who can endure failure and tribulation but can't handle success. Such was the example of Nabal, which is recorded in 1 Samuel 25:2–13. Though David was on the run from the vengeful King Saul, he and his men had voluntarily protected Nabal's family, lands, and goods as they resided in the region. Nabal was later asked to help David in a time of need, but the wealthy landowner flatly refused. David was a great warrior, the Lord's anointed, and the future king. Even the Philistines spoke of David with reverence (1 Sam 21:11), yet Nabal scornfully described David as insignificant. We would do well to consider the description of Nabal. His name literally means "fool." Indeed, "the fool has said in his heart there is no God" (Ps 14:1). In this case, there is no God because a different god reigns, otherwise known as money. In discussing the foolish builder in chapter 4, we likened the disobedient to the atheist. We can add to their company the greedy individual who is unwilling to part with his wealth. God views all these fools in much the same way.

There are many more passages that illustrate the many ways in which the thorns of materialism choke the life of God's people. Long could we talk about camels going through the eyes of needles, and the rich young ruler who owned so much (in truth, it owned him).[4] There is much to say about prodigals living in pigpens (Luke 15:11–32). We could discuss Ananias and Sapphira's deceitful greed, and God's eye-opening response (Acts 5:1–11). Or Peter's rebuke of Simon the sorcerer when he tried to purchase the power of God (Acts 8:9–13). We could talk about greedy ministers who use the pulpit for profit.[5] Let us not forget the painful parable in which many were invited to a great dinner but responded with excuses rather than attendance (Luke 14:15–24). One was focused on his possessions, one was busy at work, and one just wanted to go home and be with his wife. Such

3. Olson, *American Church in Crisis*, 99.

4. Matt 19:16–26; Mark 10:17–31; Luke 18:18–30.

5. Mal 2; Mark 7:13; 2 Cor 2:17; 2 Pet 2:3, Jude 1:11.

excuses may sound reasonable, even legitimate, but many have become "enemies of the cross of Christ" and are headed for destruction because they have set their minds on earthly things and allowed their appetite to become their god (Phil 3:18–19).

The attempt to find such fulfillment has eradicated what Swenson defines as "margin." To illustrate, imagine a circle inside a larger circle. The inner circle represents everything you are currently doing, and the outer circle represents everything you have the time, energy, and resources to do. Margin is the area between completion and capacity. That space is increasingly diminished as people desperately try to achieve more and obtain faster. We tend to live on the edge of human limits, which is a dangerous place to reside. The closer the lines of completion and capacity become, the closer you are to a physical, spiritual, or emotional breakdown. "We must have some room to breathe. We need freedom to think and permission to heal. Our relationships are being starved to death by velocity. No one has the time to listen, let alone love."[6]

That is not to say that achievement is evil, but it must remain subservient to the greater goals and needs of social, emotional, and spiritual health. If we neglect these priorities, "our final reward will fittingly be all the unhappiness money can buy."[7]

In addition, such pursuit must be mitigated by godly faith and patience (Heb 6:12). We live in a microwave society that wants everything our way, right away. The impetuous nature often results in decisions that bring lifelong and life-changing consequences. This is a lesson Esau learned the hard way. That skilled hunter was set up for life. God promised Esau's grandpa, Abraham, that all the nations of the earth would be blessed through Abraham's son, Isaac (Gen 22:18). Isaac's firstborn son was Esau, which meant the birthright was his. This granted Esau authority, and guaranteed him a double portion of the inheritance. If Isaac had nine sons, his possessions would be divided into ten parts, and Esau would receive two of those ten parts. But Isaac had only two sons, which meant Esau would get two-thirds of Isaac's vast wealth.

One day, Esau stumbled in from work. He was physically, spiritually, and emotionally exhausted—and was met by his younger brother, who had a nice bowl of stew in hand (Gen 25:29–34). Jacob, whose name is translated "deceiver" or "supplanter," offered the stew in exchange for his brother's

---

6. Swenson, *Margin*, 22.

7. Swenson, *Margin*, 25.

birthright. Overcome by desperation, the short-sighted Esau sold out. He surrendered that which was most precious to satisfy a temporal appetite. The result was immediate and telling: Esau *despised* his birthright (25:34). That verb (*bazah*) is also used to describe the way David despised the Lord in his adultery with Bathsheba (2 Sam 12:10).[8] Let that sink in.

Now, allow me to ask, what would you exchange for your birthright? To put it in the words of Jesus, what would you take in exchange for your soul?[9] The idea may seem ludicrous on the surface, but the truth is we trade our treasures in heaven when we become fully invested in the pleasures of this world. Therefore, hold fast to what you have, and invest in heaven's "self-storage" plan.[10]

Unfortunately, this was not Eli's attitude when the thorns of ungodly appetites sprouted in Shiloh (1 Sam 2–4). Sin had a firm grip on his household; Eli knew it, and he did little to stop it. The priest had grown comfortable sitting around the sanctuary and getting fat off of the offerings.[11] He had become immobile and ineffective.

Eli's sons, Hophni and Phinehas, were all about their own kind of comfort. They had little reverence for God's presence, and instead used religion to satisfy their insatiable appetites. The brothers had sex with many women who came to serve at God's house, and they robbed God of the best sacrifices offered there. This dastardly duo had grown so comfortable with God that when trouble hit, in the form of a Philistine army, they didn't hesitate to grab the holy ark of the covenant and carry it into battle.[12] The brothers were not obedient to God's word, yet expected God to fight their battles. God was nothing but a way to obtain what they wanted. They had a relationship of comfort, not commitment. That relationship did not end well.

The enemy destroyed many of God's people and drove many others from their promise. Hophni and Phinehas were among those slaughtered. The ark of God was captured. When the news came to Eli, who was too fat

---

8. Walton, *NIVAC*.

9. Matt 16:26; Mark 8:36–37.

10. Isa 55:1–2; Matt 6:19–21; Rev 3:11.

11. It is worth noting that Shiloh means "a place of rest."

12. If you have seen Indiana Jones, you know the power of the ark. We're talking face-melting annihilation. The Nazis weren't the only ones on the receiving end. In Joshua's writings, the ark caused the Jordan to split and was there when the walls of Jericho fell. Later in 1 Samuel 5, the god Dagon was toppled before the ark, and the Philistine people were hit with a terrible plague.

to fight, he fell over and died. When Phinehas' wife heard the news, she gave birth and named her son Ichabod, which means "the glory has departed."

That is what results when we serve our appetites over the Almighty. It is the difference between Immanuel (God with us) and Ichabod (the glory has departed), between whether God dwells or departs. Compromised Christians who succumb to secular or material appetites may be spiritual and may see Jesus as a great man or a great teacher—they may even declare with their lips that he is God—but they will never experience Jesus in his true divinity.[13] For them, the glory has departed.

Appetites of the flesh is a significant issue in the Western church. As Paul warned, men have become lovers of self and lovers of money (2 Tim 3:2). Procrastination and worry have become top temptations for three-in-five Americans.[14] That same poll found that more than half (55 percent) say they are tempted to overeat. Forty-four percent spend too much money—the same number that said they spend too much time on media entertainment. Roughly one-in-four struggle with gossip and jealousy, while slightly more than one-in-ten admit to being tempted to lie or cheat, or to indulge in drugs or alcohol. And most Americans (59 percent) say they do nothing to avoid the tempting situation.

Enlightenment principles have certainly created a culture that openly embraces unbiblical behaviors, and postmodernity's rejection of objective truth has fostered a far greater allowance for what was once fringe behavior. This morality of self-fulfillment is perhaps most evident in the evolving opinions toward pornography. In ranking "bad things," teens and young adults said failure to recycle and the significant consumption of electricity or water is more immoral than viewing porn.[15] Indeed, the prevalence of point-and-click pornography has brought the issues of temptation and morality to a whole new realm, and the church is not immune. Though pornography use is significantly lower among Christians than non-Christians, the Barna Institute rightly classifies this as a crisis within Christendom. One in five youth pastors and one in seven senior pastors—more than fifty thousand US church leaders—admit they currently use porn. Two out of

13. Matt 15:18; Mark 7:6; John 1:5, 3:19, 14:19.

14. Barna Group, "Changing Shape of Temptation," bar graph titled "What Tempts Us?"

15. Barna Group, *Porn Phenomenon*, 81.

three youth pastors and more than half of senior pastors say porn is a current or past struggle.[16]

It is critical that the believer not let power, possession, pleasure, or plaudits become a driving force, lest the individual become entangled with the thorny affairs of this life (2 Tim 2:4). How do we clear our spiritual gardens of such? That can get a bit tricky, especially if we use strange fire to burn the thorny bushes.

The fear of indulgence has long-driven many to legalistic extremes. For example, in 197 AD, Tertullian renounced "all [the world's] spectacles" and went on to name "the madness of the circus, the immodesty of the theatre, the atrocities of the arena, the useless exercises of the wrestling-ground."[17] He further urged believers to instead be "knit together" in unity and discipline.

At roughly the same time, Clement of Alexandria instructed that "even laughter must be kept in check" and "whatever things are natural to man we must not eradicate from them, but rather impose on them limits and suitable times."[18] Food is to "minister to life, not to luxury." Clement called for moderation in consumption, and a rejection of different varieties "which engender various mischiefs," to include "the useless art of making pastry."[19] He took a similar approach to wealth, which he felt was provided by God for man's use.[20] "For if no one had anything, what room would be left among men for giving?"[21] The fortunately blessed should not flaunt wealth, but "for elegance and ornament, [wear] the fair dispositions, love, faith, hope, knowledge of the truth, gentleness, meekness, pity, gravity."[22]

Tertullian had little objection to possessions. He noted that Christians are "one in mind and soul, [and] do not hesitate to share our earthly goods with one another. All things are common among us but our wives."[23] Nearly two centuries later, Ambrose pulled those reigns even tighter and presented the abundance of riches as poverty in his *Letter to Priests*. "Exalt not yourself as rich; He sent forth His apostles without money," he wrote.

16. Barna Group, *Porn Phenomenon*, 77–78.

17. Tertullian, "Apology," locs. 44229–31.

18. Clement of Alexandria, "Instructor," locs. 29219–21.

19. Clement of Alexandria, "Instructor," loc. 28750–933.

20. Clement of Alexandria, "Who is the Rich Man," loc. 41155.

21. Clement of Alexandria, "Who is the Rich Man," loc. 41144.

22. Clement of Alexandria, "Who is the Rich Man," loc. 41048.

23. Tertullian, "Apology," loc. 44260.

"And the first of them said: 'Silver and gold I have none' [Acts 3:6]. He glories in poverty as if escaping contamination. 'Silver and gold,' he says, 'I have none,' nor gold and silver. He does not know their order, for he does not know their use."[24]

Such humbling poverty became a hunger for prosperity not long after Christianity became the established religion of the Roman Empire. This is most evident when Thomas Aquinas answered the pope's use of aforementioned Acts passage. The Dominican friar had an audience with Pope Innocent II and happened upon him while the pope and other officials counted a sizeable sum of money.

"See, Thomas," the pope said, "the church can no longer say, 'Silver and gold have I none.'"

"True, holy father," Aquinas responded. "But neither can she now say, 'Arise and walk.'"[25]

Indeed, Christian history is an ebb and flow of pursued holiness and pathetic haughtiness when it comes to engaging the fleshly appetites. Various approaches have been taken; for example, while the Rule of Saint Benedict used poverty and discipline to cleanse monks of vices and sins, and to provide their outward, inward, and upward development, John Calvin relied on austerity when he attempted to build Augustine's City of God (or something close to it) in Geneva. People were held to a moral code that demanded sober and upright living. There was no dancing, card playing, obscenity, or drunkenness. People did not smile too much, either. Not for lack of those things, but because too much happiness was, itself, a vice.

Of course, one cannot talk of legalistic excess in Christian history without mention of my own Pentecostal/Holiness tradition. When it comes to avoiding the worldly, we really take the cake. Of course, we can't eat it, because that sugary sweetness is nothing but worldly. But if we pray that God sanctify it to the nourishment of our bodies, then consumption is allowed. Maybe. That remains a matter of theological debate.[26]

The law was laid down from the movement's inception at the turn of the twentieth century: no drinkin', no dancin', and no tobaccy. There are, however, a few caveats to be made here. No drinking often included restrictions on soft drinks, coffee, and tea. Dancing was okay if it was in the Spirit.

---

24. Wogaman and Strong, *Readings in Christian Ethics*, 493.

25. Bruce, *NICNT*, 77–78.

26. Of course, I am being facetious here, which may be a sin in some holiness venues. If so, perhaps we can discuss reconciliation over a slice of red velvet cake.

The issue of tobacco proved a bit more intricate. For example, the Christian Union gave members the "privilege to interpret for yourselves as your conscience may dictate" when it organized in 1886, so the use of tobacco and snuff was permitted. By the time this group became the Church of God (Cleveland, Tennessee) twenty years later, such use was strictly forbidden.[27] Denomination elders "wrangled about the scope of the evil" for years to come. "Was it moral to grow tobacco if that was the only way to earn a living? Was it permissible to work in a store that sold cigarettes?"[28]

The Church of God, like many other Pentecostal and Holiness adherents, also censured "the reading of novels, newspapers, and comic books; 'worldly music' was attacked, to include ragtime, tunes played on the fiddle, and classical violin . . . [t]emperance and patriotic songs might be acceptable under certain circumstances, but in general one should stick with Christian tunes."[29] Women wore no makeup; their hair was uncolored and basically uncut (trimmed for neatness, but not lacking length). Worldly accoutrements such as neckties, jewelry, hat pins, and brass buttons were frowned upon, as beauty was to be internal, not external.[30]

This abbreviated history was not meant to demean anyone's faith or practice. I offer these to show that God-loving men and women have long-strived to break free from the stranglehold caused when fleshly appetites go unchecked. While the methods could be argued, their motives were pure. Still, I would argue that any expression of holy living will always work best from the inside out.[31]

Indeed, there is a better way to avoid such entanglements, and it comes through sacrificial giving. Don't worry, I am not about to pass the offering plate.[32] In fact, I am not talking about money at all. To cut away the thorns

27. Phillips, *Quest to Restore God's House*, locs. 2077–86.

28. Wacker, *Heaven Below*, loc. 1871. For the record, my wife has a Pentecostal pedigree; her family bleeds Church-of-God blue, and she earned money throughout her teenage years by cropping tobacco (taking it off the stalk). This decision elicited no acknowledgement from her grandparents, who read the newspaper every day, but avoided "worldly" books, movies, and television.

29. Wacker, *Heaven Below*, locs. 1894–98.

30. 1 Tim 2:9–10; 1 Peter 3:3–5.

31. Matt 15:11–20; 23:25–28; Mark 7:14–23; Luke 11:39. For more on this, see my discussion on imitation vs. transformation in chapter 3.

32. Perhaps I should. There are numerous scriptures that present giving as the antidote to materialism. Suffice it to say, if there is anything you own that God cannot have, then you cannot have God. Unfortunately, big offerings have become the modern indulgence for many. By using the term "indulgence," I speak not of excessive participation,

that feed on fleshly appetites, we must present ourselves as a living and holy sacrifices to God, not conformed to this world, but reformed by renewed minds (Rom 12:1–2). We must lay aside every encumbrance and the sins that so easily ensnare (Heb 12:1–2). We must not let sin reign, not obey its lusts, and not present ourselves as an instrument of unrighteousness. Instead, we must present ourselves to God "as those alive from the dead, and your members as instruments of righteousness to God. For sin shall not be master over you, for you are not under law but under grace" (Rom 6:12–14).

This is our reasonable service.

---

but the financial offering for which the pope remits temporal punishment in purgatory. The sale of such indulgences was a catalyst to the actions of Martin Luther, which ultimately led to the Protestant Reformation. Similarly, some seem to give large offerings in the belief that this somehow covers their sinful behavior.

12

Many Are Creating God in Their Image

THE THORNS WE CUT away in the previous chapters are indicative of and contributory to the greatest garrote of all: the idol. Strange fires stoke the kilns into which we pour our golden greed. Sadly, many Christians are ignorant of the idols they construct because these idols are called by names such as "Jehovah" and "Jesus," but these gods bear little resemblance to the God of the Bible.

This scenario can be seen during the exodus from Egypt. While Moses was on the mountain with God, the people grew tired of waiting on God's blessing. They pressured Aaron, the high priest; in response, he received an offering and used the gold to fashion a golden calf (Exod 32:1–10). A whooping and hollering church service followed at the foot of the mountain. They called the golden calf "Elohim" and "Jehovah." Aaron declared, "This is your god, O Israel, that brought you out of the land of Egypt!"

God did not provide what they wanted in the manner they expected and within a time they felt reasonable, so the people of God made god into what they wanted him to be. Heavily influenced by their Egyptian worldview, they formed a golden calf who placed no requirements on them; they could worship in his presence, comfortable in the knowledge that he was blind and indifferent to their sin.

Many will follow suit this Sunday. Like Aaron, there are pastors and preachers who seek to please the people rather than please God. Like Aaron, they will be happy when the people pile up the gold, and the people will be happy when their worship is affirmed as authentic. Together, they will craft a god in the likeness of the world from which they were delivered; one who is blind to their sin and promises to provide what they want when they want it.

You see, idols are not formed by hands. They are formed by hearts. This is the fate of every Christian—even those who are growing and bearing fruit—if they do not remain in a committed relationship with God. Failure to embrace his eternal word will allow the weeds of worldly wisdom to creep in, and weeds left unchecked will crack concrete foundations. Those weeds will rob the Christian of the living water and life-giving light needed to resist the ravenous appetites of the flesh. The strange fire of diluted doctrine will allow, and even affirm, the believer, when he acts on those impulses. Now we are right back in Eden, where man first tried to dethrone the Almighty.

You will be like God.

Indeed, the most dangerous idol is the one who stares back at you from the mirror every morning. Unchecked thorns will cause you to create God into your image, rather than be reformed into his image.[1] Oh, you may call him "Jehovah" or "Jesus," but this god is made according to your preferences as you want him to be—blind and indifferent to your sin.

This self-orientation is a satanic seed planted in a peaceful garden long ago, and it has restricted the breath of life ever since. In Athanasius' view, the dissolution of physical, spiritual, and psychological integrity was initiated when Adam and Eve "began to regard themselves . . . [and] fell into lust of themselves, preferring what was their own to the contemplation of what belonged to God."[2] Adam and Eve were in right standing with God and were secure so long as God remained preeminent. This is necessary because God sustains and gives meaning to all things.[3] The serpent offered a different worldview to choke out such contemplation. The discussion that followed openly distorted God's word and will, and the couple's true standing was soon revealed. Left naked and ashamed by ungodly appetites, they

---

1. Stop making God in your image! This was a central argument of Karl Barth's theology which was, in some respects, a sustained response against philosopher Ludwig Feuerbach. The latter argued in *The Essence of Christianity* (1841) that religion is the projection of humanity's infinitude onto the divine. Barth countered with his fourteen-volume *Church Dogmatics*, which defined Christianity as God's self-revelation in Jesus Christ.

2. Athanasius, "Against the Heathen," loc. 491426.

3. For more on this, see the fuller development given in chapter 1.

knew "they had become stripped of the contemplation of divine things, and had transferred their understanding to the contraries."[4]

Having lost the contemplation of God, mankind lost unity with God, and entered a cataclysmic devolution. We still are able to see divine qualities in the creation, and even move toward what we perceive to be good, but these are distorted truths that originate from the alienated perspective. By moving toward what we perceive to be good, we think we are maintaining spiritual integrity and dignity, but we are not. We are "made not merely to move, but to move in the right direction."[5]

Kinnaman, the president of Barna Group, said that many Christians are headed in the wrong direction because they "are using the way of Jesus to pursue the way of self."[6] Many Christians lament the way in which secularism has spread through society and brought with it many ills, yet "a majority of churchgoing Christians have embraced [secularism's] corrupt, me-centered theology."[7] The results are telling. Three out of four US adults have some Christian background, but roughly three-in-five are inactive in their faith. One-third of college-aged adults want nothing to do with religion, and 59 percent of Christians will quit church at some point in their twenties.[8]

Faith's loss of influence is exacerbated by spiritual leaders who create golden calves of their own. They call their idols "church," and adorn them with steeples and stained glass; these idols are designated among the sacred, but their methods (and messages) are far more secular. Biblically illiterate ministers ignite strange fire week after week. Many have adapted their practices to accommodate the strengthening individualism that seeks only to advance one's self-interest. Emotion-driven therapeutic and results-driven managerial models of leadership have penetrated the foundations and consumed these congregations. "Caring deeply about how people feel and pressing for measurable congregational growth are often highly rewarded skills among clergy. Yet when they dominate, faith becomes a weak sibling, doing little work as a community enacts its faith in daily life."[9] Without the "vital divine presence that transforms our lives and orients

---

4. Athanasius, "Against the Heathen," locs. 491430–32.

5. Athanasius, "Against the Heathen," loc. 491455.

6. Kinnaman and Lyons, *Good Faith*, 251.

7. Kinnaman and Lyons, *Good Faith*,

8. Kinnaman and Lyons, *Good Faith*, 13, 30.

9. Scharen, *Faith as a Way of Life*, 7.

our living towards a good beyond ourselves, we are left with a thin faith aimed at helping us to improve our circumstances or at least feel better about them."[10]

Though far more common than in days past, such error is nothing new. One example is found in Revelation 3:1–6, in which Jesus sent word to a cutting-edge congregation in Sardis. The church was on the move and had a great reputation in the community. Imagine how they felt when a letter from the Lord arrived in the inbox. No doubt Jesus was going to give them his seal of approval! Not quite. When Jesus looked at this church, all he saw was death. All of their hard work amounted to nothing because they were building their own kingdom. They had not done as commanded. It was time to straighten up. His counsel was clear: remember what you have received and honor it! Remember what you have heard and obey it! Repent of your wrong! Do this, and I will present you by name to my Father in the presence of his angels. Fail to do it, and I will erase your name from the Book of Life.

If Jesus were to send written correspondence to every church today, I wonder how many would receive a letter similar to that of Sardis? Suffice it to say, "God made men upright, but they have sought out many devices" (Eccl 7:29). They fear the Lord, but also serve the gods and customs of the land (2 Kgs 17:33).

It is with good reason that the first commandment is the first commandment. There is no sin so offensive to God as idolatry. The false god diminishes God's majestic and righteous character, and substitutes its own presence and purpose in our lives. Similarly, no sin is as disastrous to the individual as idolatry. By its nature, idolatry projects a divine who is created in, and increasingly conforms to, our fallen image. Therefore, we must become "so strong in our union-communion relationship with God that we need not create idols."[11] We must be careful to not create God in our image, and thus become an idol unto ourselves. To do so is to worship in the orthodoxy of Christless Christianity. As Gause explains, "God must be honored as the only God. Any substitution for this God is idolatry. Any

---

10. Scharen, *Faith as a Way of Life*, 38. Attempts to placate the masses have only backfired. In addition to the decrease in Christian practice noted earlier, only one-fifth of US adults strongly believe that clergy are a credible source of wisdom and insight (Kinnaman and Lyons, *Good Faith*, 15).

11. Rediger, *Fit to be a Pastor*, 124.

reduction of His glory is sacrilege. Any desecration of His Name, Word or Presence is profanity."[12]

In our time together, we have discussed why "many" is the scariest word in the Bible. In light of this, we addressed the most important question in the Bible: "what must I do to be saved?" As we near the conclusion, we now identify the most dangerous temptation in the Bible. It is the temptation to be like God; to remove God from his rightful place and enthrone yourself at the center of your universe.

It is the promise of a kingdom without a cross.

Jesus faced this temptation no fewer than three times in his earthly ministry. The first occurred when Jesus, having been baptized and empowered for ministry, was driven by the Spirit to battle Satan in the wilderness. The devil in an instant showed him all the kingdoms of the world and their glory, and he offered them to Jesus if he would but bow to Satan.[13] Take your place on David's throne, rally the nation around you, institute your Messianic kingdom—you can rule right now, there is no need to endure all of the pain and agony, no need for the sacrifice and struggle. All you have to do is replace *thy will* with *my will.*

Why would Satan make such an offer? Because any kingdom that lacks a cross still belongs to him. The cross is the answer to alienation. It is the means by which God bridges the gap that stands between, and thus reconciles unto himself. That is why Satan is happy to grant any kingdom, so long as it lacks the cross.

But Jesus had come for a cross, not a crown, and sent Satan packing.

The deceiver soon adapted his temptation, and certainly had home-field advantage when it was leveled a second time.[14] The setting for this climactic clash was the region of Caesarea Philippi, which lay twenty-five miles north of the Sea of Galilee. The land had long been consumed by the worship of false gods. It was a stronghold of the pagan god Ba'al. Later, a one-hundred-foot stone altar was carved to honor the Greek god Pan—a half-man, half-goat who sported a goatee beard, horns upon his head, and was so fond of music that he was never depicted without his reed in hand (cf. Ezek 28:13). Other gods were worshipped in this region, as well. Herod the Great built a massive marble temple to honor the Roman emperor, the

---

12. Gause, *Living in the Spirit*, 12.

13. Matt 4:1–11; Luke 4:1–13.

14. Matt 16:13–23; Mark 8:27–33; Luke 9:18–22; cf. John 6:68–69.

self-declared "god" of the secular world. Herod's son Philip then enlarged the city and renamed it in honor of Caesar.

There, in the enemy's camp, Jesus enjoyed a moment of quiet solitude and prayer. The disciples soon joined Jesus, and no doubt their arrival brought comfort and familiarity. The path that lay before him would prove increasingly difficult. The cheering crowds and popularity that had accompanied his ministry would diminish; each step would be met with intensifying pain and persecution, sacrifice and betrayal. The "way of suffering" that culminated with Jesus' crucifixion atop Golgotha did not begin at Pontius Pilate's praetorium. The first steps of that torturous trek were taken in Caesarea Philippi.

"Who do the people say that I am?" Jesus asked.

"Some say John the Baptist," one disciple answered.

"Some say Elijah," a second added.

"Yes, and others say Jeremiah, or one of the other prophets."

The disciples nodded in agreement. They were glad to report how the people held Jesus in the highest regard, but the disciples failed to realize that the Galileans' lofty estimations fell well short of Jesus' actual worth.

"But who do you say that I am?" Jesus asked the twelve.

No doubt the disciples' thoughts raced as they searched for the correct answer. The answer found Simon Peter.

"You are the Christ, the Son of the living God," Peter said. The disciples were awestruck by the realization: Jesus is not simply a man anointed and favored by God. He *is* God.

"Blessed are you, Simon, son of Jonah, for man has not revealed this to you, but my Father who is in heaven."

It is interesting to note that Jesus defined blessing not as the answer to prayer, but the ability to hear God in prayer. And Simon was blessed, indeed. Peter's confession of what he heard was foundational; Christ would build his church on that confession, and the gates of hell will not overpower it.

In what is known as the first prediction of the passion, Jesus then began to explain that he must go to Jerusalem, suffer many things, be crucified, and be raised the third day. We understand this to be describing the eternal turning point for all mankind, but it challenged everything the disciples knew and believed about Scripture, the prophets, and the Messiah. This was not what they understood. This was not what they expected. This was not what they had hoped for. The twelve were greatly affected and struggled to understand what Jesus was saying (Luke 9:45). Indeed, the cross is foolishness to Greeks and a stumbling block to Jews (1 Cor 1:23).

Peter, who had just received an unprecedented revelation, now heard a voice so similar that he could not discern this voice from God's voice.[15] Satan convinced Peter to put his faith in what *he* believed God's plan to be instead of embracing what *God* revealed his plan to be. Peter then declared this word as though it were another from God.

"God forbid it, Lord! This shall never happen to you."

Matthew and Mark describe Peter as "rebuking" the Lord, which means to censure severely; to admonish or charge sharply. Peter had the audacity to look God in the face and tell him no. Peter had the audacity to tell God that he was wrong.

It was never proper for a disciple to challenge, let alone rebuke, his rabbi. But does not this brazen bellow echo the temptation Jesus overcame in the wilderness? We just told you that you have the support of the people! Surely God would not allow this! We will not let such wrong come upon you! There must be another way!

Jesus had not entertained Satan's offer in the wilderness, but the people who are close to us have more influence on our lives then we sometimes admit. Might he consider the impassioned plea of a loving friend? Might he listen to a trusted brother? Might Jesus listen to such reason? He would not. Peter had offered strange fire that was mindful of the things of men, not of God. Well-meaning as he may have been, Peter had allowed Satan to speak through him, and Jesus was not about to allow this manipulation to stand unanswered. He commanded Satan to get out of the way and defined this temptation as an offense. In this, Jesus used the Greek word *skandalon* that we discussed in chapter 5. This was a trap designed to persuade Jesus to take an easier path.

We know why Satan would tempt Jesus in such a way—he desires a kingdom without a cross. But what made him think that he even had a shot at pulling it off this time? Because the desire was already in Jesus' heart.[16] Do you struggle with such a claim, even though Jesus was tempted in all things as we are (Heb 4:15)? If so, consider this: Jesus himself would ask the Father if there was another way.

15. Though it originates from the opposite end of the spiritual spectrum, the temptation of Satan can easily be confused with God's voice for one who lacks discernment (2 Cor 11:3, 14; Eph 5:6; 2 Tim 3:13; Jas 1:16; 2 John 1:7; Rev 12:9).

16. cf. Jas 1:14–15. Also note Augustine's treatment of Adam and Eve's temptations, as discussed in chapter 1

Jesus confronted this temptation a third time in the Garden of Gethsemane.[17] If there was satanic activity, it is not recorded in Scripture. Nevertheless, it is evident that self-preservation could have easily succumbed to self-orientation. Jesus knew what awaited him. He would be rejected and despised, beaten and ridiculed. He would be saturated in the vile and putrid sins accumulated by a creation. Worst of all, the Son would experience the deepest sense of separation when abandoned by the Father.[18] The profound pain of this separation is captured in the outcry of Jesus. It is the only prayer in which he did not use the relational terms "Father" or "Abba." Instead, he lamented, "My God, my God, why have you forsaken me?"[19]

The weight of the world was upon the Nazarene as he entered the garden to pray. His tanned and troubled face was wet with perspiration, yet his mouth was desert dry. The agonizing anticipation caused capillaries to burst, and the blood to mingle in beads of sweat that lined his brow. As Stott right observes, "the agony in the garden opens a window on to the greater agony of the cross. If to bear man's sin and God's wrath was so terrible in anticipation, what must the reality have been like?"[20]

Innumerable thoughts battled for Jesus' attention, but he asked the Father only one question: is there another way? More to the point, could Jesus inaugurate the kingdom without a cross? We know God's answer by Jesus' response, and by Jesus' response we know our responsibility.

We cannot enter God's kingdom but through the cross.

The cross marks the beginning of our growth in holiness, and the first steps toward fulfilling God's plan for our lives. We have discussed three thorns that choke out godly life and fruit: biblical illiteracy, strange fire, and selfish appetites. From these are built the idols we worship. Now, consider the manner in which Jesus overcame his temptation. In the first instance, he overcame with the word. In the second instance, the strange fire that was mindful of the things of men was overcome by the authority of Spirit fire, captured in the command that Satan depart. In the third instance, self-orientation was thwarted by selfless obedience. It is fitting that this final victory took place in a garden. In Eden, precedence was given to *my will* rather than *thy will*. In Gethsemane, *my will* surrendered to *thy will*, and the results speak for themselves.

17. Matt 26:36–46; Mark 14:32–42; Luke 22:39–46.
18. Moltmann, "On the Suffering of God," 192–93.
19. Matt 27:46; Mark 15:34.
20. Stott, *Cross of Christ*, 80.

We are left to ask, what will be our response in times of similar testing? I pray that we will echo the words of Paul: "I have been crucified with Christ; and it is no longer I who live, but Christ lives in me; and the life which I now live in the flesh I live by faith in the Son of God, who loved me and gave Himself up for me" (Gal 2:20). This will be our testimony if we hold fast to the inspired word, are led and empowered by Spirit fire, and commit to selfless obedience. In doing so, we will not be counted among the "many on that day" who will be told to depart our Lord's presence.

Yet, there will be many.

Hell was never God's plan for you (2 Pet 3:9). In Idleman's view, "it's not so much that God won't let us into heaven; it's that we won't let ourselves in. If we can't learn how to say 'Thy will be done,' then finally God must sadly say, 'Okay, then *thy* will be done.'"[21] Our eternal home is determined by the g/God we choose to serve. Heaven is not populated with people who hate hell, but rather people who love God. Conversely, as the anonymous author of *Theologia Germanica* rightly said, "nothing burns in hell but self-will."[22]

We are being transformed into the image of the g/God we serve, either the Spirit leading to life or sin leading to death. The Christian is transformed into the glory and image of Christ, a process that is not completed until we reach heaven.[23] Those who reject Christ are transformed into the likeness of sin.[24] This transformation, which Athanasius would describe as dissolution into nothingness, is completed in hell, the abode of eternal alienation.

Life and death, heaven and hell—it all comes down to the choices we make. Created in God's image, we are creatures of free will. Love can have it no other way. The choice we face is nothing new. Though the methods and messages have changed throughout history, it is the same choice that has echoed throughout the ages: thy will or my will? Secular and satanic reasoning presents the greatest good as finding yourself within yourself, and then living your life in light of that truth. Our Father presents the greatest good as finding yourself in Christ, and glorifying God through participation in his life and truth.

No one can serve two masters. Choose well.

---

21. Idleman, *Gods at War*, 208.

22. Winkworth, *Theologia Germanica*, 57.

23. Rom 8:18; 1 Cor 13:12; 15:49–57; 2 Cor 3:18; 4:17; Phil 3:20–21; 1 John 3:2–3.

24. Gen 6:12; Ezek 28:17; Rom 1:18–31; 12:2; Eph 4:22.

Appendix 1

Truth You Can Trust

THERE ARE MANY VARIATIONS when one discusses the divine inspiration of Scripture. I hold the verbal plenary inspiration theory over the intuition, illumination, and dynamic theories of inspiration, so long as allowance for accommodation be made. I concur that the dictation theory can be supported, but only in certain passages (i.e., the Ten Commandments and much of Revelation). I also contend that the encounter theory, which promotes continuing revelation through the Spirit in community, is of critical worth.

The verbal plenary theory finds inspiration extended to words and ideas. The Holy Spirit selected the words used, but human authors wrote in their own distinct style. Since the authors' words are God-breathed, they are without error.[1] This is understood in light of accommodation, the assertion that God accommodated biblical language to the common language and understanding of the day without forfeiting the perfection and purity of his word.[2] As Sunshine rightly notes, "[f]or an infinite, perfect, and holy God to interact with finite, infallible, and fallen humanity, he must accommodate himself to our ability to understand him, coming down to our level so that we can grasp what he says and does."[3] For example, Jesus described the mustard seed as the smallest of all seeds (Mark 4:30–32). It is not, but it was in the understanding of his audience. Similarly, Jesus conveyed the

1. Barrett, *God's Word Alone*, 225.
2. Barrett, *God's Word Alone*, 86.
3. Sunshine, "Accommodation Historically Considered," 238.

idea that seeds die before germinating (John 12:23–24), stars are small and can all fall to earth (Matt 24:29–30), Sheba is at the ends of the earth (Matt 12:42), and would spend three days and nights in the heart of the earth, (Matt 12:40).

This organic (as opposed to mechanical) inspiration sees God not merely communicate information through the human author, but allow the perspective, tone, and voice of the author as well.[4] To view inspiration otherwise is to reduce the prophet to a passive mouthpiece; a puppet with a pen. Hellenistic Jewish writers tended to take such an approach when using language common to pagan understanding, but this is contrary to the active participation of the prophets with God.[5]

While prophecy implies double agency, it does not imply equal agency.[6] However, one must use caution here; to remove the human aspects of inspiration in an attempt to preserve inerrancy is tantamount to hermeneutic Apollinarianism. There is equal danger when one attempts to omit the sinful nature of humanity in the act of inspiration, which posits an immaculate conception (albeit temporary) among the Scripture writers.

Such tendencies are most evident and inevitable when one attempts to reconcile absolute inerrancy, which demands agreement between biblical and scientific truth. Other views better address this conundrum. For example, full inerrancy regards scientific and historical references as phenomenal; that is, they are reported the way they appear to the human eye, and therefore true. Limited inerrancy regards the Bible as inerrant and infallible in its salvific doctrinal references, while scientific and historical references reflect the understanding of the time.[7]

While absolute inerrancy stresses the divinity of Scripture, the Historical-Critical Method stresses its humanity. This method is based on the presupposition that human reason is the final arbiter in all truth and is obtained through rational thought—and therein lay the problem. Scripture collects a sanctified reality; a collection of supernatural truths that cannot be measured by natural means, and especially one that has a closed-world view in which there is no room for God to interact with the world. The

---

4. Barrett, *God's Word Alone*, 233 in referencing Abraham Kuyper and Herman Bavinck.

5. Blocher, "God and the Scripture Writers," 501–2. Here, Blocher heavily quotes the research of Richard J. Bauckham (cf. Exod 3:11; 4:10–16; Jer 1:6–7; 23:16–22; Isa 49:5; Amos 3:7; Hab 1; Acts 2:30–31; 1 Cor 14:32; 2 Pet 1:21).

6. Carson, *Enduring Authority*, 505.

7. Erickson, *Introducing Christian Doctrine*, 69–70.

approach assumes a standardized history; a view that past events happened the same way they will happen today and tomorrow. This ignores, and even excludes, any possibility of divine intervention or supernatural activity. This is a critical omission for a book of faith. Although the Bible does, at times, convey historical information, this is not the primary intent.

This "hermeneutic of suspicion" went far beyond the method of doubt espoused in the early twelfth century, when Peter Abelard looked to reverse the emphasis on Augustine's "faith seeking understanding." This hermeneutic had the goal of liberating reason from the authorities of Scripture and tradition and was bolstered by the rule of Cartesian doubt, which accepts nothing as certain that can in any way be doubted. The idea of method follows from this rule.[8]

Ironically, the historic accuracy of the Bible as determined by textual criticism is without equal. For example, there are roughly seven hundred manuscripts of Homer's Iliad—the best represented of all ancient writings apart from the New Testament—and there are far more significant variations in those manuscripts than in Holy Scripture. In comparison, there are roughly five thousand, three hundred partial or complete Greek New Testament manuscripts as well as sixteen thousand second-century editions that were translated into other languages. Scholars have estimated a textual purity between 98.33 and 99.9 percent. The accuracy in which the words of Scripture have been maintained is unequaled in history.[9] On this point Charles H. Welch, in his book *True from the Beginning*, quotes from the third edition of the Encyclopedia Britannica: "This argument is so strong that, if we deny the authenticity of the New Testament, we may with a thousand times greater propriety reject all the other writings in the world."[10]

While few would dismiss the historic accuracy by which Scripture has been maintained, many are quick to reject any truth it purports. However, a willingness to acknowledge truth only when it has been "verified" by historiography or archaeology is naïve at best. Historiography and archaeology are paralyzed by personal opinions, and both are incomplete as a new finding occurs daily. In addition, historiography can neither confirm nor deny reality, and neither historiography nor archaeology can prove meaning. As

---

8. Gadamer, *Truth and Method*, 284.

9. Hindson and Caner, *Popular Encyclopedia of Apologetics*, 400.

10. Welch, *True from the Beginning*, 16. There are numerous historical affirmations of the Old Testament's accuracy, as well. These include the Ras Shamra Tablets, the Ebla Tablets, and the Dead Sea Scrolls.

theologian Paul Tillich once outlined, historical criticism is nothing more than historical research that shows preference for the probable.[11]

A response to the Historical-Critical Method would be deficient without mention of Hans-Georg Gadamer and his biblical hermeneutic. Established amid the emergence of neo-orthodoxy, his paradigm is a marked maturation of Christian thought that stands in stark contrast (even opposition to) Enlightenment methods that dominated much of twentieth century scholarship. Gadamer flatly rejected the assertion that method is the arbiter of truth. Instead, he proposed a "fusion of horizons" between text understood in context and personal lifeworld.[12] This fusion would enable the individual to anticipate the future in light of the past. Reason is not contrary to tradition in this view, yet true authority must be earned by the historic witness and respected in the contemporary setting.

To counter the naïveté of historicism, Gadamer teamed the existential philosophies of Martin Heidegger with a revival of Augustine's "faith seeking understanding." Like Socrates, Gadamer approached truth dialectically, which is the antithesis of method. From German philosopher Edmund Husserl, he adopted the intentional horizon of consciousness within the "lifeworld." This horizon is "the range of vision that includes everything that can be seen from a particular vantage point."[13] Horizons can be narrow or broad, depending on the individual. More value is placed on that which is nearer to the individual when the horizon is narrow. As the horizon broadens, the individual can better see the significance of everything within that horizon. To use a modern phrase, he is able to see the forest *and* the trees.

Thus, Gadamer's approach is to "approach the testimony of the past under its influence," acknowledge one's own presuppositions, then fuse the investigator's horizon to that of the historic to bring contemporary and future understanding. This begins by looking at the past in proper context.

It can be argued that text taken out of context leaves you with a con. The deficiency of context is the failure of the historical-critical method, in Gadamer's view. I would agree, and I argue that full inerrancy is maintained within the historical-grammatical context in which the Bible was written.

---

11. Tillich, *Systematic Theology*, 101.

12. With respect to Gadamer, I would suggest that a truer understanding must go beyond the horizons of past and present to consider the horizons of the author, text, and reader(s) of the past, as well as the author, text, and reader(s) in the present.

13. Gadamer, *Truth and Method*, 302.

The universal message does not change, but our understanding and application of that message does see progressive development amid an evolving modern context. It is therefore necessary to appropriate and apply the proper hermeneutic response.

There is great worth in considering the approach of Karl Barth, who held that the word, or *logos*, takes on three forms: Christ, Scripture, and the proclamation of the gospel. In his view, "[t]he Bible is God's Word to the extent that God causes it to be His Word, to the extent that He speaks through it."[14] Scripture is a witness to Christ, who is the Word of God, the revelation.[15] Scripture becomes revelation when the Spirit uses it to make Christ known.[16] Therefore, revelation cannot be chained down to Scripture because revelation is an event, and necessary for the truth of God to be known.[17]

Barth criticized fundamentalism for its Biblicism, which he said turned Scripture into a paper pope. Indeed, the church must be careful to avoid *nuda scriptura* (what Vanhoozer refers to as *solo scriptura*), which holds to "the Bible, the whole Bible, and nothing but the Bible." Correct hermeneutics demand a mutual endeavor of word and Spirit; an external principle (the inspired Scriptures) and an internal principle (illumined Scriptures).[18] Scripture is not alone, but is above reason, experience, and tradition; it is the final, but not the exclusive authority. While supplemental sources maintain a ministerial role, Scripture alone holds the magisterial role.

As Vanhoozer rightly asserts,

> naïve Biblicism [is] a belief that the Bible contains everything God has to say to human beings, that it is comprehensive in the issues it covers, that any reasonable person can understand its plain sense without reliance on confessional schemes, that its teaching remains universally valid, and that it therefore serves as the Christian's authoritative handbook for all time and for all subjects, including science, politics, and philosophy.

14. Barth, *Church Dogmatics 1.1*, 109.

15. Barth, *Church Dogmatics 1.2*, 457–63.

16. Barth, *Church Dogmatics 1.1*, 109–20.

17. With that said, Barth held the errancy of Scripture was certain because biblical authors were human and sinners. Thus, fallibility applies to its historical, scientific, and spiritual aspects (Barth, *Church Dogmatics 1.2*, 533). As noted earlier, I do not go to this extreme.

18. Vanhoozer, "Beyond What is Written," 763.

Its Achilles heel is the inability to provide definitive instruction and direction amid divergent interpretations. In addition, Biblicism downplays the difference between "then" and "now" as it tends to assume universal relevance—it asserts a text without a context.[19] Evangelicals are quick to study what Scripture meant in the original historical and cultural context, but the challenge is to know what to do with the original meaning today.

Proper theology and hermeneutics, in Vanhoozer's view, will go beyond the word of God, not in the sense of leaving it behind or going against it, but rather extending it through patient interpretation and prayerful reflection. Moving beyond what is written is necessary and inevitable; neither history nor culture stand still, and neither should the church. The challenge is to know how to preserve the same gospel in different settings, as proper theology and hermeneutics is more a matter of formation than information.[20]

Pentecostal renewal thus demands the development of a pneumatic hermeneutic—a Spirit/Scripture/community methodology that facilitates renewal of the biblical model on which the church is founded, as well as the experiential transformation (and reformation) of the individual and community.[21] This trialectic hermeneutic, as espoused by Amos Yong, works to merge the hermeneutical horizons of the ancient text and the contemporary interpreter. This revelatory synergism reveals what was meant by the biblical authors with a view to understanding what God wants to say to us today, and it allows for multiple meanings in light of the reader's experience.[22]

When rightly applied, a pneumatic hermeneutic may "yield legitimate understandings according to the theology of the cross, inasmuch as they properly assess the power of experience for negotiating meaning as penultimate and the text of Scripture as ultimate."[23] Such primacy of Scripture is not foreign to Pentecostalism; from its inception, the Pentecostal experience is rightly and strongly rooted in biblical evidence and understanding. What is needed is a return to those roots.

---

19. Vanhoozer, "Beyond What is Written," 763–64, 768.

20. Vanhoozer, "Beyond What is Written," 769–74.

21. Spawn and Wright, Spirit & Scripture, 74, 117, 133.

22. Spawn and Wright, Spirit & Scripture, 73. For more on this, I recommend Keener, Spirit Hermeneutics, and Archer, A Pentecostal Hermeneutic.

23. Courey, Wittenburg to Do With Azusa, 226.

Appendix 2

Salvation: Choice or Chosen?

THOUGH MANY WILL POINT to Jakob Arminius as the originator of such understanding, the foundation for the soteriological role of free will was laid in the early ecumenical councils, when Cyril argued that Jesus' humanity was central to the dual nature of Christ, an understanding embraced at the Council of Ephesus in 431 AD.

Over the next two centuries, discussion of Christ's two natures raised an inevitable question: did Christ have one will, or two? Sergius proposed a solution for the monothelite (one will) controversy in which Christ's two natures were united in a single activity or energy. Two wills implied the possibility of one standing contrary to the other, he argued.

It is here that history came to know Maximus the Confessor. He was not a bishop, nor a priest, nor even a deacon, yet he changed Christendom, and became known as the father of Byzantine theology to boot. Maximus did this because he "was forced by the unfolding theological and political drama of his day to look at the agony of Christ with fresh eyes."[1]

Maximus launched an exegetical appraisal of Christ's petition that the Father remove the cup of suffering (Luke 22:39–42). Maximus built upon Cyril's view of Christ's unique humanity, and noted that, from the onset, Christ was without sin—the cause of our rebellion against God. When Jesus said, "the ruler of this world is coming, but he will find nothing in me" (John 14:30), he meant that he would find none of the things that display

---

1. Wilken, *Spirit of Early Christian Thought*, 124.

the "contrariness of our will that debases our nature."[2] Simply put, there was nothing in Christ contrary to God, despite Sergius' objections.

To further assert the reality of two wills, Maximus echoed Cyril's formulation of the resurrection ("If he conquered as God, to us it is nothing") and argued that if only a divine will determines his actions, then Christ's flesh is "lifeless and irrational." If Christ does not have a human will, he cannot be fully human.

Pope Martin I joined Maximus in this understanding, but this rare amalgamation of Eastern Orthodoxy and Roman Catholicism did little to convince Byzantine Emperor Constans II. He instead imposed heavy penalties on anyone who asserted a doctrine of two wills or two energies. The debate came to a head at the Rome Synod of 649. To the tradition of Cyril, Maximus and Martin added the arguments from Chalcedon regarding Christ's two natures, as well as other patristic references. The emperor responded not with a biblical hermeneutic, but with orders to arrest the pope. Incarceration was avoided for several years, but an imperial order ultimately saw Martin deposed, arrested, and sent to Constantinople in chains. Charged with treason, he was detained for three months. Eventually, the emperor paraded him before a jeering crowd while he removed Martin's pallium, the two strips of lamb's wool marked with six black crosses worn over the pope's shoulder. Martin was exiled, and essentially abandoned by the church in Rome. Starvation, cold, and mistreatment ultimately claimed his life. Martin died a martyr on September 16, 655 AD—the last pope to receive that title.[3]

Maximus was imprisoned and exiled for his role. He continued to uphold the apostolic tradition even while on trial. "I have no teaching of my own," he said, "only the common teaching of the Catholic Church. For I did not promote any formula that should be considered my own teaching." His right hand was cut off and his tongue ripped out in an effort to force him to recant. He did not, and he died in exile in 662 AD.[4]

The assertions Martin and Maximus made were ultimately validated at the Council of Constantinople in 680–681 AD. As they rightly argued, Christ had an unspoiled human will amid the divine will, and the victory of Christ is ours only if it was obtained in his humanity. However, the next significant step in this progression would not be made for one thousand years.

2. Wilken, *Spirit of Early Christian Thought*, 128.
3. Wilken, *Spirit of Early Christian Thought*, 133–34.
4. Wilken, *Spirit of Early Christian Thought*, 135.

Because Jesus had to make a willful choice to obtain victory, willful choice is needed for us to accept the victory. Indeed, if Jesus' declaration ("not my will") is the catalyst to imputation of sin leading to propitiation, our echo of that declaration is the catalyst to imputation of righteousness resulting from propitiation (2 Cor 5:21). Such understanding would come to be understood by Arminius, who exegeted numerous passages in his attempt to reconcile double predestination.[5] The rejection of free will in Reformed soteriology was and remains largely predicated on the foreknowledge of God (Rom 8–9). As most will rightly note, the Hebrew *yada* and the Greek *ginosko* goes beyond cognitive knowledge and speaks to intimate knowledge. However, the inclusion of intimate knowledge is removed from definition in each of the five times the prefix *pro* ("before") is added to the Greek verb in the New Testament. Therefore, the foreknowledge does not speak to God's "forelove" of the elect, but "knowledge beforehand."[6]

This understanding was not lost on Arminius. The prolific exegete soon gained a significant following, which led to the creation of the Remonstrance, a doctrine asserting that Christ died for all, he offers saving grace to all, grace can be rejected, and the elect can fall from grace. Leading Arminians were arrested and ultimately exiled when they refused to recant. The Synod of Dort (1618–1619) unanimously rejected the Arminian Remonstrance and responded with five canons summed up in the pneumonic TULIP (total depravity, unconditional election, limited atonement, irresistible grace, perseverance of the saints).

Freedom of the will was a prevalent battle in Lutheran theology, as well. For Martin Luther, right standing with God comes by the surrender, rather than the operation, of free will.[7] The requirements of the moral law are endless, and man is incapable of any work that could overcome the sinful condition. Furthermore, it is possible to obey such requirements "while remaining a quite wicked person."[8] Therefore, efforts to fulfill the moral law are fruitless and lead only to bondage. Indeed, "the gospel, the Christian

---

5. These include John 3:16–21; 1 Tim 2:3–4; 2 Pet 3:9.

6. Louw and Nida, *Greek-English Lexicon*, 28.6, 30.100. Had this been the intent, the better word selection would be *problepó*, as in Hebrews 11:40. Cf. Acts 26:5; Rom 8:29, 11:2; 1 Pet 1:20; 2 Pet 3:17.

7. Luther defined this surrender of free will as faith—and proper faith is not a matter of simply offering right words or religious activity to achieve surrender. Proper faith is not the mental assent to certain understanding, or even the right application of sacraments. It comes by grace alone.

8. Wogaman, *Christian Ethics*, 118.

faith, and even God himself are denied if the freedom of the will is asserted as the power of man to choose his salvation for himself."[9]

Within the dynamics of free will and submission, as well as theologies of the cross and glory, resides the foundations of Luther's "two kingdoms." Steeped in the influence of Augustine's doctrine of "two cities," Luther advances the thought by marking a distinction between God and the world. Unlike the cities of God and Satan, these kingdoms share an inseparable connection and are arguably symbiotic, as the relationship shared by these kingdoms is one of movement, activity and conflict.[10] One kingdom marks man's relationship to God, while the other marks his relationship to fellow man. For the Christian, to exist before God and to exist before the world is not mutually exclusive, but necessarily simultaneous until the coming of Christ. The "Christian is perfectly free lord of all, subject to none," yet "a perfectly dutiful servant of all, subject to all."[11] As such, believers must "function within both kingdoms, practicing one ethic in our life before God and a different ethics in our life before the world."[12] The reason for this, in Luther's view, is that believers are *simul justus et peccator* (sinners and justified at the same time). Yet this ontological assessment marks a significant tension in the reformer's doctrine.

While Luther affirms that man is "abundantly and sufficiently justified by faith inwardly," the believer must (in subjugation to the Spirit) discipline the attitudes and actions so that the outer man will conform to the inner man. Though the Christian is free from all works, Luther speaks of the need to empty oneself, take the form of a servant, and serve and help his neighbors. "This he should do *freely*, having regard for nothing but divine approval."[13] In this, the obligation and initiative clearly resides with the individual, who is to act without compulsion for reward and approval not from neighbor, or onlookers, but from God. In fact, Luther will declare

9. Ebeling, *Luther*, loc. 2274.

10. Ebeling, *Luther*, 1779.

11. Wogaman and Strong, *Readings in Christian Ethics*, 123.

12. Wogaman and Strong, *Readings in Christian Ethics*, 122.

13. Wogaman and Strong, *Readings in Christian Ethics*, 125–26; emphasis mine. The editors are quoting Luther's treatise *Concerning Christian Liberty*. The reformer also addressed the distinction between works and grace in *On the Bondage of the Will* (an essentially Augustinian account of bondage either to sin or grace), and *The Heidelberg Disputation* (1518). Regarding the latter, the first section (theses 1–12) states the demands of God's law and human powerlessness to fulfill it. The second section (theses 13–18) addresses the limits of free will.

"wicked" those who would choose to rest in the sufficiency of faith and do no works.

The tension is this: if divine approval is sufficient motivation for the outer man, why is it not for inner man? If willful actions are essential to satisfy divine requirements for the outer man, why are they unnecessary (even contrary) for the inner man? Since the Great Commandment (Matt 22:34–40) addresses our relation with God and with others, why would the individual find willful obedience to please God in the latter, but not in the former?

Pressured by many to respond, Desiderius Erasmus presented free will not as a means to achieve divine favor, but something that works in participation with the divine. In his view, "grace does not work *through*, so much as *in*, free choice."[14] Erasmus viewed human will as a source of freedom, not of bondage, when in cooperation with God's grace, which is the primary of the two.[15] Rather than seeing man as incapable of doing anything good, the Catholic humanist asserted that "there is nothing that man cannot do with the help of the grace of God and that therefore all the works of man can be good."[16]

While Erasmus is seen as having struggled to equal Luther's exegetical prowess, his views were supported by far richer references to the patristic sources.[17] He charged Luther and company with having "immeasurably" exaggerated original sin to say that "even though justified by faith, a man cannot of himself do anything but sin . . . . [a]nd yet the same people assert that even when he has received grace, a man does nothing but sin."[18] On the contrary, God's grace is not a divine response to utter human depravity, but "divine assistance to a humanity that has not been totally corrupted by the fall."[19]

Erasmus certainly did not attribute to the human being the ability to redeem himself. For him, everything is grace. The free will that is attributed to the human being is the ability to turn toward grace. If one does not allow for this, Erasmus would argue, it would eliminate any human responsibility

---

14. Wogaman and Strong, *Readings in Christian Ethics*, 136.

15. Wogaman and Strong, *Readings in Christian Ethics*, 121.

16. Wogaman and Strong, *Readings in Christian Ethics*, 134. Here, the editors are quoting from Erasmus's work, *On the Freedom of the Will*.

17. Miller, *Erasmus and Luther*, 42, 148, 191.

18. Miller, *Erasmus and Luther*, 137.

19. Wogaman, *Christian Ethics*, 135.

and any ethical demand with it. In addition, human evil would have to be attributed to God, and "it would be the highest level of sin if one were to insult God by accusing him and holding him accountable as the originator of sin."[20]

The differences espoused by Luther and Erasmus have not abated with time, and the topic remains of great relevance to Christian ethics. The debate between providence and participation stands at the heart of this enigma. Erasmus rightly questioned whether Luther's "freedom" could become an excuse for complacency and inaction. Furthermore, how is there reward without merit, or judgment without a weighing of merits? Why does God demand unceasing prayer and labors for that which he has already decreed? If God works all good and all evil, then a man who cannot author good works cannot author evil works. How, then, can he be judged in either capacity?[21] How one answers these questions will determine how one lives out his or her Christian existence in relation to God and others. Though of the greatest importance, these questions have found no consensus in the five centuries since.

The question is one of balance between freedom and providence. This struggle is evident in the views of Reformed theologian Wayne Grudem, who stated that "God causes all things to happen, [but] he does so in such a way that he somehow upholds our ability to make *willing, responsible choices*, choices that have *real and eternal results*, and for which we are *held accountable*."[22] Grudem's theologies are largely consistent with Luther's in that salvation is completely a work of grace, while subsequent actions and obedience are required yet ordained. He goes so far as to say that humans are not free to make decisions apart from God's will but are free to make willing choices with real consequences.[23] How is this possible? Grudem's explanation is simple: Scripture does not explain this to us.[24] In the view of Luther, Calvin, Grudem and others, the believer is free to make a choice, but God has already ordained that choice. The believer (not God) is responsible for that ordained choice. In fact, even though God has ordained the evil choice, he is neither the author of that evil nor responsible for its results.

20. Bayer, *Martin Luther's Theology*, 188, 195.
21. Wogaman and Strong, *Readings in Christian Ethics*, 121, 134–36.
22. Grudem, *Systematic Theology*, 321.
23. Grudem, *Systematic Theology*, 331.
24. Grudem, *Systematic Theology*, 322.

Erasmus would likely charge these with having neglected the willful obedience required by Scripture.[25] That is not to say that the believer is responsible for any success in the fulfillment of God's ordained plan—it is God who made the way, revealed the way, and gives the believer everything necessary to remain in the way.[26] Erasmus would also take issue (as he did with Luther) with the view of evil in the context of providence. Grudem notes that God does indeed cause evil events to come about and evil deeds to be done, but he argues that God is removed from actually doing evil.[27] God brings about, but is not the author? Scripture does not bear this out. The omniscient and omnipotent God uses the willful actions of evil persons to influence others and help bring about his ultimate purpose, but he does not originate these for his purposes.[28]

The complexities of Luther's views on providence and free will have not been resolved, and Erasmus' views on providence and participation have not been fully embraced. As such, this topic remains a primary relevance to Christian ethics as believers seek to determine right actions and attitudes toward God and others, and thus find right standing with God.

25. Deut 28:14; Josh 1:7; 1 Sam 12:20; Prov 4:27; Matt 7:13–14; John 3:20–21, 36; Acts 5:32; Rom 1:5; 2:4–11; 16:26; Eph 2:10; 4:2–24; 2 Thess 1:8–10; Heb 5:8–10; Jas 4:17; 1 Pet 4:16–18; 1 John 1:6; 2:3–6; 2 John 4–6, 9. In these and others, we see that obedience is a critical element of salvation.

26. Jer 10:23; 1 Cor 4:7; 15:10; Jas 1:17.

27. Grudem, *Systematic Theology*, 328.

28. Gen 50:20; Rom 8:28; Jas 1:17; 1 John 1:5.

Appendix 3

The Salvation/Sanctification Symbiosis

SANCTIFICATION IS BOTH SYMBIOTIC with and subsequent to salvation, as it provides the complete positional and conditional separation of God's people for committed service unto him; a restorative repositioning that demands a cleansing from and empowered avoidance of whatever displeases God, whether that is internal or external to the believer. This is a participatory process in which the divine initiative is shared by Christ and the Holy Spirit, while the human responsibility is achieved by the Holy Spirit and the believer. Therefore, sanctification is both definitive and progressive; that is, it occurs at a certain point in time, yet is a lifelong process.

To be sanctified is of utmost importance, for without this, no one will see God (Heb 12:14). Sanctification speaks of a multifaceted process by which believers in Christ are made holy through separation, purification, and perfection/maturation.[1] Biblical holiness is neither objective legality, nor is it measured by one's ability to follow the letter of the law. Rather, it is the work of the Holy Spirit to help and empower the believer "to live in the kind of God-pleasing way that God wanted to see in Israel when he gave the law."[2]

The fundamental meaning of the Hebrew *qadash* is "to set apart" or "to consecrate." This speaks specifically to the removal of persons or things from the realm of the common or profane (the familiar picture is that of the priests and holy vessels of the tabernacle and temple). Yet it must be

1. Williams, *Renewal Theology*, 83–85. Cf. Lev 16:30; 22:21; Deut 7:6; Ps 24:3–4.
2. Horton, "Pentecostal Perspective," 96.

understood that their holiness was not simply a matter of position, but also condition. As Stanley Horton rightly notes,

> it was not their separation from ordinary use that made them holy. They were not holy until taken into the tabernacle and used in the service of God. So, we are saints, not merely because we are separated from sin and evil, but because we are separated to God, sanctified and anointed for the Master's use.[3]

Such use required the priests and holy vessels be purified through ritual observances. Later writings (particularly the Psalms and Prophets) extended the concept of holiness to all of God's people and presented it in ethical terms—a call to righteous behavior centered on the preeminence of love, compassion, and mercy (Ps 15:1–2), and the need to act justly and walk in humility (Mic 6:8).

The priesthood of new covenant believers finds them positionally sanctified, or set apart, upon conversion; they are "in Christ," and therefore seated in heavenly places.[4] However, our fallen condition demands continued sanctification and growth in Christlikeness.[5] Indeed, the Greek rendering of *hagios* strengthened the ethical emphasis of holiness noted in the Old Testament passages, as it required the sanctified to demonstrate the holy character of God in internal attitudes as well as external actions.[6]

Thus, sanctification is, for the individual, a position and a proposition; a verb as well as an adjective. It is positional in the sense of the believer's right standing with God, and conditional in the sense of continuing development of Christlike character.[7] The holiness it achieves is therefore more than a legal standing as it enables and necessitates the deliverance from sinful actions and attitudes.

The exegetical cornerstone of this understanding is found in Hebrews 10:14, which tells us that "by one offering He has perfected for all time those who are sanctified." The Greek word *teleioó* ("perfected") is rendered in the perfect tense, which notes a completed action. This is further established by

3. Horton, "Pentecostal Perspective," 132.

4. 1 Cor 1:30; Eph 2:4–6; Col 2:11–12; Heb 2:10–11; 13:12.

5. 1 Cor 3:1; Eph 4:22–24; Col 3:5–10; 1 Thess 4:3–4; Heb 10:14; 2 Pet 1:4–8; 3:18; 1 John 1:7.

6. Matt 5–6; 1 Pet 1:14–16.

7. This approach to positional and conditional sanctification is anchored in the theologies of John Calvin (where it is most commonly referred to as definitive and progressive), but has acceptance and development well beyond the Reformed tradition.

the subsequent *diénekés* ("forever, continuously, and for all time"). Indeed, Jesus' sacrifice was "once for all" (Heb 9:28), and our positional sanctification is immediate and complete as a result. However, the Greek *hagiazó* (sanctified) is presented in a continuous form of the verb, which notes the need for continued cleansing and purifying by the blood of Jesus, Spirit of God, and the word of God.[8]

As such, sanctification relates to the beginning, the continuation, and the goal of the Christian life.[9] Yet to fully appreciate this definition, it is necessary to understand the purpose, which is found in the symbiotic relationship sanctification shares with salvation.

The initiation of salvation will see three distinct events: justification, in which guilt is removed and eternal punishment abated;[10] regeneration, in which the believer's old sinful nature is replaced;[11] and positional sanctification, in which the believer is set apart unto God.[12] While all three works are initiated at the cross of Christ, none of them end there. Indeed, Calvary marks the beginning, not the culmination, of the salvation experience.

The anchor of salvation is love, not holiness. Were salvation a matter of inviting Christ into our lives, it would require a holiness we are unable to achieve. By inviting us into his life, Christ demonstrates a love we cannot comprehend. That love enables unity and fellowship with the triune God and his extended family of believers. Still, divine love demands holiness.

Sin breaks the covenant of unity as it places self-orientation over godly love and fellowship. As there is no singularity in the tri-unity of God, there can be none in the fellowship shared with God and those restored to his image (Matt 22:34–40). Therefore, reformation necessitates the purification of heart, which was a primary purpose of Christ's passion.[13] Such purity will result in conformity to Christ, who is the perfect image of God.[14] Purity enables conformity, and conformity enables unity.

8. Cf. John 17:17; Rom 15:16; 1 Cor 6:11; 2 Thess 2:13; 1 Pet 1:2, 22.

9. Williams, *Renewal Theology*, 86.

10. Isa 53:6; John 3:16–18; Rom 3:23–24; 4:25; 5:1; 1 Cor 15:17; Gal 3:13, 24; Titus 3:7; 1 Pet 2:24.

11. John 3:3–5; Rom 6:1–14; 2 Cor 5:16–17; Gal 2:20; 6:14–15; 1 Pet 2:24; 2 Pet 1:4.

12. 1 Cor 1:30; Gal 2:20; Eph 2:1–6; Col 2:11–12; Heb 2:10–11; 10:10; 13:12.

13. Matt 5:8; Titus 2:14.

14. Conformity through sanctification is seen in Romans 8:29, 2 Corinthians 3:18, and Ephesians 4:15. Jesus is identified as the perfect image of God in John 14:8–9, 2 Corinthians 4:4, Colossians 1:15, and Hebrews 1:3.

More to the point, complete unity requires the participants have the same purposes, perspectives, and way of life. There can be no unity if one is sinful and the other holy.[15] Unity demands the persons have one heart. This unity of heart (upward and outward) is the purpose of the salvation/sanctification symbiosis (Ezek 36:26–27), and it is the desire of God.

Therefore, sanctification by faith is the logical next step from justification by faith. This is not only a lifelong process, but a moment-by-moment obedience to God's will, through which God's grace eradicates the sinful affections and tendencies that reside even after justification. Restoration of the *imago Dei* enables God to set apart a holy people for intimate fellowship.[16] This work enables a return to communion with God (1 John 1:3–4), responsibility to God, and stewardship for God.[17]

Thus, sanctification works by and for divine love, and that love becomes the true test of one's holiness. As such, our holiness is centered in "loyalty rather than legality."[18] As Macchia further asserts, this truth is evident throughout the Old Testament, where "righteousness" is rarely used in a legal or forensic context, but instead speaks of covenant faithfulness. The challenge to obey is never softened, but one is ultimately made to depend on the mercy of God for the gift of righteousness. This is because the law cannot create singleness of heart in devotion to God, give new life, or fulfill righteousness. This responsibility falls to the Spirit-filled Messiah.[19]

With that said, it must be understood that condemnation and corruption are neither synonymous nor overcome in the same manner. Condemnation speaks of our legal standing, and is overcome by justification, which is a legal act of God. As a result, there is no condemnation to those who are in Christ (and thus have been "set apart" in positional sanctification). Judicial justification not only brings propitiation, or a turning away of God's wrath, but it brings God himself into the life of the believer. The indwelling of the Holy Spirit enacts experiential sanctification—the systematic

15. Amos 3:3; 2 Cor 6:14; cf. Acts 2:14, 42–47; 4:32–36; 2 Cor 13:14.

16. Eph 5:25–27; 1 Thess 5:23; Heb 13:12.

17. Gen 1:26–27; 2:16–17; Titus 2:13–14. If justification was salvation's ultimate goal, Jesus would have gone straight to the cross (and we could ignore what he did and taught for the previous three-and-a-half years). To have a true understanding of sanctification, it is necessary to see God's purpose in restoring believers to the original image and likeness in which we were created, and Jesus is the perfect(ed) example (Rom 12:1–2; 2 Cor 3:18).

18. Macchia, *Justified in the Spirit*, 105.

19. Isa 11; 42:1; 61:1–3.

dismantling of the corruption that remains (which is necessary, as even our new nature is challenged by rebellion and fallenness).[20] In the same way the Spirit vindicated the cursed, crucified Son in resurrection and exaltation, he now vindicates those who are in Christ.[21]

It is little wonder that the fact that sanctification is the work of the Holy Spirit receives the greatest attention among New Testament writers, according to Horton. "It takes precedence over witnessing, evangelism, giving and every other form of Christian service. God wants us to be something, not just to do something. For only as we become like Jesus can what we do be effective and bring glory to him."[22] Yet to be successful, this conditional sanctification must be seen as a cyclical, synergistic endeavor with the Spirit. Sanctification that was made *possible* by the blood of Christ is now made *personal* by the Holy Spirit.

The role of the individual falls squarely in the context of free will, as sanctification stands as a progressive transformation that transpires amid a delicate balance between divine sovereignty and human responsibility. The difficulty is in defining and applying sanctification without emphasizing one to the neglect of the other. This is a challenge in Reformed theology. While John Calvin's view of free will is often misinterpreted and misrepresented (the "theologian of the Holy Spirit" certainly saw sanctification as a non-negotiable aspect of faith, and one which required the believer's submission and participation), Reformed theology has failed to fully address the professing Christian who behaves like a worldly person and consistently fails to bear the fruits of repentance and the Spirit. The Wesleyan and Arminian would see this as a sanctification issue, while many within the Reformed tradition would contend that the person is not truly saved. Such a position is difficult to maintain, as their own doctrine of sanctification demands participation, which affords the opportunity to reject God's correction and direct. However, efforts to reconcile this are deficient.

As was the example of our Lord, Christians do not serve out of strength but out of submission.[23] Conditional sanctification is often achieved

---

20. Ps 138:8; 1 Cor 6:11; Phil 3:12; 2 Thess 2:13; Titus 3:5; Heb 12:10; 1 Pet 1:1–2.

21. Macchia, *Justified in the Spirit*, 172; Rom 3:21–26; Gal 3:13–14; Heb 10:14.

22. Horton, *What the Bible Says*, 258.

23. Hoekema counters the use of the term "cooperation," arguing that it implies God and the believer each do their respective part of the work. He (like most Reformed theologians) prefers the term "participation," which supports the perspective that *because* God works, we work. In his view, "sanctification is a supernatural work of God in which the believer is active" (Hoekema, "Reformed Perspective," 71–72).

through God's discipline and our growth through discipleship.[24] The reception of such can be difficult, and sometimes rejected, especially in light of Stott's pointed observance that "[w]hat provokes our anger (injured vanity) never provokes his; what provokes his anger (evil) seldom provokes ours."[25]

Still, sanctification is proactive as much as it is reactive. The believer does not passively wait, but is directed to actively pursue perfection through obedience and imitation.[26] Within these passages, we find the Greek word *epiteleó* (perfecting). Its root word, *teleo*, means "progressively bringing to its goal." Thus, the believer's task is to bring holiness to its goal.[27] As Williams rightly asserts, sanctification is a progressive transformation; "not a movement toward sanctification (for believers are already holy) but a growth in it, a gradual process of transformation."[28]

The inherent difficulty in this sanctifying process brings us back to its ultimate purpose: unity with God and fellow believers. While sanctification is primarily achieved through the participatory work of discipline, obedience, imitation, and conformity, the believer is also sanctified by union with Christians, and union with God through his eternal truth.[29] The latter brings faith, the final agent of sanctification.[30] Thus, our positional sanctification enables a participatory sanctification through which we obtain "a heart perfected in love, a personal restoration to the moral image of God, and the responsibility and power to express that love in relationship with God and neighbor."[31] As we enter the loving depths of that *koinonia*, we find that God (through the word and faith) and fellow believers enable further sanctification. This internal work of sanctification must precede Spirit baptism, the external empowerment for ministry. Before God can fully work through us, he must be allowed to work in us. In this, the Holy Spirit is

---

24. 2 Cor 7:1; Heb 12:10.

25. Stott, *Cross of Christ*, 171.

26. 1 Cor 11:1; 2 Cor 7:1; Eph 5:1–2; Phil 2:5–13; Heb 12:14; 1 Pet 2:21.

27. This process is further defined in the following passage: Rom 12:1–2; Phil 3:12–16; Heb 12:1–2; Jas 1:2–4; 1 John 2:5; 4:12–18. In addition, the word "faith" in the Old Testament can most often and more accurately be rendered "faithful," as an obedient response was expected. This understanding is not lost on New Testament writers, and undeniably expressed by James' timeless declaration that "faith without works is dead."

28. Williams, *Renewal Theology*, 89; 2 Cor 3:18; Heb 12:1–2.

29. John 17:17; Eph 4:16; cf. 2 Tim 3:16–17.

30. Acts 26:18; 1 John 5:4.

31. Dieter, "Wesleyan Perspective," 21.

God's provision for the holy living and effective service, through which the great commandment can be fulfilled.

Appendix 4

Power through Weakness

THE APOSTLE PAUL WAS forced in Corinth to contend with a superficial and naïve Christianity that sought health and wealth, protection and provision. Paul's message instead focused on the cross, and power through weakness. When his authority was challenged, the apostle taught that signs and wonders are insufficient proof of God's power and purpose resting on the individual (2 Cor 13:1-4). Instead, it is the transformed lives of believers that provided (and continues to provide) true validation of ministry.

The Corinthian opinion that Paul's previous visit lacked spiritual boldness and power served as a backdrop for his comments. Paul had earlier threatened to address wrongdoers "with a whip" (1 Cor 4:21), but he was perceived as timid and ineffective when he actually faced the Corinthians (2 Cor 10:1-10). False apostles and would-be leaders soon emerged, and quickly assailed Paul's seeming weakness "to justify their own emphasis on health, wealth, and the miraculous as expressions of Christ's 'power' in their midst."[1] These charlatans were quick to boast of their own worth.[2] Questions regarding Paul's credentials and conduct soon became demands for proof that Christ really spoke through Paul. They demanded a display of power—no doubt something on the level of what happened to Elymas, who was struck blind for trying to thwart Paul (Acts 13:11), or the salvation of the Macedonian jailer after empowered praise opened the prison doors (Acts 16:25-40).

1. Hafemann, *NIVAC*; 2 Cor 10:10; 11:6-11; cf. 1 Cor 4:8.
2. 2 Cor 10:7b-12; 11; 12:21b-23.

To demand godly power as proof is blatant error. Any effort to evaluate, assess the claims, or test the credentials of Christ and his designated ministers in this way is to reduce Christ to a powerful genie who performs spectacular tricks on command. "As long as people are assessing him, they are in the superior position, the position of judge. As long as they are checking out his credentials, they are forgetting that God is the one who will weigh them."[3]

While some might charge Paul with causing this conundrum by showing restraint rather than power in his second visit, such an argument is without merit. The fault lay squarely with the Corinthians. The demand for proof revealed the self-serving nature of their faith, a woeful lack of spiritual discernment, and utter confusion about apostolic sufficiency and authority. As such, they would receive proof that Christ's power was working through Paul through the warning the apostle gave concerning his pending third visit.

Paul's warning included a little boasting, which may seem out of character. To boast in one's own anointing or ministry is tantamount to theological error in Paul's perspective, as a minister ought to boast only in the Lord, and what the Lord had done. Yet the apostle knew that Corinthian culture considered boasting a prized, even honorable activity. Indeed, his opponents had boasted to glorify themselves and assert supremacy over others (2 Cor 11:18). Therefore, the apostle joined the boasting battle—but he would boast of his weakness, a topic that would have elicited extreme contempt among his proud readers (2 Cor 11:30).

Throughout his famous "theology of suffering" (2 Cor 10–13), Paul noted that he was able to match their proclaimed powers, experiences, and labors, but they were unable to match his record of suffering and persecution on behalf of Christ. Though he pointed to signs, wonders, and miracles as "signs of an apostle" wrought among the Corinthians (2 Cor 12:12), Paul placed greater worth on times of perceived weakness; times in which he was imprisoned, flogged, lashed, stoned, shipwrecked, imperiled, hungry, thirsty, and stripped naked (2 Cor 11:23–29).[4]

Paul declared weakness to be the source of godly power and the mark of true ministry. Just as holiness is the proof of justification, weakness is the proof of power. The evidence of this truth is the spiritual fruit among

3. Savage, *Power Through Weakness*, 20.
4. Brown, *INT*, 542.

believers—Christ is not weak in dealing with you, Christ is powerful in you (2 Cor 13:3).

The term ἀσθένεια and its cognates occur fifteen times in 1 Corinthians, fourteen times in 2 Corinthians, and eight times in Romans, but only seven times in all of Paul's other letters. As noted by Hawthorne, Paul develops his concept of weakness in four ways:[5]

- Anthropologic: weakness presupposes that a person's whole being is dependent on God. Limitations include the inability of human beings to obtain God's favor by themselves (1 Cor 9:22).

- Christological: weakness is the platform from which the power of God is exhibited in the world. Weakness is the place where God's power is perfected (2 Cor 12:9).

- Ethically: weakness is the catalyst of servanthood. Due to the priority of love over knowledge and gift, believers must hold their Christian freedom in check in deference to the sensibilities of weak Christians (1 Cor 8–10). A failure to help the weak (1 Thess 5:14) is a failure to recognize the mutual dependence of every member of the unity that is characterized in Christ's body (1 Cor 12:12–13).

- Theocentric: God depends neither on human strength nor human achievement, but instead seeks out the weak, the ungodly, and the hostile to redeem them and fit them as vessels of his own strength.

Paul identifies himself as a testimony to this. If he had achieved anything, it was only because of God's power working through a weak but consecrated vessel (cf. 2 Tim 2:20–21). Therefore, Paul did not deny, justify, or excuse his own weakness, but rather embraced it as the conduit through which the power of God worked. In three pericopes in which Paul reflected on power, he also addressed the hardships that beset his ministry.[6] Such hardship and weakness enabled the power of Christ to be revealed in miracles, in Paul's preaching, and in the conversion of sinners who were washed, sanctified, and justified.[7]

The Corinthians sought δοκιμή ("proof"). The word δοκιμή carries the idea of "passing the test," and Paul's use of the word signals that he was

---

5. Hawthorne et al., *Dictionary of Paul*, 966.

6. 2 Cor 4:7—5:10; 6:3–10; 11:16—12:10.

7. Gräbe, *Power of God*, 154. References to miracles: 2 Cor 12:12; Rom 15:19; Gal 3:5. Reference to preaching: 1 Cor 2:4. Reference to conversion: 1 Cor 6:11.

not the one to be tested—they were. The test was not to offer proof through miracle, but to see the present proof through ministry. Christ was among them, and they must therefore repent. In using the present clause, ἐπεὶ δοκιμὴν ζητεῖτε τοῦ ἐν ἐμοὶ λαλοῦντες Χριστοῦ ("since you seek proof that Christ is speaking through me"), the apostle has "conceded to the church the right to examine his work. In fact, he welcomed this opportunity. But the nub of the debate is that the criteria chosen by the Corinthians to evaluate his work are wrong."[8]

To the wayward believers who demanded proof of his power and calling, the apostle responded in force. Paul defended his apostolic authority with the promise of pending charges, a threat that was presented amid contrary revelations highlighted by the promise that the apostle would not show restraint in dealing with wrongdoers, as he had in his second visit. That restraint had been given with reason. In order to preach Christ, who embodied the love of God, Paul had to be patient in his love and endure all things. Because the love of God was manifested in the self-giving of Christ, the love of Christ could be shown in no other way.[9] In such understanding, Paul would rejoice when Christ was proclaimed even by those who sought to harm him (Phil 1:17–18).

However, such patience cannot come at the expense of obedience to Christ. Paul therefore issued a warning that he, in his pending third visit, would not spare any of those causing division or committing sexual immorality (2 Cor 13:2). Paul also included "any of the others" (literally, "all the rest"), which referred to any he might find guilty of sin upon arrival. Included in this "hit list" were those who had shown leniency toward or ignored these sinful behaviors. "To Paul's mind there are no 'innocent bystanders' in what has happened at Corinth."[10]

In light of such unwillingness by the Corinthians, Paul was unwilling to spare anyone. Martin asserts that φείδεσθαι is a military term that speaks to sparing an enemy in battle, though the opportunity to take the life is present.[11] Such would not be the case in Corinth. Though Paul would not spare those who deserve punishment, the perfect προημαρτηκόσιν points to persistence in sin, which indicates Paul would not punish those who repent.

8. Martin, WBC; 2 Cor 10:12; 11:12, 17; 12:11–18.

9. Brown, INT, 449–50; 2 Cor 1:6; 4:10; 1 Thess 2:8.

10. Garland, NAC.

11. Martin, WBC.

Still, Paul's purpose is to reveal neither a demonstration nor evidence of godly power, but rather the source of that power. True power for ministry comes by following the example of Christ: divine power is experienced in the midst of sufferings that results from exposed weakness. This parallel—the crucifixion of Christ "in weakness" with Paul's own weakness—demonstrates a continuing participation in Jesus' death, and therefore a continuing participation in Jesus' power. As Gräbe asserts:

> While Christ lives (and rules) by the power of God who raised him from the dead, he also lives and rules as the crucified. The resurrected remains the crucified, the crucified is the resurrected. Paul's apparent weakness must be understood as the weakness of one who has been crucified with Christ (cf. Rom 6:6, Gal 6:14) and one who carries around the "death of Jesus" in his own body (2 Cor 4:10–12) . . . so that the life of Jesus and power of God may also be revealed in our body.[12]

The crucifixion is stated in the aorist, an unqualified past-tense verb. Christ's life by the power of God, as well as the apostle's weakness, is related in the continuous present tense. Paul's life with Christ through the power of God is related in the future tense. Therefore, when one follows the way of the cross, the weakness that is necessary only has a temporary nature, while the subsequent power has continuous life leading to eschatological fulfillment. Both elements, power and weakness, constitute an indivisible unit and belong inseparably to the Christ event.[13] Thus Paul could boast of "weakness" (2 Cor 12:19) because it aligned him with Christ's death, which enabled him to experience the power of the resurrection. This is of great significance because many in the modern church, like the Corinthians, desire the power of God to overcome our weaknesses. Paul let the power of God work through his weakness. He did this by being crucified with Christ; by dying to the world's system that puts its trust in itself.

Indeed, God's power is not revealed *as* weakness, but rather *in the midst of* weakness, and through the broken existence of our earthen vessels (2 Cor 4:7–12). The more a believer surrenders his plaudits and preferences, the more room there is available for God's power to manifest. This is exemplified in the ministry of Paul. The apostle had committed to follow the example of the Lord, who set aside his rights and prerogatives as God,

12. Gräbe, *Power of God*, 155. As the author later notes, Jesus is not only the crucified and risen, he is especially the crucified Risen (242).

13. Gräbe, *Power of God*, 156, 259.

was not willing to punish those who opposed him, and humbled himself to the point of death on a cross (Phil 2:1–11). For Paul, this is power at its purest.

Though the Corinthians found Paul's weakness distasteful, he showed it to echo the crucifixion of Christ. As Garland notes, "if this displeases or mystifies them, then there is some serious flaw in their faith. They do not understand the full implications of the cross and resurrection."[14] Indeed, weakness is not the lack of power. It is the submission to power that enables one to live in that power. By sharing in Christ's weakness, the believer enters into the paradox of Jesus Christ: comfort from suffering, life from death, strength from weakness, wisdom from foolishness.

In this understanding, Paul uses the verses that follow the selected pericope to turn the tables. The readers have demanded proof of his apostolic authority, but the question at hand is not whether Christ is speaking *in Paul*, but whether Christ is living *in them*. The answer would be achieved through self-examination, conviction of Holy Spirit and apostolic authority, repentance, and prayerful support.

Such instruction and example remains invaluable in the modern church and society, which bears remarkable similarities to Corinth in the time of Paul. Its people were sinking into an abyss of individualism and self-glorification. The people worshiped wealth; poverty was regarded as a disgrace and a dishonor. The projection of wealth and status was crucial. Most remarkable, however, is the similarities shared between religious attitudes of Corinth and the common era. The surge in religious interest was superficial. People wanted contact with the supernatural; amulets, curse tablets, astrology, miracles all filled the atmosphere of enchantment as the people became engulfed in superstition. Salvation played an important role in first-century religion, but Greek philosophy was wrapped in an erroneous understanding of "being and becoming." It led hearers to despise the ever-changing material world and radically oppose the idea of bodily resurrection (as Paul learned the hard way in Acts 17:32). Therefore, salvation dealt with matters of health, wealth, protection, and sustenance.[15]

As Paul expressed and exhibited, God's power was instead manifested in the weakness of Christ. Because Paul willfully walked in that same weakness, he carried that same power. Paul accepted suffering as a necessary consequence; he carried in his body the death of Jesus, so that the life of

14. Garland, *NAC.*

15. Savage, *Power Through Weakness,* 28

Jesus might also be revealed in his body (2 Cor 4:10). If the church (Corinth and modern) would similarly submit in weakness, it would see in Paul and obtain for itself the power both have demanded.[16]

While most try to overcome their weaknesses, God is satisfied to use weakness for his own special purposes. "God's means of working, rightly understood, is not making people stronger, but weaker and weaker, until the divine power alone is seen in them."[17] As such, weakness is not the mark of an inferior or false apostle, but rather the essence of a true believer—and the transformed lives that result are the true validation of ministerial authority.

16. Martin, *WBC.*
17. Hawthorne et al., *Dictionary of Paul,* 967.

Appendix 5

How Two Wills Presents the True Christ and True Victory

THE DEVELOPMENT OF DYOTHELITISM, or Christ having two wills, was the natural outflow of the dual-nature theology that became central to Nicene Christianity. As the latter developed, there emerged an intense Antiochene desire to protect the full humanity of Christ and thus safeguard freedom of the will and ensure the Word's transcendence was not compromised.[1] The divine and human natures were incompatible in the Antiochene prosopic union. However, Nestorius could not bring an ontological union of Jesus' full divinity and full humanity through an anthropomorphic interpretation of the incarnation, as Christ's human experiences would jeopardize the integrity of his divine status. For Cyril, union of the two *hypostasis* was the interpretive key that would explain how the impassible God could truly be born, suffer, and die. This understanding proved invaluable to the development of Chalcedonian Christology, solidified at Council of Ephesus in 431 AD. The doctrine presented a union of two natures: the infinite, uncreated divinity with the finite, created humanity. Each nature retains full integrity and is expressed through one person, namely, the incarnated Word.

In defending Christ's united dual nature against Nestorius's tendency to divide the two, Cyril argued that the resurrection was evidence that Christ "presented himself to God the Father as the first fruits of humanity.

---

1. Kalantzis, "Is There Room For Two," 97.

He opened up for us a way that the human race had not known before."[2] Humanity was incapable of destroying death, but Christ overcame the world and conquered death and corruption. Christ now extends to us the power of His resurrection. As Cyril famously noted, if Christ conquered as God, to us it is nothing; but if he conquered as man, we conquered in him. It is therefore his humanity that makes Christ unique, in that he triumphed over death as a man. Not an ordinary man, mind you, but the new Adam, who pioneered a new path for all of humanity.

As subsequent discussion and debate escalated in the seventh century, an inevitable question emerged: did Christ have one will, or two?[3] The Patriarch Sergius proposed a solution in which Christ's two natures were united in a single activity or energy. Two wills implied the possibility of one standing contrary to the other, he argued. Furthermore, to maintain unity amid a salvific *oikonomia* would require the human will to be overruled by the divine.

To minimize their differences and maximize theological and political unity within the East, Emperor Heraclius and Sergius came into agreement in 638 AD and issued the *Ekthesis* (Exposition of Faith), an edict that decreed everyone must accept the teaching that Jesus had one will in two natures. However, this imperial imposition resulted in further difference as factions debated whether this one will would be human or divine. Heavily influenced by the Alexandrian school, most leaned toward the latter. Others continued to argue (ineffectively) for the necessity of two wills, but that fledgling effort seemed all but silenced by the sound rejection offered by Sergius.

Maximus arose to insist that Christ had two wills while under the spiritual direction of Sophronius, who was most likely the abbot of the Eukratas monastery near Carthage in North Africa, but would later become patriarch of Jerusalem. To assert otherwise would be tantamount to Apollinarianism, in his view. Maximus' argument was centered on exegetical appraisal; specifically, on Christ's petition that the Father remove the cup of

---

2. Wilken, *Spirit of Early Christian Thought*, 118–20.

3. Competing theologies brought immediate confusion to this issue. For example, Pope Leo the Great, in his 449 AD Tome to Flavian, bishop of Constantinople, maintained Christ's two natures as unified, but attributed Christ's miraculous activity to the divine nature and all else to the human nature. While this fell (barely) short of Nestorianism, the explanation made Christ's human nature different from ours, and thus vitiated its integrity.

suffering (Luke 22:39–42) and Paul's declaration that "I no longer live, but Christ lives in me," (Gal 2:20).[4]

The heart of Maximus's theology is captured in *Disputation with Pyrrhus*, an account of his debate with Constantinople's former patriarch in 645 AD. Maximus, like Cyril, saw Christ's humanity as essential yet unique. In response to Monothelite objections, Maximus argued that nothing in Christ was contrary to God because Christ was without sin, the cause of our rebellion against God. This was due to the manner of his incarnation.

Maximus asserted that Adam's disobedience disabled his deification; the one born immaterial was condemned to a material mortality. As Behr powerfully notes, "when Adam sinned, he was condemned to birth."[5] The sin was twofold, in Maximus's view. The first aspect was culpable, as Adam's free choice willfully rejected the good; the second, occasioned by the first, was innocent as human nature unwillingly put off its incorruption.[6]

Maximus thus differentiated between the gnomic and natural will. The former speaks to the process of deliberation that culminates in a decision but is a result of our sinful state. The latter is the will humans have by design; one that is oriented toward God and moves toward its teleological fulfilment. Maximus held that Christ maintained the pure integrity of a natural will but lacked a gnomic will due to the Holy Spirit's role in the incarnation.[7] The manner in which the Spirit overshadowed Mary circumvented the issue of original sin and subsequent condition (Luke 1:35).

According to Behr, the Lord neither knew the mutability of my free choice nor did he become my sin. Rather, he became the "sin that I caused." Christ assumed the corruption of human nature that was a consequence of the mutability of my free choice. He became a human being naturally liable to passions and used the "sin" that I caused to destroy the "sin" that I commit.[8]

---

4. Maximus interpreted the prayer in Gethsemane as "Not what I as man will, but what you and I as God will." He also employed a variety of passages that portray Christ as having a human and a divine will, to include Mark 7:24; 14:35; Luke 13:34; John 1:18; 4:34; 5:19–30; 6:38–40; 8:28–29; 12:49–50; 14:31; 15:9–10; Romans 5:19; and Hebrews 5:7–10; 10:5–10.

5. Behr, *Cosmic Mystery of Jesus Christ*, loc. 2551.

6. Behr, *Cosmic Mystery of Jesus Christ*, loc. 2755.

7. It is worth noting that Maximus had ascribed to Christ a gnomic will perfectly fixed on the good in his *Commentary on the Lord's Prayer*, but later rescinded that attribution in *Ad Thalassium* 21 and 42.

8. Behr, *Cosmic Mystery of Jesus Christ*, locs. 2770–74.

Despite the lack of a gnomic will, Christ still possesses two wills: "a 'natural' divine will reflective of the good pleasure of the God whose Son he is, and a 'natural' human will."[9] Thus, to liberate and return humanity to its divine inheritance, the *Logos* entered an incarnation that united not the fallen with the divine, but prelapsarian perfection with the divine. As Maximus noted in *Ambiguum*, this "modeled the perfect co-existence of intelligent soul and material body."[10]

Furthermore, Christ rectified our liability to passions in his assumption of natural passibility. He did this not by turning evil *to* good, but by refusing to voluntarily turn *from* the good. This thwarted evil and turned our expected end (death) toward a transformative deification. In short, Christ turned willing aright. This enabled Christ, who had no gnomic will, to redeem the gnomic wills of sinners.

> For the Saviour to lack gnome does not mean that he is missing some essential component of humanness, but that he is free from the twistedness of the human condition as it is experienced by sinners, who cannot discern properly what goodness is but are subject to the confusion of a moral existence that is not what it is intended to be.[11]

Indeed, Jesus (the only authentic human) demonstrates that true freedom is not a matter of absolute choice separate from external constraint. On the contrary, self-orientation stands as testimony to the fact that humans are not so free as they may suppose. Authentic freedom, and thus authentic existence, resides in lifelong commitment to the Father. The Holy Spirit creates, sanctifies, and sustains such humanity, of which Christ is the perfect(ed) example. Through the Spirit, the Christ was "living out his mission in a distinctly human way, willing as a truly human being, but willing in a way that is never at odds with a divine purpose."[12] The effect is the same for those who follow Christ's example. As Maximus rightly noted, the Spirit redirects the gnomic will so that it might be converted toward God and deification.[13]

Therefore, Jesus had a natural human will as a result of his incarnation, but one void of sinful control—a nature similar to that of Adam and

---

9. Davidson, "Not My Will," 192.

10. Behr, *Cosmic Mystery of Jesus Christ*, loc. 309.

11. Davidson, "Not My Will," 195.

12. Davidson, "Not My Will," 201.

13. Maximus, "Ad Thalassium 6," 103–4.

Eve before their fall. Jesus was capable of sin, otherwise his victory over temptation would mean nothing to us. However, sin had no control over him, and therefore, his human will would not stand in opposition to God as does the human will prior to justification and reformation. Maximus elaborated with Jesus' own comment that "the ruler of this world is coming, but he will find nothing in me" (John 14:30). In Maximus's view, this meant Satan would find none of the things that display the "contrariness of our will that the bases are nature."[14]

Natural human will was also evident in Christ's display of weakness when he pleaded to be spared death, Maximus argued. This is not to suggest that his human will could have been in opposition to the Father's will; on the contrary, the work of salvation is a work of God, but could not be carried out without human cooperation, as this redirects the natural will of human beings transformed by Christ's salvation and Spirit.

Such understanding was not without its challengers, whose questions were varied and valid: how does one find unity of purpose amid the human struggle and divine plan? In becoming a man who is perfected through obedience, does the Son of God become estranged from proper fellowship with the Father? Did Christ's submission imply that the Son was of lesser status than the Father? Does having two wills mean Christ had two self-determining faculties? Does this render Christ a schizophrenic? Does it commit the heresy of Nestorianism and divide Christ into two persons?

Similar questions persist. Wolfhart Pannenberg argued that two wills must necessarily conform to one another, thus making one of them (namely, the human) superfluous.[15] Moreland and Craig argued that the Bible never speaks of Jesus as having two wills, and so there is no reason to do so.[16] Macquarrie suggested that two wills in one person would be a "pathological condition" and some kind of split-personality disorder.[17] Schleiermacher seemed unhappy with any solution, as he held that one will leaves either the divine nature or human nature incomplete, but two wills results only in agreement, not unity.[18]

Such assertions persist because most fail to consider or develop the asynchronous relationship shared between the natural human and natural

14. Wilken, *Spirit of Early Christian Thought*, 128.

15. Pannenberg, *Jesus—God and Man*, 294.

16. Moreland, *Philosophical Foundations*, 611.

17. Macquarrie, *Jesus Christ in Modern Thought*, 166–167.

18. Schleiermacher, *Christian Faith*, 394.

divine wills in Christ. The Son had access to the divine mind shared with the Father and Spirit, but that human mind knew only what the divine mind chose to reveal through the Spirit (Luke 2:52; John 5:19–20). The human mind is not capable of comprehending, let alone containing the fullness of such knowledge. Furthermore, to bear the fullness of divine knowledge would "dehumanize" the Son of Man, as he would have a divine understanding beyond that of the humanity with whom he would sympathize and set free.

In this we see the symbiotic relationship between kenosis and theosis espoused by Gregory of Nazianzus. The Son of Man descended to become flesh, and the flesh ascended to be transformed. Deification is initiated at the moment of union—for the incarnated *Logos*, and for the *logoi* alike. This enabled the Son of Man, in his humanity, to recapitulate human history and destiny.

Christ's passion event, specifically its final eighteen hours that stretched from Gethsemane to Golgotha, stand as the climax of this process. Christ was faced with continuous choices, came to know divine will through the Spirit's continuous revelation, and was able to fulfill that will through the Spirit's continuous anointing. Indeed, Jesus' obedience to the point of death was not only an act of humility, but a necessarily willed act, as unwilling obedience is not obedience at all (Phil 2:8; cf. Isa 1:19).

For this reason, Maximus found his greatest defense of Dyothelitism in Gethsemane. There, Jesus was presented many "goods," and had to discern between charity and cupidity to properly order and thus rightly choose the greatest good. Jesus was driven by the fundamental desire to live, which is a good and godly quality, but was not the ultimate good. Redemption was the ultimate good, the motion of the soul that would fully demonstrate love of God, self, and others. Still, questions and conundrums beyond our comprehension clouded such understanding. Redemption was the ultimate good, but was there another way to achieve it? Perhaps the wilderness temptations echoed in Jesus' mind: *are you really the Messiah? Would the Father really let you be hurt? Is there a way to obtain the kingdom of God without a cross?*

In deference to Augustinian thought, sin usually enters the equation when we designate something that is good as ultimate good. This begs the following question: could Jesus choose the good (preservation of life) over the ultimate good (redemption), and thereby sin? It was an epistemological possibility—the human mind certainly thought it possible, which was a necessary condition to achieve willful obedience. However, it was a metaphysical impossibility—the Son, the second person of the Trinity, was not going to walk away (though his human mind did not know or understand such theological depth).[19] "Viewed one way, the humanity particularized by the Word clearly 'cannot' sin, in so far as his humanity is naturally one with the divinity that assumes it, whose will it is to carry out a redemptive purpose within it. Viewed another way, his humanity is nevertheless genuinely vulnerable and weak, and only by the Spirit's power is the Word's perfect incarnate obedience lived out."[20]

It is no wonder that Jesus agonized as he considered the various "goods" that battled for dominance. This struggle was evident in his petition regarding the cup of suffering (Luke 22:39–42), that he was "overwhelmed with sorrow to the point of death" (Mark 14:34; Matt 26:38), that his sweat was "like drops of blood falling to the ground" (Luke 22:44),[21] and in the subsequent descriptions of weakness attributed to our high priest (Heb 4:15; 5:2). Amid this struggle was the search for divine will, and the need to recognize this as ultimate good. The revelation of the Spirit was certain: the Father willed that redemption come through crucifixion.[22]

Jesus first experienced a natural human fear of death, but the combination of progressive deification and Spirit-anointing enabled his human will to align with this revealed divine will, even to the point of death.[23] The difference between Jesus' human and natural wills is clear: the former desired to avoid death, while the latter desired to save all through an atoning death. Christ's willful submission brought perfect harmony and concurrence to both, and it revealed him able both to will and effect our salvation.[24]

Ultimately, the Spirit's power and the Word's perfect obedience was fully displayed at Golgotha. There, upon the cross, crescendos the Spirit's work of deification that strengthened and enabled Jesus to complete the otherwise unbearable and impossible task. In his crucifixion and death, Jesus experienced the isolation, abandonment, and darkness of hell. Though

19. Coulter, "Basic Ideas."

20. Davidson, "Not My Will," 202.

21. Luke is likely describing a rare phenomenon called hematohidrosis, or hematidrosis, in which extreme stress and fear cause capillaries to rupture. Blood then enters the sweat glands, which causes the appearance of one sweating blood. See Manonukul, "Hematidrosis."

22. And with that came the promise of resurrection (Isa 53; Ps 16:10).

23. Watts, "Two Wills," 464.

24. Behr, *Cosmic Mystery of Jesus Christ*, locs. 3947–83.

not a metaphysical alienation, Jesus' humanity did experience the full reality of sin's consequence, a struggle he was able to endure only through the power of the Spirit. Yet Christ completed the work of salvation not because the Spirit established Jesus' divinity, but because the Spirit enlivened and enabled Jesus' humanity.[25]

The Spirit's work is evident throughout Jesus' life. Christ was conceived by the Holy Spirit (Luke 1:35), increased in wisdom by means of the Spirit (Luke 2:40–52), was anointed for ministry by the Holy Spirit at his baptism (Matt 3:16; Mark 1:10; Luke 3:22; John 1:32), and was raised from death by the Spirit (Rom 8:11). This Spirit-led endeavor not only enabled Jesus to know and complete the divine will, it enabled the glorification subsequent to (and arguably resulting from) Jesus' obedience unto death. In this, Jesus became Spirit-bearer to his church (Acts 2:33). The bestowal of this same Spirit upon his people united Christ to the church and the church to the divine life. The church's participation in the triune life by means of the Spirit gives shape to a properly Christian anthropology and enables the fulfillment of the salvific goal. For Maximus, the influence of Christian Platonism was evident and appropriate. The lower does not create or give meaning to the higher; fulfillment is found when the lower is taken into the higher, which imposes itself for the lower's development and plurality of meaning. This is necessary, as the higher always supplies the lower with its meaning and ultimate telos (which is always external and prior to the lower). Therefore, as corruption entered through human autonomy, restoration is achieved by human self-determination—a submission to deification through which the individual is taught and empowered to refrain from all but God's will, and therefore master what had been one's master. "Difference is thus by Maximus not considered as the solution to the problem of human freedom, but as the problem itself; the solution therefore consists in the disappearance of difference and God becoming all in all."[26]

In this scheme, Maximus

> highlights the divine pedagogy that oversees the errant impulses and affections of embodied human beings. We must either learn severely, by God's direct purgation and reorientation; or we must learn through our own present experiences to train ourselves

---

25. McFarland, "Spirit and Incarnation," 154.

26. Alfsvag, "God's Fellow Workers," 178.

against evil passions; or else, as Maximus further explains, we must look to imitate the example of the truly virtuous.[27]

The result is that human will fully submits to God (which, for Maximus, is humanity's natural state). This willful submission is so complete that God alone is active, but this should not be mistaken as the obliteration of the human will, "as that would amount to the destruction of human nature rather than its salvation."[28]

Though Maximus did not espouse a pneumatic Dyothelitism, the trinitarian matrix in which he presented deification amid the Dyothelite structure certainly lends itself to this fuller definition. In addition, the trinitarian *oikonomia* of Jesus' passion event (which is viewed through this paradigm) presents a right and robust soteriology that moves well beyond the confines of penal satisfaction and into the Spirit-led transformation that reforms the believer into the *imago dei* in order to transform the believer into the *imago Christi*.

While there are modern challenges to Maximus's approach, these typically fail to differentiate the gnomic and natural will inherent to his paradigm. This must be rightly assessed, and such understanding necessitates use of Augustine's double account of the Son (the Son is equal to Father in the form of God, less than the Father in form of man, and the reader must discern which is addressed in any particular passage). When Dyothelitism is considered in its proper context, Christ's incarnation is seen to heal human passibility and thus pioneer a new path in which willful submission enables Spirit-led growth through empowered, transformed, and disciplined reasoning. This fulfills the Father's pedagogical plan to overcome passions and peccability, and to realign the soul's natural desire for God.

Indeed, a proper deification sees the believer taken into that which already exists—the only way to become united to Christ is to become Christlike. Jesus' agony in the garden stands as the prototype of genuine natural human will.[29] In following the example of Jesus' movement, the Christian becomes his true self, and stands in true union with God. Thus, human beings, "who in a historical fall abused their freedom to turn toward what was worse, in Christ are able to move toward God who draws them by grace

---

27. Behr, *Cosmic Mystery of Jesus Christ*, loc. 343.

28. McFarland, "Naturally and By Grace," 426.

29. Matt 26:39; Mark 14:34; Luke 22:42; Phil 3:20–21; Heb 2:10; 5:7–9.

into his divinizing life."[30] Humans are divinized by the grace of God who became human. They are a portion of God; the *logoi* of the *Logos*.

30. Behr, *Cosmic Mystery of Jesus Christ*, loc. 278.

Bibliography

à Kempis, Thomas. *The Imitation of Christ*. Translated by Robert Jeffery. London: Penguin, 2012.

Alfsvag, Knut. "God's Fellow Workers: The Understanding of the Relationship Between the Human and the Divine in Maximus Confessor and Martin Luther." *Studia Theologica* 62 (2008) 175–93.

Ambrose of Milan. "Letter to the Priests." In *Readings in Christian Ethics*, edited by J. Phillip Wogaman and Douglas M. Strong, 48–50. Louisville: Westminster John Knox, 1996.

American Bible Society. "State of the Bible 2017." https://1s712.americanbible.org/cdn-www-ws03/uploads/content/State_of_the_Bible_2017_report_032317.pdf.

Anderson, Paul N. *The Riddles of the Fourth Gospel*. Minneapolis: Fortress, 2011.

Anselm of Canterbury. *Cur Deus Homo?* Translated by Sidney Norton Deane. Fort Worth: RDMc, 2005.

Aquinas, Thomas. "On the Satisfaction of Christ." In *The Christian Theology Reader,s* edited by Alister E. McGrath, 302. Chichester, UK: Wiley, 2016.

Archer, Kenneth J. *A Pentecostal Hermeneutic: Spirit, Scripture and Community*. Cleveland, TN: CPT, 2010.

Athanasius. "Against the Heathen, Part I." In *Nicene and Post-Nicene Church Fathers, Second Series, Volume IV: Athanasius: Select Works and Letters*, edited by Philip Schaff, locs. 491378–943. The Complete Ante-Nicene, Nicene, and Post-Nicene Church Fathers Collection. London: Catholic Way, 2014. Digital edition.

———. "On the Incarnation of the Word." In *Nicene and Post-Nicene Church Fathers, Second Series, Volume IV: Athanasius: Select Works and Letters*, edited by Philip Schaff, locs. 492308–3461. The Complete Ante-Nicene, Nicene, and Post-Nicene Church Fathers Collection. London: Catholic Way, 2014. Digital edition.

Augustine. *The City of God*. Translated by Marcus Dods. Peabody, MA: Hendrickson, 2009.

Barna Group. "2017 Bible-Minded Cities." https://www.barna.com/research/2017-bible-minded-cities/.

———. "Barna Survey Examines Changes in Worldview Among Christians over the Past 13 Years." https://www.barna.com/research/barna-survey-examines-changes-in-worldview-among-christians-over-the-past-13-years/.

———. "The End of Absolutes: America's New Moral Code." https://www.barna.com/research/the-end-of-absolutes-americas-new-moral-code.

———. "New Research Explores the Changing Shape of Temptation." https://www.barna. com/research/new-research-explores-the-changing-shape-of-temptation/.

———. *Porn Phenomenon: The Impact of Pornography in the Digital Age.* Carol Stream, IL: Tyndale, 2016.

Barrett, Matthew. *God's Word Alone: The Authority of Scripture.* Grand Rapids: Zondervan, 2016.

Barth, Karl. *Church Dogmatics 1.1: The Doctrine of the Word of God.* Translated by G. T. Thompson et al. Edinburgh: T. & T. Clark, 2010.

———. *Church Dogmatics 2.1: The Doctrine of God.* Translated by T. H. L. Parker et al. Edinburgh: T. & T. Clark, 2004.

Bayer, Oswald. *Martin Luther's Theology: A Contemporary Interpretation.* Grand Rapids: Eerdmans, 2008.

Bee Gees. "Stayin' Alive." *Saturday Night Fever: The Original Movie Soundtrack.* RSO Records. CD. Recorded 1977.

Behr, John, et al. *On the Cosmic Mystery of Jesus Christ.* Popular Patristics Series 25. Yonkers, NY: St. Vladimir's Seminary Press, 2011. Kindle edition.

Bivens-Tatum, Wayne. *Libraries and the Enlightenment.* Los Angeles: Library Juice, 2012.

Blocher, Henri A. G. "God and the Scripture Writers: The Question of Double Authorship." In *The Enduring Authority of the Christian Scriptures,* edited by D. A. Carson, 497–541. Grand Rapids: Eerdmans, 2016.

Bonhoeffer, Dietrich. *The Cost of Discipleship.* New York: Touchstone, 1995.

———. *Life Together.* New York: HarperCollins, 1954.

Brown, Raymond E. *An Introduction to the New Testament.* New Haven, CT: Yale University Press, 2010.

Bruce, F. F. *The Book of Acts.* NICNT. Revised edition. Grand Rapids: Eerdmans, 1988.

Bureau of Labor Statistics. "Economic News Release." https://www.bls.gov/news.release/ atus.t12.htm.

Calvin, John. "John 1:6–13." http://www.ccel.org/ccel/calvin/comment3/comm_vol34/ htm/vii.ii.htm.

Carson, D. A., ed. *The Enduring Authority of the Christian Scriptures.* Grand Rapids: Eerdmans, 2016.

Centers for Disease Control and Prevention. "Heart Disease Facts." http://www.cdc.gov/ HeartDisease/facts.htm.

Chandler, Diane J. *Christian Spiritual Formation.* Downers Grove, IL: InterVarsity, 2014.

Chandler, Matt. *The Explicit Gospel.* Wheaton, IL: Crossway, 2012.

Chrysostom. *Saint Chrysostom, Homilies on the Acts of the Apostles and the Epistle to the Romans.* Vol. 11 of *The Complete Ante-Nicene, Nicene, and Post-Nicene Church Fathers Collection,* edited by Philip Schaff. Grand Rapids: Eerdmans, 1989.

Clement of Alexandria. "The Instructor, Book II." In *The Ante-Nicene Fathers, Volume 2: Translations of the Writings of the Fathers Down to A.D. 325,* edited by Philip Schaff, locs. 28750–9949. The Complete Ante-Nicene, Nicene, and Post-Nicene Church Fathers Collection. London: Catholic Way, 2014. Digital edition.

———. "Who is the Rich Man that Shall be Saved?" In *The Ante-Nicene Fathers, Volume 2: Translations of the Writings of the Fathers Down to A.D. 325,* locs. 41011–486. The Complete Ante-Nicene, Nicene, and Post-Nicene Church Fathers Collection. London: Catholic Way, 2014. Digital edition.

Coulter, Dale M. "Basic Ideas of Jewish Monotheism." Lecture, Regent University School of Divinity, April 10, 2018.

Courey, David J. *What Has Wittenburg to Do With Azusa?* New York: Bloomsbury, 2015.

Davidson, Ivor J. "'Not My Will But Yours Be Done': The Ontological Dynamics of Incarnational Intention." *International Journal of Systematic Theology* 7:2 (April 2005) 178–204.

Dieter, Melvin E. "The Wesleyan Perspective." In *Five Views on Sanctification*, edited by Stanley N. Gundry, 11–46. Grand Rapids: Zondervan, 1987.

Ebeling, Gerhard. *Luther: An Introduction to His Thought.* Minneapolis: Fortress, 2007.

Erickson, Millard J. *Christian Theology.* Grand Rapids: Baker Academic, 2013.

———. *Introducing Christian Doctrine.* Grand Rapids: Baker Academic, 2001.

Frost, Michael, and Alan Hirsch. *The Shaping of Things to Come.* Grand Rapids: Baker, 2013.

Gadamer, Hans-Georg. *Truth and Method.* Translated by Joel Weinsheimer and Donald G. Marshall. 2nd revised edition. New York: Continuum, 2006.

Gane, Roy. *The NIV Application Commentary: Leviticus, Numbers.* Grand Rapids: Zondervan, 2004. Digital edition.

Garland, David E. *New American Commentary Volume 29: 2 Corinthians.* Nashville: B. & H. Academic, 1999. Digital edition.

Gause, R. Hollis. *Living in the Spirit: The Way of Salvation.* Cleveland, TN: CPT, 2010.

Gonzalez, Justo. *A History of Christian Thought, Vol. III.* Nashville: Abingdon, 1975.

Gräbe, Petrus J. *The Power of God in Paul's Letters.* Tübingen, Germany: Mohr, 2008.

Greenslade, S. L., ed. and trans. *Early Latin Theology Selections from Tertullian, Cyprian, Ambrose, and Jerome.* Library of Christian Classics 5. Philadelphia: Westminster, 1956.

Grudem, Wayne. *Systematic Theology: An Introduction to Biblical Discipline.* Grand Rapids: Zondervan, 1994.

Hafemann, Scott J. *The NIV Application Commentary: 2 Corinthians.* Grand Rapids: Zondervan, 2000. Digital edition.

Hamer, Dean H. *The God Gene: How Faith Is Hardwired into Our Genes.* New York: Random House, 2005.

Harvard Health School. "Anxiety and Physical Illness." http://www.health.harvard.edu/staying-healthy/anxiety_and_physical_illness.

Harvard University. "Serve and Return." http://developingchild.harvard.edu/science/key-concepts/serve-and-return/.

Hawthorne, Gerald F., et al., eds. *Dictionary of Paul and His Letters.* Downers Grove, IL: InterVarsity, 1993.

"Heroic Redmond Defies the Pain Barrier." https://www.olympic.org/news/heroic-redmond-defies-the-pain-barrier.

Hindson, Ed, and Ergun Caner. *The Popular Encyclopedia of Apologetics.* Eugene, OR: Harvest, 2008.

Hoekema, Anthony A. "The Reformed Perspective." In *Five Views on Sanctification*, edited by Stanley N. Gundry, 59–90. Grand Rapids: Zondervan, 1987.

Hollinger, Dennis P. *Choosing the Good: Christian Ethics in a Complex World.* Grand Rapids: Baker Academic, 2002.

Horton, Stanley M. "The Pentecostal Perspective." In *Five Views on Sanctification*, edited by Stanley N. Gundry, 105–35. Grand Rapids: Zondervan, 1987.

———. *What the Bible Says About the Holy Spirit.* Springfield, MO: Gospel, 1976.

Idleman, Kyle. *Gods at War.* Grand Rapids: Zondervan, 2013.

Kalantzis, George. "Is There Room For Two? Cyril's Single Subjectivity and the Prosopic Union." *St Vladimir's Theological Quarterly* 52.1 (2008) 95–110.

Kärkkäinen, Veli-Matti. *Pneumatology: The Holy Spirit in Ecumenical, International, and Contextual Perspective.* Grand Rapids: Baker Academic, 2002.

Keener, Craig S. *The NIV Application Commentary, Revelation.* Grand Rapids: Zondervan, 2000.

———. *Spirit Hermeneutics: Reading Scripture in Light of Pentecost.* Grand Rapids: Eerdmans, 2016.

Kinnaman, David, and Gabe Lyons. *Good Faith: Being a Christian When Society Thinks You're Irrelevant and Extreme.* Grand Rapids: Baker, 2016.

Kluger, Jeffrey, et al. "Religion: Is God in Our Genes?" *Time Magazine*, October 25, 2004.

Köstenberger, Andreas, et al. *Truth Matters: Confident Faith in a Confusing World.* Nashville: B. & H. Academic, 2014.

Ladner, Gerhart B. *The Idea of Reform: Its Impact on Christian Thought and Action in the Age of the Fathers.* Whitefish, MT: Literary Licensing, 2011.

Lane, Tony. *A Concise History of Christian Thought*, Grand Rapids: Baker Academic, 2006.

Leahy, Robert L. *The Worry Cure: Seven Steps to Stop Worry from Stopping You.* New York: Crown, 2005.

Lewis, C. S. *God in the Dock: Essays on Theology and Ethics.* Cambridge, UK: Eerdmans, 1970.

———. *Mere Christianity.* New York: HarperCollins, 1980.

———. *Surprised by Joy.* London: Geoffrey, 1955.

Lienhard, Joseph T., ed. *Ancient Christian Commentary on Scripture, Old Testament, Vol. III: Exodus, Leviticus, Numbers, Deuteronomy.* Downers Grove, IL: InterVarsity, 2001.

Lipka, Michael. "A Closer Look at America's Rapidly Growing Religious 'Nones.'" http://www.pewresearch.org/fact-tank/2015/05/13/a-closer-look-at-americas-rapidly-growing-religious-nones/.

———. "Why America's 'Nones' Left Religion Behind." http://www.pewresearch.org/fact-tank/2016/08/24/why-americas-nones-left-religion-behind/.

Lockyer, Herbert. *All the Parables of the Bible.* Grand Rapids: Zondervan, 1963.

Loke, Andrew Ter Ern. "On Dyothelitism Versus Monothelitism: The Divine Preconscious Model." *Heythrop Journal* 57.1 (2016) 135–41.

Louw, J. P., and E. A. Nida. *Greek-English Lexicon of the New Testament Based on Semantic Domains.* New York: United Bible Societies, 1988.

Lyons, Gabe. *The Next Christians.* New York: Doubleday, 2010.

Macchia, Frank D. *Justified in the Spirit: Creation, Redemption, and the Triune God.* Grand Rapids: Eerdmans, 2010.

Macquarrie, John. *Jesus Christ in Modern Thought.* London: SCM, 1990.

Manonukul, J., et al. "Hematidrosis: A Pathologic Process or Stigmata. A Case Report With Comprehensive Histopathologic and Immunoperoxidase Studies." *The American Journal of Dermatopathology* April 30.2 (2008) 135–39.

"Marathon Man Akhwari Demonstrates Superhuman Spirit." www.olympic.org/news/marathon-man-akhwari-demonstrates-superhuman-spirit.

Martin, Ralph P. *Word Biblical Commentary, Volume 40: 2 Corinthians.* Dallas: Word, 2012. Digital edition.

Maximus. "Ad Thalassium 6." In *On the Cosmic Mystery of Jesus Christ*, edited by John Behr, translated by Robert Louis Wilken and Paul M. Blowers. Yonkers, NY: St. Vladimir's Seminary Press, 2011. Kindle edition.

————. *Disputation with Pyrrhus*. Translated by Joseph P. Farrell. South Canaan, PA: St. Tikhon's Seminary Press, 1990.

McFarland, Ian A. "'Naturally and By Grace': Maximus the Confessor on the Operation of the Will." *Scottish Journal of Theology* 58.4 (November 2005) 410–33.

————. "Spirit and Incarnation: Toward a Pneumatic Chalcedonianism." *International Journal of Systematic Theology* 16.2 (April 2014) 143–58.

McGee, Robert S. *The Search for Significance*. Nashville: Nelson, 1998.

McGrath, Alister E. *Christian Theology: An Introduction*. Chichester, UK: Wiley, 2017.

McKnight, Scot. *Kingdom Conspiracy: Returning to the Radical Mission of the Local Church*. Grand Rapids: Brazos, 2014.

MercyMe. "I Can Only Imagine." *The Worship Project*. INO Records. CD. Recorded 1999.

Miller, Clarence H. *Erasmus and Luther: The Battle Over Free Will*. Indianapolis: Heckett, 2012.

Mohler, R. Albert, Jr. *We Cannot Be Silent: Speaking Truth to a Culture Redefining Sex, Marriage, and the Very Meaning of Right and Wrong*. Nashville: Nelson, 2015.

Moltmann, Jürgen. *The Crucified God: The Cross of Christ as the Foundation and Criticism of Christian Theology*. Minneapolis: Fortress, 2014.

————. "On the Suffering of God." In *The Christian Theology Reader*, edited by Alister E. McGrath, 192–93. Chichester, UK: Wiley, 2016.

Moreland, J. P., and William Lane Craig. *Philosophical Foundations for a Christian Worldview*. Downers Grove, IL: InterVarsity, 2003.

National Severe Storms Laboratory. "Severe Weather 101—Thunderstorms." http://www.nssl.noaa.gov/education/svrwx101/thunderstorms.

Newbigin, Lesslie. *Proper Confidence: Faith, Doubt, and Certainty in Christian Discipleship*. Grand Rapids: Eerdmans, 1995.

Niebuhr, H. Richard. *The Kingdom of God in America*. Middletown, CT: Wesleyan University Press, 1988.

Olson, David. *American Church in Crisis*. Grand Rapids: Zondervan, 2008.

Osborne, Grant R. *Exegetical Commentary on the New Testament*. Grand Rapids: Zondervan, 2010.

Palmer, Michael D. *Elements of a Christian Worldview*. Springfield, MO: Logion, 1998.

Pannenberg, Wolfhart. *Jesus—God and Man*. Translated by Lewis L. Wilkins and Duane Priebe. 2nd ed. Philadelphia: Westminster, 1982.

Pearcey, Nancy. *Total Truth: Liberating Christianity from Its Cultural Captivity*. Wheaton, IL: Crossway, 2004.

Pew Research Center. "U.S. Religious Knowledge Survey." http://www.pewforum.org/2010/09/28/u-s-religious-knowledge-survey/.

Phillips, Wade. *Quest to Restore God's House—A Theological History of the Church of God (Cleveland, Tennessee): Volume I, 1886–1923, R.G. Spurling to A.J. Tomlinson, Formation-Transformation-Reformation*. Cleveland, TN: CPT, 2017.

Pinnock, Clark H. *Flame of Love: A Theology of the Holy Spirit*. Downers Grove, IL: InterVarsity, 1999.

Porter, Stanley E. *Idioms of the Greek New Testament*. 2nd ed. Sheffield, UK: Sheffield Academic, 1994.

Rainer, Thom. "The Main Reason People Leave a Church." *The Thom Rainer Blog*, January 21, 2013. http://thomrainer.com/2013/01/21/the-main-reason-people-leave-a-church/.

Rediger, G. Lloyd. *Fit to be a Pastor*. Louisville: Westminster John Knox, 2000.

Savage, Timothy B. *Power Through Weakness: Paul's Understanding of the Christian Ministry in 2 Corinthians*. Cambridge: Cambridge University Press, 1996.

Savitsky, Eric, and Brian Eastridge, eds. *Combat Casualty Care: Lessons Learned from OEF and OIF*. Washington, DC: Office of the Surgeon General, 2012.

Scharen, Christian B. *Faith as a Way of Life*. Grand Rapids: Eerdmans, 2008.

Schleiermacher, F. D. E. *The Christian Faith*. Translated by H. R. Mackintosh and J. S. Stewart. 2nd ed. Edinburgh: T. & T. Clark, 1928.

Schlosberg, Jason. "Battle of Kruger." YouTube. 8:24. May 3, 2007. https://www.youtube.com/watch?v=LU8DDYz68kM.

Shank, Robert. *Life in the Son*. Minneapolis: Bethany, 1989.

Skinner, B. F. *Beyond Freedom and Dignity*. Indianapolis: Hackett, 2002.

Spawn, Kevin L., and Archie T. Wright, eds. *Spirit & Scripture: Exploring a Pneumatic Hermeneutic*. London: T. & T. Clark, 2012.

Stassen, Glen H., and David P. Gushee. *Kingdom Ethics: Following Jesus in Contemporary Context*. Downers Grove, IL: InterVarsity, 2003.

Stott, John. *Confess Your Sins: The Way of Reconciliation*. Grand Rapids: Eerdmans, 1964.

———. *The Cross of Christ*. Downers Grove, IL: InterVarsity, 2006.

Sunshine, Glenn S. "Accommodation Historically Considered." In *The Enduring Authority of the Christian Scriptures*, edited by D. A. Carson, 238–65. Grand Rapids: Eerdmans, 2016.

Sussman, Dalia. "Poll: Elbow Room No Problem in Heaven." http://abcnews.go.com/US/Beliefs/story?id=1422658.

Swenson, Richard A. *Margin: Restoring Emotional, Physical, Financial, and Time Reserves to Overloaded Lives*. Colorado Springs: NavPress, 2004.

Tertullian. "Apology." In *The Ante-Nicene Fathers, Volume 3: Latin Christianity: Its Founder, Tertullian*, edited by Philip Schaff, locs. 43220–4566. The Complete Ante-Nicene, Nicene, and Post-Nicene Church Fathers Collection. London: Catholic Way, 2014. Digital edition.

Thiselton, Anthony C. *The Living Paul: An Introduction to the Apostle's Life and Thought*. Downers Grove, IL: InterVarsity, 2011. Digital edition.

Tillich, Paul. *Systematic Theology, Vol. II*. Chicago, University of Chicago Press, 1957.

Tozer, A. W. *The Crucified Life*. Ventura, CA: Regal, 2011.

Turner, David L. *Baker Exegetical Commentary on the New Testament*. Grand Rapids: Baker Academic, 2008.

Vanhoozer, Kevin J. *Faith Speaking Understanding: Performing the Drama of Doctrine*. Louisville: Westminster John Knox, 2014

———. "May We Go Beyond What is Written After All? The Pattern of Theological Authority and the Problem of Doctrinal Development." In *The Enduring Authority of the Christian Scriptures*, edited by D. A. Carson, 747–94. Grand Rapids: Eerdmans, 2016.

———. "On the Challenge of Postmodernity for Theology." In *The Christian Theology Reader*, edited by Alister E. McGrath, 60–62. Chichester, UK: Wiley, 2016.

Volf, Miroslav. *Free of Charge*. Grand Rapids: Zondervan, 2005.

Wacker, Grant. *Heaven Below: Early Pentecostals and American Culture*. Cambridge, MA: Harvard University Press, 2001.

Walton, John H. *The NIV Application Commentary, Genesis*. Grand Rapids: Zondervan, 2001. Digital edition.

Watts, Thomas A. "Two Wills in Christ? Contemporary Objections Considered in the Light of a Critical Examination of Maximus the Confessor's Disputation with Pyrrhus." *The Westminster Theological Journal* 71.2 (Fall 2009) 455–87.

Welch, Charles H. *True from the Beginning*. London: Berean, 1934.

Wesley Center Online. "The Sermons of John Wesley—Sermon 40, Christian Perfection." http://wesley.nnu.edu/john-wesley/the-sermons-of-john-wesley-1872-edition/sermon-40-christian-perfection/.

Wesley, John. "A Plain Account of Christian Perfection." In *The Works of John Wesley*, edited by Thomas Jackson, locs. 431–1290. Kansas City: Beacon Hill, 1978.

Wilken, Robert Louis. *The Spirit of Early Christian Thought*. London: Yale University Press, 2003

Williams, J. Rodman. *Renewal Theology: Systematic Theology from a Charismatic Perspective, Vol. 2*. Grand Rapids: Zondervan, 1990.

Winkworth, Susanna, trans. *Theologia Germanica*. Mesa, AZ: Scriptoria, 2010.

Wogaman, J. Philip. *Christian Ethics: A Historical Introduction*. 2nd ed. Louisville: Westminster John Knox, 2011.

Wogaman, J. Phillip, and Douglas M. Strong, eds. *Readings in Christian Ethics*. Louisville: Westminster John Knox, 1996.

Subject/Individual Index

Scripture Index

1 Corinthians

Made in the USA
Middletown, DE
12 January 2020